The Lamp in the Desert

THE LAMP IN THE DESERT

The Story of the University of Arizona

by

DOUGLAS D. MARTIN

With a New Foreword by President Ann Weaver Hart

SENTINEL PEAK

TUCSON

Sentinel Peak
An Imprint of The University of Arizona Press
www.uapress.arizona.edu

Special Commemorative Edition Published 2014

Printed in the United States of America
20 19 18 17 16 15 7 6 5 4 3 2

Cover designed by Leigh McDonald
Cover image: © Special Collections, The University of Arizona Libraries, University of Arizona Photograph Collection

Photographs for *The Lamp in the Desert* have been provided by the Associated Students of the University of Arizona Photo Division, and by various commercial photographers including Ray Manley, Lynn Sanders, and George Geyer of Tucson, and by Bachrach.

L. C. Catalog Card Number 60–10878

♾ This paper meets the requirements of ANSI/NISO Z39.48–1992 (Permanence of Paper).

Contents

Foreword to the Special Commemorative Edition

THERE IS A GREAT DEAL of excitement this year at the University of Arizona. Our one-hundredth homecoming is this fall, renovations to our historic and beloved Old Main have been completed, and we have embarked on a new era of discovery and learning with a forward-looking strategic plan supported by the largest fundraising campaign in the UA's history.

Clearly, we have much to be proud of in the present. We also have a great deal to be proud of throughout the UA's distinguished past, and Douglas R. Martin's The Lamp in the Desert: The Story of the University of Arizona is a wonderful reminder of that past. Martin's work is a record of the vast changes that took place from the UA's founding in 1885 to the middle part of the twentieth century; it is also a piece of history itself, and as such it is a reminder of how much has changed since the book's original publication in 1960.

For instance, as you will see in the pages to follow, Dr. Richard A. Harvill, one of my predecessors as UA president, wrote the foreword for that edition. He noted the size and reach of the UA: 12,000 students, 59 schools and departments, 21 divisions of research and public service, with over 100,000 alumni around the nation and the world. Today, the UA has well over 200,000 living alumni, we operate 54 research centers and outreach stations, and nearly 40,000 students study in 21 colleges that are made up of 112 departments, schools, and interdisciplinary degree programs.

Though the size of the university has changed, its land-grant mission to support all Arizonans through education and partnership has remained consistent. The UA's mission is reflected in this commemorative edition, which preserves the interpretation—and reinterpretation—of Arizona's complicated and sometimes violent history. When Martin writes of the troubles that early supporters had in getting the University started, he refers to the conflicts between settlers from the eastern United States and the local Apache tribes by talking about white men and red men, terms that sound out-of-date at the least. Yet at other times, Martin seems to reveal an awareness of the injustices that were part of the formation of our state, as when he writes about the challenges posed to the UA's creation by shifting priorities in the territorial government: "Goodwin was thinking of the future, but he had no illusions about the present. He knew survival came first and that there would be no survival unless the Apache was either controlled or wiped out. Whether the white man had given provocation by his rather ruthless action against the Apache did not seem to concern Governor Goodwin" (13).

My point here is not to belittle the past or those who were part of it. Instead, I want to suggest that in reading and enjoying this book, we all have a means to recognize the University of Arizona's role as an engine of change, opportunity, and learning for every member of our state. Of the 112 academic units that now make up the University of Arizona, one is the American Indian Studies Department, just this year transformed from a Graduate Interdisciplinary Program into an academic department that will offer undergraduate degrees starting in fall 2014. This change does not erase the good or the bad elements of our collective past, but the opportunities that it will create for all students who come to the UA is due at least in part to knowing and learning from our history. Professor Martin's book is a piece of that history as much as it is the story of it. It deserves to be read and appreciated for the imperfect and therefore human achievement that it is. Professor Martin treats the UA's history with care and expertise from those early days, through many years of new buildings, expanding academic programs, growing pride in UA athletics, and much more. As President Harvill wrote in 1960, the University is grateful to have its story told in such an enthusiastic and thorough way—I sincerely hope that everyone who finds this book has the time to read it, enjoy it, and to learn from it.

President Ann Weaver Hart
University of Arizona, 2014

Foreword to the First Edition

THE UNIVERSITY OF ARIZONA was founded in 1885. Today, among universities located in desert areas, it is one of the two or three most complete and largest in the world. It enrolls 12,000 students and is organized as ten colleges, fifty-nine schools and departments, and twenty-one divisions of research and public service. The homes of more than one hundred thousand former students are distributed among every community in Arizona, every state and territory of the nation, and some seventy other countries.

As a state university, and as a member institution of the world-renowned system of land-grant colleges and universities of the United States, the University has, throughout its history, been dedicated to the service of the people of Arizona. At the same time, its educational and research programs have been of national and international significance. Today, with the development of desert areas of ever-increasing concern, it is rapidly gaining recognition internationally for its research on problems of arid lands.

The history of the region in which the University is located has influenced markedly its development and its traditions. Archaeological evidence reveals that prehistoric Indian peoples lived in southern Arizona more than 10,000 years ago. The city of Tucson, in which the University is located, was founded in 1776 as a Spanish presidio, and the San Xavier Mission, founded in 1700, still stands as a reminder that what is now Arizona was Spanish territory for nearly three hundred years.

Just over a hundred years ago, prior to the Gadsden Purchase, southern Arizona was a northernmost area of Mexico. Then came the early American period and the railroads, then the cattle and mining industries, and irrigated agriculture, and the development of the great state which we know today.

The story of the University of Arizona is closely interwoven with the history of the state and, in The Lamp in the Desert, Professor Douglas D. Martin has told this story dramatically and with delightful touches of humor. He has told it with realistic understanding, both of pioneer days and of developments since those days, and the University of Arizona is deeply grateful to him.

Richard A. Harvill
March 12, 1960

Preface

BECAUSE THE STATE is the campus of the University, *The Lamp in the Desert* is dedicated to the people of Arizona. It was written for and to them and is neither a textbook nor a thesis, but a story of human courage, dreams, and deeds.

In writing the book an effort has been made to avoid burying history under masses of dates and details that annoy and delay everyone except the scholarly researcher. There is a place for such books in the libraries, but this book was meant to be read for pleasure as well as information.

It is published in celebration of three-quarters of a century of partnership between a frontier commonwealth and its educators and students; seventy-five years in which they worked together not only to conquer the appalling problems of survival in a semi-arid land, but also to found a desert college that became a University and finally one of the nation's great institutions of advanced education.

It has been impossible to use all the material found, but this was inevitable and would be the case if there were three volumes instead of one. A supplementary book which will present the history and growth of the colleges, institutes, and laboratories, will be published later in the Diamond Jubilee year.

Acknowledgment must be made of the support of President Richard A. Harvill, the faculty, the alumni, and the library staff without which little could have been accomplished. Much credit is due Dr. David Patrick, vice-president; Miss Patricia Paylore, and Miss Phyllis Ball of the library; and Mr. C. Zaner Lesher, Registrar Emeritus, all of whom read the manuscript and made valuable suggestions. Nor can one overlook mentioning the tireless supervision which Miss Mary Lauver, secretary to the Dean of the College of Liberal Arts, gave to the seemingly endless revisions and typing of these chapters. Thanks should also be given to Henk Moonan of the University Photography Division.

Finally, one must make an honest bow to those historians and reporters whose recorded observations have preserved the past so that it could be reviewed by future generations. Every effort has been made to follow their footsteps, but if there have been times when the way was lost and an error was made, the fault is not theirs.

Douglas D. Martin
Professor of Journalism
The University of Arizona

The Lamp in the Desert

CHAPTER 1

1863–1886

THE ANTHROPOLOGIST can trace man back to about 10,000 or 12,000 B.C. in Arizona and has reasons for believing he was here thousands of years before that period. Herbert Howe Bancroft, great Western historian, says the first white man to enter Arizona was Fray Marcos de Niza, a Franciscan, who appeared in A.D. 1539. One year later Coronado led a strong Spanish military force up the valley of the San Pedro in search of the "Seven Cities of Cibola," all of which were said to be storehouses of gold and gems. The prospects of finding treasure that was greater than the riches captured by Cortez had all Mexico in a high fever, but Coronado came back from his search without finding anything he thought of value. So the dream died and Mexico lost interest in her northern lands for almost a century and a half.

Then a man who cared nothing for wealth and who had dedicated his life to the conversion of heathen Indians came up from Sonora in 1687. He was the great Jesuit, Padre Eusebio Francisco Kino, missionary, explorer, and tireless builder. Start the clock now and begin dating modern Arizona history from Kino's time, for he was the first to bring the white man's culture into the red man's lands. Indians burned his missions after he died in 1711, but much that he had taught remained. His maps reformed the world's conception of the geography of the Southwest, and great forces moved along the trails he had opened. The land passed from Spain to Mexico and from Mexico to the young United States. War split the Northern and Southern states. The Southern forces invaded the valley of the Santa Cruz and the troops of the North drove them out.

It all took a long time and again a century and a half ticked by before civilization made another notable advance in the frontier lands. Then, in the midst of a snowstorm at Navajo Springs, which was a desolate spot twenty-five miles inside the northeastern boundary of Arizona, time drew a ring on the calendar around December 29, 1863 as the clock struck four.

From that hour on, Arizona had a legally constituted government, established by an Act of Congress.

Standing bareheaded in the falling snow, Governor John N. Goodwin and other officials appointed by President Abraham Lincoln took their oaths of office as the American flag was unfurled and the military escort saluted.

Richard C. McCormick, Territorial Secretary, read the official proclamation and although the blizzard swept the words away, there was a printing press in a baggage wagon which spread them across the mountains, through the valleys, and over the deserts:

> I, John N. Goodwin, having been appointed by the President of the United States, and duly qualified, as Governor of the Territory of Arizona, do hereby announce that by virtue of the powers with which I am invested by an Act of the Congress of the United States, providing a temporary government for the Territory, I shall this day proceed to organize such government. The provisions of the Act and all acts and enactments established thereby, will be enforced by the proper Territorial officers after this date.
>
> A preliminary census will forthwith be taken, thereafter the judicial districts will be formed, and an election of members of the Legislative Assembly, and other officers ordered by the Act, be ordered.
>
> I invoke the aid and co-operation of all citizens of the territory in my efforts to establish a government whereby the security of life and property will be maintained throughout its limits, and its varied resources be rapidly and successfully developed.

To the printed proclamation there were added in pen and ink the words, "The seat of government will for the present be at or near Fort Whipple."

Navajo Springs was a strange place in which to announce the formation of the Territory. It had no inhabitants, there were no permanent shelters, and worse still, there was a great scarcity of wood for the camp-fires and water for men and horses. The elevation was 4,400 feet and the day was cold. The temperature would drop lower as night fell. But time was running out for the officials of the new government. If their salaries were to start the first of the year, they had two days left in which to take their oath of office on Arizona soil and Fort Whipple was 170 miles away.

The party had been long on the road. They had left Fort Larned, Nebraska, on October 15 and headed for Santa Fe, moving from one army post to another under the protection of government troops. They lived off the country when they could, depending on venison roasts, buffalo steaks, antelope, and prairie chicken. After they had reached the treeless plains where there was no wood, even the Governor had to go out with a flour sack and help gather buffalo chips for the camp-fires.

When the officials finally reached Santa Fe, they were welcomed by Brigadier General James H. Carleton, commander of the Military Department of New Mexico and Arizona, and Carleton had a bill of goods to sell. He was planning a new military post in Northern Arizona which he had named Fort Whipple, and insisted it would be just the place for the new territorial capital, even though the country was a wilderness.

Tucson, to the south, was the only town of any consequence in the Territory but Carleton hated it. As commander of the "California Column" of Union volunteers that had marched east in 1862 to recapture New Mexico and Arizona from the Confederates, he had occupied Tucson, which he found strongly pro-southern.

There were good reasons for the sentiments of the people. The federal government had deserted Arizona in 1861, destroying its forts, burning its stores and moving the garrisons east to face the forces of the Confederacy. This left the land and people at the mercy of the Apaches. Tucson citizens reacted by holding a mass meeting in which they declared that since they had been deserted by the government the people now considered their country was part of the Confederacy. To show they were in earnest they elected Granville H. Oury as a delegate to the Confederate Congress in Richmond. Oury was never seated, but this did not soften Carleton's anger. In his book these people were rebels and he didn't like them.

The townspeople didn't like Carleton either, although he protected them from their red enemies. In some respects he drove them with a hard bit, levying heavy tribute on the gamblers and saloon-keepers for the care of his sick and taxing the merchants for the cost of feeding his troops. All men were ordered to take their choice between an oath of allegiance to the Union and leaving town; nine were sent to the military prison at Fort Yuma on charges of having terrified the citizens.

Carleton's most unpopular act appears to have been the seizure of the Mowry mines near Tubac and the arrest and imprisonment at Yuma of Sylvester Mowry. A former West Pointer, Mowry was an able and popular man who had been sent to Washington before the Civil War broke out to argue that Arizona should have a territorial government.

Carleton charged him with having furnished ammunition to the Confederate troops that had occupied Tucson and a court martial ordered him confined in the army prison on the Colorado. The government reviewed the case and ordered Mowry released, thus in effect reproving the general for his action.

So it is understandable that Carleton's memories of Tucson were not pleasant. Now, as military commander of all New Mexico and Arizona, he had no sympathy for the old pueblo town, which he called an "insignificant village away in the sterile region toward the southern line of the Territory," and did not approve of it as the seat of the new government.

Another reason was that Carleton had sent scouts to investigate rumors of rich gold placer strikes in Little Chino Valley near the present site of the city of Prescott and had found such rumors were true.

Gold meant a rush of prospectors and miners, and to Carleton this meant a town, which, in turn, meant a fort. His imagination ran away with him at this point and he saw the center of population shifting from the south to Fort Whipple. If the territorial capital should be located there, Tucson would certainly be doomed.

The general hurried his opinions off to Washington and painted a glowing picture of the wealth of the lands around his new post. He wrote in one letter:

> Providence has indeed blessed us. Now that we need money to pay the expense of this terrible war, new mines of untold millions are found and the gold lies here at our feet for the mere picking of it up. The country where it is found is not a fancied Atlantis; it is not seen in golden dreams; but it is a real tangible El Dorado, that has gold that can be weighed by the steelyards—gold that does not vanish when the finder is awake.

Actually the entire Yavapai County district is said to have produced only $4,000,000 from 1863 to 1900.

After pointing to the magnificent outlook, Carleton then asked for a full regiment of cavalry to protect his fort and the seat of civil government, as well as a road from the Rio Grande to the new placer fields. The War Department cut him down to two companies of cavalry.

Governor Goodwin may have wished he had followed the well-known trail from the Rio Grande to Southern Arizona as he shivered over his campfire at Navajo Springs. Congress, in the enabling act, had intentionally omitted naming any special locality for the capital, so there was nothing in the law that said the Governor could not establish himself in a warmer climate than the one he would find at Fort Whipple. Certainly he didn't hurry to reach his capital, for he spent three weeks on the way. Then he rode in with his party and received the proper salute of nineteen guns, but apparently he was not very happy over the site.

Jonathan Richmond, a young man from Michigan who accompanied the official party with the intention of serving as a clerk for Associate Justice William T. Howell, wrote his parents that "offers of prayers and thanksgiving should have been made, but upon viewing the site which Major E. B. Willis (who with three companies had preceded us by two weeks) had selected for a military post and, if suitable, for a capital, we concluded to let the thing slide."

The Governor didn't like the location any better in May than he had in January, and as a result the fort was moved to a new mining camp on Granite Creek. This was called Prescott and there the territorial government began to function as though everyone knew what he was doing and exactly how to do it.

Milton B. Duffield, United States' Marshal, was ordered to begin taking the census that Goodwin had promised, and while this was in progress the Governor took to the trails to survey his domain. He visited the mining districts that had aroused Carleton's enthusiasm, went east to Verde Valley, and then down to Tucson where he performed an unusual ceremony.

The town had no authorized officials, and leading citizens petitioned the chief executive to establish a city government having power to maintain law and order. Goodwin not only obliged them by appointing a mayor and councilmen, but surprised the community as well by ignoring politics and selecting the most capable men.

Fears that the Governor would be bitter toward men who had sympathized with the South proved needless. The great war was approaching its climax in the East and Goodwin had no intention of fanning dying embers into a new blaze on the frontier. The result was that his city government functioned well and sometimes vigorously, for it occasionally used a whipping post.

Pushed by a chief who was in a hurry to get things done, Marshal Duffield turned in his census report on May 24. The Governor issued a proclamation dividing the Territory into three judicial districts and called for an election on July 18 to select members of the First Legislature. The boundaries of the districts were simple. The First District lay south of the Gila River and included Tucson. The Second District bordered the Colorado River and took in Arizona City and the mining camp known as La Paz. The Third District lay north of the Gila and so included Prescott and Fort Whipple.

Duffield's count showed that Arizona had 4,573 citizens, about 33 per cent less than the advocates of territorial government had claimed when the measure was before Congress. Opponents of the enabling act had laughed at the claims that Arizona had 6,500 white citizens. They had charged that most of the residents were half-breed Indians and Mexicans who had no interest in citizenship, and had said the whole deal was a plot to provide offices for jobless politicians.

The Arizona faction, however, clung to its estimate and insisted that 6,500 was the correct total, until Senator Benjamin F. Wade gave the bill his approval on condition that Tucson should not be made the capital. After that the measure passed the Senate by a vote of 25 to 12 on February 24, 1863.

Duffield and his assistants had scraped the bottom of the barrel to get their total. The 750 soldiers in the Territory were included. So were people whose only claim to citizenship was two weeks' residence. Of course, hundreds of Mexicans were included also.

The law was that unless within one year after the signing of the Guadalupe-Hidalgo Treaty, an Arizona Mexican declared he did not want to become an American citizen, he had no further choice. He was then an American whether he liked it or not.

Tucson was the largest town and the census gave it 1,568 citizens, including 268 officers and men of the First California Cavalry. Writers and travelers of that day said frequently the town had practically no "white" people at all. Jonathan Richmond, the Federal Court clerk, wrote with great scorn that after the delegates had departed to attend the first session of the Territorial Legislature in Prescott, only six white men remained.

Richmond, like many others of his time, didn't consider Mexicans as a white race because of their Indian blood. This was the height of ignorance or snobbery and probably a triple-distilled essence of both. The contribution of the Mexicans is indicated by the fact that they had built the only church and school in the Territory and a good many of them were superior products of a finer culture than the one they encountered in their new land.

The census showed that ninety-two citizens of Tucson were native Americans and in addition it listed thirty-nine men from England, Scotland, Ireland, Wales, France, Germany, and Denmark. Since this was an actual count and not a casual observation, it will have to be accepted as the final authority; and if one reads the census for something besides totals he will learn much about the people and their lives in this hard frontier land.

About one quarter of the whites, 1,080 to be exact, worked in or about the mines in capacities ranging from superintendents to cooks. Farming was highly profitable if a man didn't lose his hair to the Apaches, but, since most men preferred to take no chances with their scalps, only 157 citizens were farmers. There were eighty-five merchants and traders. Ten men said they were saloon keepers or whiskey dealers, three claimed to be school teachers, and two admitted being gamblers.

The remainder of the people followed the occupations and trades common to a frontier land. They were ordinary laborers, teamsters, traders, shoemakers, harness makers, blacksmiths, carpenters, and gunsmiths—with a very light sprinkling of lawyers, doctors, and priests.

Most of the citizens who were to be ruled by and asked to pay for the new government were desperately poor or, as economists put it, "there was limited capital in the country." Both statements are generalizations and to get the real picture one must turn again to the census, which showed that out of the total 4,573 people registered, only seventy-four men, most of whom were merchants, were worth $1,000, 130 had more than $500, and 357 claimed $100 or more. To sum it all up and state it briefly, 4,000 citizens of the new Territory had less than $100 each.

The largest fortune was reported by Mark A. Aldrich, who gave his occupation as farming, but who was also a partner of Solomon Warner in the first American store opened in Tucson. Aldrich claimed a personal estate of $48,000. As for the 4,000 citizens with less than $100, the census takers didn't include people with less than $4.00, and so hundreds reported that they had nothing.

The census made provisions for reporting the value of real-estate holdings but, judging from the figures, very few thought their holdings were worth much. One J. C. Jackson, an engineer at the Mowry mines, valued his holdings at $10,000 and this was the top figure for the Territory. From that point the valuations dropped to the twenty-four cents reported by Thomas J. Goodman, a miner, and then vanished.

The election following the census was apparently a very calm and orderly event, and when it was over the elected representatives of the people met on September 26, 1864, to open the First Legislature, and the wheels of government began to turn.

It is worth taking time today to consider the frontier statesmen who now stepped forward to direct the affairs of the nation's youngest Territory. Governor Goodwin was a graduate of Dartmouth and a lawyer who had been a congressman from Maine. Richard C. McCormick, the Territorial Secretary of State, was a noted war correspondent. He was destined to be appointed and then elected Governor after Goodwin resigned. William T. Howell, Associate Justice, was a lawyer who had been President Pro Tem of the Senate and Speaker of the House in the Michigan Legislature. He compiled the first code of Arizona law and had it ready for the Legislature when it met.

Coles Bashford, of Tucson, president of the Council, as the upper house of the Legislature was called, was a graduate of Wesleyan Seminary and the first lawyer admitted to practice in Arizona. He had been a district attorney in the State of New York, had helped form the Republican party in Wisconsin, and had been elected Governor of the state. President Grant twice appointed him Territorial Secretary of State for Arizona. Charles D. Poston was Superintendent of Indian Affairs, but resigned when he was elected delegate to Congress. Poston is known in history as the "Father of Arizona" because he fought successfully for territorial standing and worked persistently to awaken eastern interests to the mineral wealth of the country. He had practiced law in Washington D. C., and Tennessee, but had gone west to become clerk of the United States' Customhouse in San Francisco. There he became an agent for mining interests and later opened mines near Tubac. Chief Justice William F. Turner was a Pennsylvania lawyer who held his Arizona office for seven years. There is little on record concerning the career of Associate Justice Joseph P. Allyn, beyond the fact that he was a world traveler and newspaper correspondent who had held minor positions in congressional offices. He served one term as associate justice, then ran for Congress against Governor Goodwin and was defeated.

Milton B. Duffield, United States Marshal, was the only man who seems to have failed to measure up to the average standards of the first Territorial officials. He had a bad habit of threatening people with sudden death. Finally, he met it himself in an argument over a mining claim.

From these brief biographies, it is easy to see that the territorial government was in the hands of administrators with experience and ability. They knew how government was organized and how it functioned. Because of their education and political training, they recognized the necessity for schools, the importance of a firm foundation in law and, finally, they remembered their responsibility to the future as well as the present.

Governor Goodwin touched on this last point in his first message to the Legislature when he said:

> We are entrusted not only with the present interests of a small constituency, and amendable to them alone, but we are the trustees of posterity, and are responsible to the millions in all time who shall come after us.

The first legislative session lasted only forty-three days, but in that time able leaders and intelligent representatives made an admirable record under difficult conditions. The most important action was probably the adoption of the Howell Code, which was based on the codes of California and New York. It was the first act passed and was the law in Arizona for thirteen years.

Above all else, however, the pioneer Legislature is remembered for its attitude toward education. There was not a public school, Protestant church, courthouse, stagecoach, or telegraph line in the Territory when Governor Goodwin delivered his first message, yet he named free schools as the first need. He said:

> Self-government and education are inseparable. The one can be exercised only as the other is enjoyed. The common school, high school and the University should all be established and are worthy of our fostering care. The first duty of a free state is to make, so far as lies in their power, education as free to its citizens as the air they breathe. . . . I earnestly recommend that a portion of the funds raised by taxation be appropriated for these purposes, and that a beginning, though small, be made. . . .
>
> The Act of July 2, 1862, [The Morrill Act] the operation of which has been extended by the present Congress has provided for the establishment of an Agricultural College in every state or territory that shall avail itself of its provisions and comply with conditions. I recommend that you take the necessary steps to enable the territory to accept this donation. . . . It is for you to determine what legislation, if any, the interests of Arizona require under this donation, or what further legislation in that direction should be asked of Congress.

It was utterly impossible to expect the poverty-ridden people of 1864 to build or support common schools, much less high schools and a university. Even if by some miracle funds were available, there were no children prepared for grammar-grade work. Goodwin was thinking of the future, but he had no illusions about the present. He knew survival came first and that there would be no survival unless the Apache was either controlled or wiped out. Whether the white man had given provocation by his rather ruthless action against the Apache did not seem to concern Governor Goodwin. He said:

> To the Apache has been transmitted for a century an inheritance of hate and hostility to the white man. He is a

> murderer by heredity, a thief by prescription. . . . They have exhausted the ingenuity of fiends to invent more excruciating tortures for the unfortunate prisoner they take, so that the traveler acquainted with their warfare, surprised and unable to escape, reserves the last shot in his revolver for his own head.
>
> They have made Southern Arizona and Northern Mexico a wilderness and desolation. But for them mines would be worked, innumerable sheep and cattle would cover these plains and some of the bravest and most energetic men that were ever the pioneers of a new country, and who now fill bloody and unmarked graves, would be living to see their brightest anticipations realized. . . . One policy only can be adopted. A war must be prosecuted until they are compelled to submit and go upon a reservation.

Since making a living and holding off the Apache were the problems that filled men's minds, it was natural for men to ask whether any education except that born of frontier experience would be of help. If not, then why worry over schools and a university?

Knowing this, as the Legislature did, it is to its credit that the Joint Committee on Education acknowledged that while a regular school system was premature, "an appropriation be made and given to these towns where the number of children warrant the establishment of schools . . ."

> Your committee recommends that a donation of $259 be made to the Mission School at San Xavier del Bac. To Prescott, Mohave and La Paz, each town $250. To Tucson, $500 providing the English language form a part of the instruction of such public schools.

The measure was passed with the condition that the towns must raise equal amounts of money, either through taxes or private gifts. None raised its share, so no schools were opened. This was not the fault of the Legislature, which earmarked $1,500 for education out of a total appropriation of $16,137.

Amenable to the hopes of Governor Goodwin, the Legislature then authorized a University of Arizona and wrote a constitution for it. It set up a Board of Regents, provided that the institution be supported by the sale of lands granted by the federal government for University purposes, and gave the Regents one year in which to find a site—free if possible. After that the Board was expected to start building or renting quarters. Provision was made for all university money to be deposited with the territorial treasurer, with the strict understanding that it could be used for no other purpose. Finally, the Legislature authorized tax levies for free education and then, conscious of the dignity of history, it authorized the establishment of a territorial library and an historical department. The latter eventually became the Arizona Pioneers' Historical Society.

Though not one free public school was opened for seven years and no high school was established for twenty years, the First Territorial Legislature made a magnificent gesture which no one can say was completely futile. For these easterners "with college on the brain" had placed the lamp of learning in the desert with sure faith that in time the people would supply oil for the bowl and teachers who would trim the wick.

Gilbert W. Hopkins, who was one of the first Regents, did not live out the year. He and William Wrightson, superintendent of the Santa Rita mines, were shot and killed by Apaches within 500 yards of Fort Buchanan. Wrightson is remembered in Arizona history as the pioneer who brought the first printing press to the Southwest and started its first newspaper, the *Arizonian*, at Tubac. Mount Wrightson (Mount Baldy in the Santa Ritas) is named after him.

Goodwin resigned to run for Congress after the Legislature adjourned, and Richard C. McCormick, the Secretary of State, was appointed to fill the vacancy. McCormick was interested principally in the Apache problem and the development of the territorial resources and told the Legislature in 1865 that "utter subjugation, even to extermination, is admitted as a necessity by all who are familiar with his [the Apache's] history and habits." He gave scant attention to education in his first term, saying merely that he thought "the existing provisions for schools" were satisfactory, although it was clear that nothing had been accomplished. Even the university was now forgotten.

The Territorial Legislature was now making so many requests for help that some army officers said it would be cheaper if the government bought up private holdings and gave the country to the Indians. General William T. Sherman had another idea. He said we had fought one war to take Arizona away from Mexico and ought to fight another to make her take it back.

What almost everyone in Washington seemed to fail to understand was that the pioneers were fighting merely to hold the land and, tough people that they were, this was about all they could do.

Governor McCormick let the Second and Third Legislatures slip by without doing anything to promote education, but when the Fourth Legislature met in 1867 and moved the capital to Tucson, he decided the time had come to make provisions for establishing and maintaining public schools. The Legislature agreed and passed an act giving county boards of supervisors the power to establish school districts wherever there was a population of 100 citizens in a four-mile area, and to levy a tax of five mills on the assessed valuation of property.

Nothing happened after this, so the Fifth Legislature tried its hand and amended the School Act to provide for election of county school superintendents and an increase in taxes. People merely ignored the law, but before criticising it must be remembered that the population was only 9,500 and that while the War Between the States was over, the war between the red and white man raged on.

To McCormick's credit it should be mentioned that he never failed to remind Congress that the benefits of the Morrill Act had not yet been extended to Arizona for the support of a university.

What the Territory needed was a leader dedicated to free public schools and it finally found him in Anson P. K. Safford, a Vermonter who became the third governor and who is remembered as the "Father of Arizona Schools."

Safford had been Surveyor General of Nevada and a member of the California House of Representatives. A tireless worker, he looked the situation over when he arrived in 1869 and decided to adopt the old maxim that if a man wants a thing well done, he should do it himself. So he planned to serve as Territorial Superintendent of Public Instruction as well as Governor.

Congress had decided that biennial sessions of the Legislature were sufficient, so there had been no legislative activity for two years when Safford greeted Council and House in 1871 with an eloquent address on education in which he said, "The object most desirable to attain is the adoption of a school system which will provide free public schools so that the poor and rich alike can share equal benefits."

Naturally, he did not neglect the Apache problem. No early governor who did that would have lasted long. In fact, Safford revealed that he personally had taken the field in command of a company raised by Tucson citizens to punish the Indians for an attack on a stage station. The company never caught up with the marauders but Safford reported, "We were in the field 27 days, and during that time these men marched above 600 miles, much of the time over a rocky, mountainous country. I believe a few companies of this class of our citizens would be found invaluable in subduing the hostile Apaches."

Safford was made of stern stuff, as his Legislature soon discovered. He was determined that the Territory's 1,923 children above the age of six years be given free schooling, and presented a definite and workable plan. He wanted it made mandatory that county officials establish school districts and levy taxes sufficient to support a school in every district for at least six months a year.

The bill was presented by Estevan Ochoa who was a member of the Legislative Council from Tucson. Ochoa was the most highly respected Mexican-born citizen in Arizona, but if the Governor expected that this would inspire the souls of American-born legislators with holy zeal he was wrong. The Legislature fought him until the final day of the session but he beat down their old cry that the people couldn't fight Apaches and build schools at the same time by stubbornly repeating one answer: "Unless we educate the rising generation, we shall raise up a population no more capable of self-government than the Apaches themselves."

Safford's bill was amended in some particulars, but when it reached his desk for his signature it provided for a Territorial Board of Education and made every probate judge a county superintendent and head of a board of three district school trustees. In addition to this, school taxes were increased and a uniform county tax was set up. It was a great victory which got education under way to such an extent that the governor was able to report to the Seventh Legislature, "Free schools have been taught during the past year in every district in the Territory for at least three months."

Pima County supervisors organized "School District Number One" in November 1867 and opened a free school for boys in a rented adobe building. It was closed in six months when the funds gave out, and the children enjoyed a long vacation which lasted until 1871. Then sessions reopened and John Spring taught 138 boys. Like all early schools this one was not coeducational, probably because both American and Mexican mothers were inclined to have their daughters taught at home. Many a girl and some boys studied under a private tutor or some older member of the family. Dr. Robert H. Forbes, Dean Emeritus of the College of Agriculture, knows of one family school he believes was in existence as early as 1857. It was taught by Ellen Pennington, the oldest daughter of Elias G. and Julia Ann Pennington. The schoolroom was attached to their Sopori ranch home and was built with portholes through which the father and the oldest sons could answer an Indian attack with rifle fire.

Governor Safford's health failed under the load he carried and he resigned in 1877, but not before he had established compulsory education and cautioned the Legislature that the schools were a "sacred trust" which, he said, "must be free from sectarian or political influences" because such control would inevitably lead "to the education of the few and the ignorance of the many."

Before he left office the Governor expressed his belief that lands granted to Arizona by the government would yield the schools $10,000 a year and his optimism may have helped to promote a general misconception of the value of these grants. One Tucson newspaper said the gift would probably bring to the university—if one were built—$750,000 almost immediately. Such ideas were common in many states and led to impolite academic brawls. Universities that had scorned anything but liberal and fine arts, medicine, and law, suddenly considered adding mechanical arts and agriculture to the curriculum in hopes of qualifying for grants.

Friends of the University of Michigan once persuaded a joint legislative committee to propose that Michigan State Agricultural College be converted into an annex of the State Reform School so that Morrill land grants could be turned over to the Ann Arbor institution. Practically everybody got into the row, but Michigan State won.

It was a long time before the University of Arizona benefited much from land grants, and as late as 1911 the president revealed that the income did not exceed $500 a year. However, though the revenue was insignificant in the early years, Arizona lands bring important returns today.

John P. Hoyt was appointed acting governor to fill the unexpired portion of Safford's term and then President Rutherford B. Hayes selected John C. Fremont, famous explorer and soldier, as governor in 1878. Fremont's achievements as chief executive did not equal the part he had played in the winning of the West, and he added no glamour to his reputation. Since Prescott had won the state capital back from Tucson in 1877, Fremont met the Tenth Legislature there when it convened in 1879.

It is said that the new Governor was contemptuous of his position as the head of a frontier territory and felt "it was not worthy of his ability or fame." Since he was an educated man, he might have carried on the work of Governor Safford, but he completely neglected public schools in his messages to the Tenth and Eleventh Legislatures. About all he did for the cause of free schools was to sign an act providing for a state superintendent of public instruction and to agree to direct a public lottery to be conducted under the cloak of raising funds to construct capital buildings and to aid public schools. The Lottery Act passed, but the lottery was never held. The *Phoenix Expositor* called it "a stink in the nostrils of honest men," and the postal authorities barred it from the mails.

Schools suffered under Fremont, but the shadow of Safford lingered in the capital and, remembering his warning that public schools must always be kept free of sectarian and political influences, the Legislature wrote the following section into the territorial school law:

> No books, tracts or papers of a sectarian or denominational character shall be used or introduced in any school established under the provisions of this act; nor shall sectarian or denominational doctrine be taught therein; nor shall any school whatever receive any of the public school funds which has not been taught in accordance with the provisions of this act.

The first Superintendent of Public Instruction was Professor Moses H. Sherman, an experienced school administrator and teacher who had been head of the schools in Prescott. Under his guidance, education began to recapture some of the ground lost since Safford's resignation.

Sherman tried to convince Washington that the Territory should be permitted to sell part of its lands and invest the proceeds in securities. In this he failed and authority to sell came only with statehood.

During Fremont's administration the Legislature learned that Congress was planning to make new land grants and immediately asked that Arizona be remembered. Since Fremont was a trifle dilatory about signing the memorial, the Territory received seventy-two sections before he picked up his pen.

The selection of the sections was left to Professor Sherman. He chose heavily timbered lands in Coconino County, recommending that the Legislature take appropriate action to keep private interests from lumbering there. Unfortunately, only fifty-seven sections were confirmed by the Federal Land Office, which ruled that the remainder had been reserved for a national forest. A 320 acre tract in the Tucson Mountains was added in 1904, but Arizona never received her full share.

The long war with the Apaches was now drawing to its bloody end under the tactics of Generals George Crook and Nelson A. Miles. Military telegraph came in 1873 and was followed by the wires and poles of Western Union. There were seventeen daily and weekly newspapers, and some of the better dailies carried wire news. It is difficult to make an accurate count of the number of newspapers that appeared in the early eighties, as Miss Estelle Lutrell found when she wrote the valuable university bulletin on newspapers and periodicals of Arizona.

Political candidates started papers and dropped them when the campaign closed. Ambitious printers opened job shops that printed newspapers for brief periods. Men with a longing to write editorials launched papers in communities that could not possibly support them. Yet it is a fact that many of these early editors contributed to increased respect for law and learning and to a growing realization that a great era of social and economic development lay within the grasp of the people.

The University of Arizona honors their memories and records their names in the Arizona Newspaper Hall of Fame. Student journalists look up from their typewriters to the plaques in their classroom and learn that while presses were small in territorial days, some of them were operated by men who knew the power and the glory of the printed word and used it well in the service of the Commonwealth.

Tucson remained the largest town in the Territory and held the territorial capital from 1867 to 1879, but other towns of appreciable size were growing up. Yuma was incorporated as a city, Gila Bend and Clifton were thriving, Morenci clung to its hillside; Safford, Ray, and Globe were born, and Wickenburg was active enough in 1866 to be mentioned as a site for the capital.

The greatest growth was in the Gila Basin and the heart of it was the Salt River Valley which was soon to outstrip the remainder of the Territory in population. A settlement was formed there in 1864. It became Helling's Mill, then East Phoenix, and finally Phoenix. Historian James H. McClintock says the name was suggested by one Darrel Duppa who made a speech at a mass meeting in 1870 in which he said that here "a new city would spring, Phoenix-like, upon the ruins of a former civilization."

Another village that took root at a ferry landing on the Salt River, nine miles from Phoenix, became Tempe. Mormon pioneers settled Mesa, and other Mormon settlements developed between the Tonto and Verde Valleys before and after 1885, while 1883 saw the opening of the fabulously rich copper mines at Jerome.

Armies of Chinese laborers laid the rails and ties of the Southern Pacific Railroad from Yuma to Casa Grande, Tucson, Benson, Willcox, and across the line into New Mexico in 1878, 1879, and 1880. In 1881 the Rio Grande and Texas Pacific (the Santa Fe) had reached the Southern Pacific tracks at Deming and pushed on to Ashfork via Wins-low. Now the people in Southern Arizona could travel over most of the route to the capital by rail, providing they didn't mind riding to Deming on the Southern Pacific, transferring to the Santa Fe, and then taking a stagecoach from Ashfork to Prescott.

The battle of the railroad tycoons for transcontinental routes is much too long and involved to be told here. What is more important is that, after having dreamed of railroads for years, the Territory had them. Once every town had wanted a fort. Now ever town wanted at least a branch railroad or, if it couldn't get that, a money-spending territorial institution. It did not take a very bright man to see that when the Apache was subdued the army would leave and the paydays that had meant so much would disappear. It was quite obvious that new sources of revenue must be tapped, and so there was a new war on when the Thirteenth Legislature convened under Governor F. A. Tritle in 1885. This was a war for commercial gain, and it was just as bitter as the war with the Apache had ever been. The battleground was the legislative chambers of the "Thieving Thirteenth," which got its name from its reckless, unnecessary, and illegal expenditures, for the Legislature had the power to hand out spoils in the form of Territorial buildings and institutions.

The two big objectives were the capital and the asylum for the insane. A university and a teachers' college were of secondary interest because no community really wanted them. The favorite quip was, "Who ever heard of a professor buying a drink?"

When the shouting was over and the smoke-filled rooms were aired out, Maricopa County was found to be the big winner. At least this was the idea at that time. Phoenix captured the asylum with an appropriation of $100,000; Tempe got the teachers' college (Arizona Territorial Normal School) and $5,000; Yuma was promised a new levee on the west bank of the Gila; Prescott retained the capital, and Florence was happy over an appropriation of $12,000 for a bridge across the Gila. The bridge was a complete waste of money, for the rolling Gila went on one of its famous rampages, churned out a new channel, and left the bridge stranded in the desert. Pima County and Tucson got the University, which they definitely did not want, and a puny appropriation of $25,000—or one-fourth as much as was provided for the asylum.

Having lost the capital to Prescott in 1877, Tucson had been determined to get it back, and its representatives went to the thirteenth session with instructions to settle for nothing less.

C. C. Stephens represented Pima County in the Council, and since he had a reputation as an able lawyer his constituents thought their chances were good of getting the capital from Prescott. However, the entire Pima delegation was delayed in reaching the capital. In Stephens' words:

> We were obliged to work our way around on the railroad to Ashfork, then stage it through the horrible rigors of an Arizona winter, making 56 miles in 48 hours, being stuck for one-third of that time in Hell Canyon without anything to eat or drink.

The result was that legislative caucuses had been held and vote trading completed before the Pima people reached the capital. Prescott, which had been wining and dining and "seeing" legislators, had the capital.

Since Stephens felt he couldn't beat the opposition, he joined it and even voted with it. In fact, his ballot helped to give the asylum and the fat $100,000 appropriation to Maricopa County. When the news got back to the citizens of Tucson that their champion had given up hope of recapturing the capital and was after the university, they reacted violently. First they called Stephens all the names in a frontier vocabulary. Then they sent an emissary of their own to Prescott with a slush fund of $4,000 and instructions to buy the necessary votes. The money was spent but nothing was accomplished.

The Tucson Citizen, which had originally supported Stephens, now was purple with indignation and ran bitter editorial attacks filled with abuse.

In one of these the editor of the *Citizen* said:

> If C. C. Stephens thinks he can kick Pima County from one end of the Territory to the other, utterly ignore her and the wants of the people as if he were an avowed enemy, instead of a servant pledged to faithfully represent her interests in the Legislature and then after all his contemptible acts seek to smooth things over by the sop of a Territorial University, that nobody asked for and which at best can only be realized in a far distant future, he will find it will not go down.

The Star was more inclined to grieve rather than rage over Stephen's conduct, saying editorially:

> No man went to Prescott with brighter hopes in whom many of the people looked to for more than C. C. Stephens. He has proved a failure thus far and has gone back on his constituents wherever it has been to his pecuniary interest to do so. The Star regrets that Mr. Stephens has not made a better record for himself for he certainly has ability.

Some of Stephens' friends in the Legislature who knew he was sitting in a very hot seat gave him help in getting a bill through the Council giving Tucson the university. The bill, however, faced strong opposition in the House and seemed certain of defeat until young Selim M. Franklin stood up on the last day of the session, proceeded to blast the members for their misdeeds, and then pleaded that they redeem themselves by creating a university. He said:

> Gentlemen, the Thirteenth Legislative Assembly is generally conceded to have been the most energetic, the most conscientious and the most corrupt Arizona has ever had. We have been called the Fighting Thirteenth, the Bloody Thirteenth and the Thieving Thirteenth. We have deserved these names and we know it. We have employed too many clerks, we have subsidized the local press to cover up our shortcomings, and we have voted ourselves additional pay in violation of an Act of Congress.
>
> But, gentlemen, here is an opportunity to wash away our sins. Let us establish an institution of learning, where for all time to come the youth of the land may learn to become better citizens than we are, and all our shortcomings will be forgotten in a misty past and we will be remembered for this one great achievement.

The bill passed, carrying an appropriation of $25,000 and Tucson's anger was hot enough to boil the waters of the Santa Cruz, as Stephens learned when he returned and called a mass meeting at which he tried to explain his actions and the circumstances surrounding them.

In her book, *Tucson*, Bernice Cosulich quoted Harry Drachman, a prominent citizen, as saying, "I heard Manlove and others cuss out Stephens; never heard such language in my life; terrible profanity." The audience drove Stephens off the rostrum with a shower of ripe eggs, rotting vegetables and, some say, a dead cat.

Tucson now tried to ignore the fact that it was the home of a university. Only J. S. Mansfeld, who had been appointed a member of the Board of Regents, bothered to qualify and but for him the university might easily have been lost. The Legislative Act had provided that Tucson, Pima County, or private citizens must contribute forty acres of land for a campus within a year or the appropriation would lapse, but the people folded their hands and no one offered a square foot of land. Mansfeld wrote appointees who had failed to qualify and said they should either take the oath of office or resign. When three of them stubbornly refused to act he persuaded the Governor to make three new appointments, and on November 26, 1886, the Board met in Tucson for its first session after having raised a fund privately to bring R. L.

Long, Superintendent of Public Instruction, down from Phoenix to make a quorum.

The Regents who attended the historic meeting were J. S. Mansfeld, a naturalized citizen from Prussia, who was a vigorous friend of schools and libraries; Probate Judge John S. Wood, whose office made him County School Superintendent; M. G. Samaniego, mail contractor and cattleman; Charles M. Strauss, a former mayor of Tucson; and R. L. Long. Dr. John C. Handy, a prominent Tucson physician and surgeon for the Southern Pacific, was chosen Chancellor. The Regents looked on him as an excellent choice because he was a college graduate and highly respected in the community.

Neither the county nor the town had shown the slightest interest in providing land for a campus. Only the indomitable Mansfeld refused to give up hope. On May 3, 1886, he walked over the desert, on the mesa east of Tucson, and on that day he selected the site he wanted. All that summer and fall he pleaded with the owners to offer the Regents forty acres of the mesquite-covered land. Almost at the last moment they agreed, and the happy Regents inspected the property and immediately accepted.

The names of the three donors might well be preserved in bronze, but the printed word has served well and so it is known that they were E. C. Gilford, W. S. Reid, and B. C. Parker. "Billy" Reid was the owner of the finest saloon in Tucson. Gifford and Parker were gamblers.

The deed to the property was filed November 27, and that act established the University of Arizona in fact. There were no students, teachers, or buildings—only a barren campus of forty acres. But all this would change. There would be thousands of students, hundreds of teachers, dozens of buildings, and the entire State of Arizona would, in effect, be the campus.

CHAPTER 2

1887–1893

THE REGENTS must have felt the worst was over when the deed to the forty-acre campus was recorded and they could turn to the tasks of selling the bonds and making contracts with an architect and a builder. How wrong they were became evident as soon as the Fourteenth Legislature met in January, 1887.

Representatives of Cochise County, which had been part of Pima County until 1881, joined with members from Yavapai and introduced bills in the Council and House to repeal the University Act. If they could repeal the act, the $25,000 appropriation would be fair game for anyone who could muster the necessary votes.

Pima County, however, had two strong men in the Legislature. They were Charles R. Drake, president of the Council, and R. N. Leatherwood of the House. Together they beat down all amendments and substitutions and finally defeated the bill.

The Thirteenth Legislature had been so harshly condemned for its extravagance in hiring clerks that the Fourteenth used only the office help provided by the federal government. This resulted in no record being kept of the stormy debates and votes on the University. The rather sketchy reports in territorial newspapers remain. About all they show is that it was a knock-down-and-drag-out fight.

The next problem was raised by "kinfolk," or, in other words, a group of thirty-six Tucsonans who hatched an idea that $10,000 of the money in the hands of the Regents should be spent in developing an artesian well.

This was a period when such wells were held to be the magic solution of the water problem in Arizona. The Legislature was continually beseeched to offer awards for successful drillings. Therefore, why shouldn't the university, which was certainly going to need a well, spend some of its money on such a project?

Judge John S. Wood, of Tucson, had offered the suggestion that the Pima Board of Supervisors, School District Number One, and the City of Tucson merge their resources and bore a well to supply their own needs. *The Citizen*, however, said that since the community had waited for the university to do something about water, it might as well wait a little longer. In fact, *The Citizen* thought it had inside information that the deal was set, for it said:

> The people all over the Territory will watch anxiously the results of the artesian well that is to be bored on the university grounds. Should they succeed in having a good flow of water, property in and surrounding Tucson will double in value. When the company that is to bore for the University has finished their contract, they will no doubt offer favorable terms to other parties desiring wells. This question ought to be demonstrated as quickly as possible, as so much depends on the result.

The Regents, who were trying to get favorable bids on both a drilled and a dug well, told their secretary to ask how much the community would contribute in cash. They got no answer to this, so they finally settled the problem for the time being by authorizing the expenditure of $100 to clear out an old Mexican well on the campus grounds. After this, *The Citizen* dismissed the whole affair by reporting:

> It is with sincere regret that we are called on to announce the abandonment of the proposed artesian well project on University grounds. The success of this enterprise would have done more to settle the water question in Arizona than all else combined.

Between arguments over the well, the Regents had carried on their efforts to get plans and bids on a suitable building and had offered a bonus of $500 to the architect whose plans were accepted. They began the search in March but it was August 31, 1887, before the following entry appeared in their minutes:

> All members of the Board expressing themselves as anxious to proceed with the erection of the building to be known as the School of Mines [Note: this was the original name of Old Main] and the plans and specifications as furnished by C. H. Creighton being incomplete and unsatisfactory, it was decided to accept those portions which could be used and advertise for building proposals.

M. H. Sullivan, a Tucson builder, bid $37,969 for the complete building and $24,893 for "certain portions of the work." If the Board accepted the second bid, the additional work would eventually cost $12,766. Sullivan got the contract on condition that he post a bond of $5,000 and give the Regents the right to order the work stopped when they ran out of money. Captain A. E. Miltmore, USA, then offered his services free as superintendent of construction. The Board gladly accepted and proceeded to break ground on October 27, 1887.

The Star gave good coverage to the event, and subscribers read the following account the next morning, under the headline, An Important Event.

> A large and impromptu assembly of citizens were present at the breaking of ground for the University of Arizona yesterday afternoon. The location of the site is on the high plateau, northeast of Tucson, near the road leading to Fort Lowell.
>
> Forty acres of ground some time ago was donated for University purposes, most of which has been cleared off and put in order.
>
> The public schools were closed yesterday afternoon and all the pupils repaired to the ground where they made a bright and cheerful appearance.
>
> A howitzer was on the ground which gave the signal for starting the proceedings.
>
> Chris Christensen had a fine team from his stables, bespangled with ribbons, which drew a brand new plough, furnished for the occasion by Messrs. Stevens & Hughes.
>
> Prof. Young, principal of the public schools was requested to select one of his pupils to 'break ground.' The professor let the choice to a vote of the advanced class and the choice fell upon Miss Milly Coker.
>
> At precisely four o'clock the howitzer roared, the horses with the plough started and Miss Milly Coker performed the ceremony of "breaking ground." She was tastefully dressed in white and looked as handsome as a summer rose and she did her task well.
>
> Hon. Charles M. Strauss, Territorial Superintendent of Public Instruction, made some very appropriate remarks and introduced Rev. G. H. Adams who offered up an earnest prayer in behalf of the important work just inaugurated.

> Hon. C. C. Stephens, the father of the bill creating the University, and who carried it through the 13th Legislature, was next introduced and made a short but very eloquent address.
>
> It was, in fact, one of the best efforts we have ever heard Mr. Stephens make, and we have heard him many times.
>
> After Mr. Stephens' address and a salute from the howitzer, the assembly was dismissed.
>
> There were about 600 who witnessed the ceremony.
>
> John Bolyn's big daisy was utilized as a rostrum for the speakers and about 50 children rode on it back to the city. They looked like a big boquet of flowers and had a jolly time singing.
>
> The MacKanlass Specialty Company furnished the music for the occasion gratis. They were out in style and rendered elegant music. Their generosity will not soon be forgotten by Tucson people.
>
> There were many pleasant incidents which we must omit, but it is sufficient to say that although the whole business was an impromptu affair, it was a success as a public occasion.

Several days later *The Star* published Stephens' address in full. It was in the style of eloquence admired in the eighties, and this time no one in the audience threw spoiled eggs, soggy vegetables, or dead cats at the speaker.

It must have been an outstanding hour in the life of the man who had been cursed for bringing an institution of higher learning to Tucson, when he arose as the principal speaker at the ground-breaking ceremony for the university he had fathered. Certainly the least that can be done now is to publish his address in this history of the University of Arizona:

> Twenty-five years are a long time in the life of a man but only a day in the life of a state. And yet it has hardly been that length of time since a few dauntless pioneers, the skirmish line of our advancing Anglo-Saxon civilization, crossed the great rivers to the east and west of us and successfully disputed step by step the possession of the relentless Apache to this wonderful land full of the crumbling monuments of a great pre-historic people, and endowed with

a more genial climate and greater natural resources than any other part of the Union.

The toils, struggles, dangers and sacrifices of the Arizona pioneer have never been and can never be written and suffice it now to say that to them we owe this most auspicious day. They broke the ground and laid the imperishable foundations of the political Commonwealth of Arizona, and today in the natural course of events of the building of a state, we, the pioneers of its thought and mental culture are breaking the ground and laying the foundations for all time of the future social, moral and intellectual Commonwealth of Arizona.

And as the achievements of the mind are greater than the deed of the body, and intellectual culture higher in the scale of life than bodily training, so greater is this day than any which has preceded it in the history of the Territory and greater than any other in moulding the destiny of the Southwestern portion of our domain.

Surrounded by bronzed and stalwart pioneers with their wives and children whose fortunes and futures are indissolubly linked with the frontier; the Apache signal fires having hardly died out from the surrounding mountains, the ancient and honorable pueblo of Tucson, beneath us in the valley bordered by the emerald fringe of the Santa Cruz, and the whole weird landscape of mountains, mesa and valley radiant with the suffused, ineffable and indescribable glory of an Arizona sunset, a moment of retrospection is in order.

In the famous, (sometimes called notorious) 13th Legislature, a portion of the delegation from Pima County, Honorable R. N. Leatherwood and myself in the Upper House and Honorable S. M. Franklin in the Lower House, fully appreciated the great advantages to our infant Commonwealth of a liberally endowed University, and that that portion of the Territory where it should be planted would derive from and through it more material wealth and progress than could be had from any aggregation of all other state institutions. But we rested not on this low plane. We looked onward and upward. With eyes of faith we saw in the comparatively near future upon this commanding site amid this magnificent panorama of nature's handiwork, the tasteful ornate yet utilitarian edifices of the University; we saw its cool verandas, its broad porches, its silvery fountains, its shaded walks, its academic groves, its crowded halls of thoughtful students, gathered from mountain and canyon and mining camp and stock range and the valleys for a thousand miles around, quaffing with sparkling eyes and eager delight of the ever-living fountain of the learning of all ages, their countenances illumined with the clear light of eternal truth, their souls hungering and thirsting for that knowledge which is more precious than rubies and above all price.

I prepared the bill with the assistance of my friend Judge DeForest Porter of Phenix [*sic*], and March 5, 1885, introduced it as Council Bill No. 76 with the invaluable assistance of my colleague, Honorable R. N. Leatherwood and other enlightened members of the Council. After a long struggle it was passed and went to the Lower House. There it was taken charge of by Honorable S. M. Franklin and despite the most violent and determined opposition he bore it as a banner aloft to victory. I shall never forget his successful strategy nor his fervid and all-persuasive eloquence.

In the 14th Legislature the enemies of the University returned in increased force and with renewed determination to destroy it, but the Honorable Charles R. Drake and the veteran Leather-wood stood as a stone wall between the foundling and the blind attacks of its blinder foes, and it was saved forever.

And to your faith, courage and persistent labors, gentlemen of the Board of Regents, many generations of scholars who shall yet tread this hallowed ground will pay homage.

And adown the ages when this seat of learning shall have won the prestige of its centuries, when its serried ranks of alumni shall successively from its halls have gone forth into life, their names adorning the cloister, the forum, the marts of trade, the halls of science and literature, their statues in the niches of fame and our bodies resolved to the dust of our mother earth and our names utterly forgotten, it may be that some pale faced dreamer of the school—its historical alumnus—will from its musty time-stained and cob-webbed

> records, rewrite our names as the obscure men of a remote age, unknown in history or in song, on the confines of a doubtful civilization, environed by all which was gross and material, who did not forget, though with dimmed vision and clouded mind, the great debt they owed to posterity and in their weak way and halting manner they tried to pay it.
>
> The world may forget its heroes but shall remember its teachers. The name of Alexander may fade from the scroll of history but the name of Plato, never; and the memory of this day and its actors we trust will live as long as men walk the earth, aspiring toward intellectual growth and progress, revering liberty of mind and cherishing independence of soul.

When it was all over both *The Star* and *The Citizen* made brief editorial comments. *The Star* said:

> Some of the people who were out at the University grounds where the ceremony of breaking the ground was performed and heard the remarks made and observed the enthusiasm displayed came to the conclusion that the 13th Arizona Legislature was not so bad after all, especially as compared to the 14th.

The Citizen remarked, "The building will present a very fine appearance from the depot and prove a good advertisement for the city." These comments weren't exactly enthusiastic, but they were the first kind words the University had received from its home town.

The Regents needed a few kind words, too, for there was trouble on the Board. Dr. John H. Handy, the Chancellor, as the head of the Board of Regents was known at this time, had been chosen with care and great hopes but had proved a hard man to work with and finally absented himself from meetings for six months without explanation.

G. J. Roskruge and Selim M. Franklin, who were serving as Regents, made and seconded a motion that Secretary Charles M. Strauss call the Chancellor's attention to his neglect and lay special emphasis on his failure to approve minutes of the meetings as prescribed by law.

No reply was received from Dr. Handy, and when the Board questioned the secretary about this on October 1, he admitted he had failed to write the letter. So the Board told him to write immediately and to include a warning that unless the Chancellor appeared at the next meeting, his office would be declared vacant. The warning was ignored and Dr. Handy was removed. J. S. Wood was chosen to fill the vacancy with the title of president of the board.

As the records show, the Regents had been patient with their chancellor. One reason was that during the months when he attended meetings, Dr. Handy had taken a deep interest in the progress made on the plans and the building. This could not be overlooked too readily and neither could the fact that the doctor was greatly admired in Tucson, even though he was a man with a violent temper. In her manuscript on the history of the University, Miss Estelle Lutrell gives Regent G. J. Roskruge as authority for the statement that Dr. Handy had quarreled with Secretary Strauss and thereafter had ignored the Board.

Three and one-half years after he had been dismissed by the Board of Regents, Dr. Handy sued for divorce and declared publicly that he would kill any attorney who took his wife's case. Despite the threat, Attorney Francis J. Heney announced he would appear for Mrs. Handy and this led to a fatal encounter which the *Weekly Citizen* reported under the headline, *THE DEADLY BULLET*.

According to the testimony of an eye-witness, Handy and Heney met on the street. Handy growled, "What are you looking at?" and caught Heney by the throat. Heney pulled a gun which was discharged as the two men wrestled. They went down in the dust still fighting, with the gun between them.

It was noon and a courthouse crowd gathered around the struggling men. "Don't shoot! Don't shoot!" some of the bystanders begged and Heney, looking up from his fight for life, answered, "If he'll let go of the gun I won't shoot."

A deputy sheriff finally pulled them apart and only then was it discovered that the doctor had been wounded. He was taken home, where he died. Heney surrendered immediately, but the hearing was deferred until after the funeral.

Hundreds turned out for the Masonic services and double lines of citizens, many in tears, filed past the coffin for almost an hour. Then the funeral cortege was formed. Led by the Philharmonic Band, two military companies, members of the Masonic Lodge, and a delegation of Arizona pioneers, unnumbered and unknown people followed the hearse to the Southern Pacific station.

Heney took the stand later in his own defense and gave his account of being threatened and then attacked. Witnesses corroborated what he said, and when the court finally ruled the homicide justifiable, the crowded courtroom broke into cheers.

The Citizen disposed of the affair with a paragraph in which it said:

> Dr. Handy had many noble traits and was skilled as a physician and surgeon, but when he boldly announced that he would kill the man who took his wife's case in the divorce suit he had entered against her, he set the law at defiance and denied to his wife under penalty of death a right accorded even criminals—a defense at the bar of justice.

Some of Dr. Handy's arguments with fellow Regents were the result of his insistence that the University building should not be over one story in height. Others wanted a two-story building that would stand up boldly on the mesa. The final result was a compromise that resulted in the structure so familiar today.

Many years after the building had been erected, C. H. Creighton, the architect, said, "We had to cut corners in those days. We sank the structure six feet below the surface so the ground itself would help support the building."

Earth removed in excavating for the first floor was not wasted but was baked into brick in a kiln on the campus. The cut stone used for the walls of the first floor came from a quarry south of the Ajo road. Lumber, however, had to be shipped by rail from San Diego.

Two theories on the architecture of Old Main have come down through the years and caused endless arguments. One is that Architect Creighton and the Board of Regents developed a "classic example of early American architecture," employing the long verandas and high ceilings that were the only cooling devices known in pioneer days.

Creighton seems to have had no such idea, for he wrote a letter to Dr. Robert H. Forbes in 1946 in which he said, "The whole building is an European adaptation, even to its curved French mansard roof."

The second theory is that there wasn't enough money to enclose the required amount of floor space within the walls, so the porches were added and the space thus sheltered was included in the total count. Here, too, a lovely story is blown sky-high by the architect, for Creighton's letter continues, "My recollection is that we did not figure on the floor space covered by the porches. The two floors of the main building made room for the space required by the bill passed by the Legislature for the needs of classrooms and other requirements." Creighton's letter is in the files of the Arizona Pioneers' Historical Society.

Plans, building, and finances kept the early Regents busy but they did not shirk their responsibilities. Week after week they visited the building to check on the quality and progress of the work and often found it necessary to call special meetings. Their chief worry was how far they could stretch the $25,000 appropriation and their worst fears were realized when they ran out of money before the roof was completed and the doors and windows were in. There was nothing they could do then but ask the Legislature for more money and they made such a convincing plea that a bill was passed levying a tax of three-fourths of a mill "for the erection and furnishing of suitable buildings and maintenance of the University."

That might have been almost enough, but the University became the victim of a legislative brawl that is famous in Arizona history. It was the by-product of the national victory of the Republican party that put Benjamin Harrison in the White House.

Governor C. Meyer Zulich was a Democrat, and Harrison made it known that he intended to replace Zulich with Lewis Wolfley, a Tucson Republican. The Territorial Democrats hoped that Zulich and the Legislature would complete their work and adjourn before Wolfley was appointed. But the Republicans countered by delaying the session ten days beyond its prescribed term. Zulich retaliated by refusing to sign the eleven final bills and hiding them in one of the pigeonholes of his desk. The University bill was among them.

Phoenix fared better than Tucson at this session of the Legislature for it won the territorial capital away from Prescott about as soon as the chaplain had concluded the opening prayer. No time was wasted in making the move. The members immediately adjourned, boarded a train for Los Angeles, took another to Phoenix—traveling, of course, on passes—and then re-opened their deliberations.

An interesting sidelight on the removal of the capital is found in the vote of the Pima County delegation which, with one exception, voted for Phoenix.

The case of the "lost laws," as they were called, was taken to the courts where the bills were validated, but in the meantime the university building remained roofless. The Regents succeeded in making arrangements with L. M. Jacobs of the Consolidated Bank of Tucson to pay pressing claims and then had to let the skeleton remain as it was.

The Board, however, did not spend all its time worrying over finances. The minutes of a meeting held in July, 1889, show that it must have found time to practice parlor magic, for without a building, a faculty, or money, it set up a paper School of Agriculture with one professor and director of a non-existent experiment station. The purpose was laudable, for the Board wanted to convince the government that Arizona was in line for the $15,000 granted annually to schools of agriculture under the terms of the Hatch Act. The means employed were devious. The Regents simply looked around the conference table, selected Selim M. Franklin, who was the only member with a college degree, and named him professor of agriculture without salary. Franklin was an attorney and knew nothing about agriculture but he took the post and, to the amazement of even the Regents, the University received an initial award of $10,000. It was pure manna from heaven.

The next year, however, was the one that must have silenced the critics who had made the University of Arizona the butt of endless dreary jokes, for it was in 1890 that the Regents became masters of legerdemain and started pulling rabbits out of hats. They not only got the full grant of $15,000 a year from the Hatch Act but also $15,000 from the second Morrill Act. The second Morrill Act gave $15,000 annually to every state and territorial institution that was teaching agriculture, increasing the grant by $1,000 a year for the next ten years. Important also was the fact that the grant permitted the use of the funds to pay teachers of English, science, and mathematics.

In addition to this federal aid, the Board had reasons to expect $15,000 from the Legislature, and it is not surprising that the secretary grew overly optimistic when he noted the good fortune in the minutes.

"It is hardly probable," he wrote, "that any further appropriations will be asked for some years to come, as almost the entire appropriation of the school will be paid from Congressional appropriations."

The Regents were entitled to a chance to gloat. They had given unlimited time and effort to what had often seemed a thankless if not a hopeless task. They had made one dollar do the work of two dollars, and part of the time they had worked with an empty treasury. Eventually, through faith and persistence, they had lifted themselves by their own bootstraps and pulled the University up with them to a peak from which they could see a sure future.

Twenty per cent of the Hatch funds was available for buildings, and with money in the bank the Board hurried work on the building and began to plan on a faculty and to look ahead to the installation of laboratories for mining and agriculture. Franklin stepped out as a professor and the Board appointed its first paid faculty member in 1890. He was Professor Frank A. Gulley, a graduate of Michigan State Agricultural College, who had been professor of agriculture in Mississippi Agricultural College for four years and director of the Texas Experiment Station for one year.

Gulley came to Arizona as Dean of the School of Agriculture, and in the months that preceded the actual opening of the new University he worked with enthusiasm and driving energy. While his principal task was to select a faculty, he did much more than that. He issued and distributed the three first bulletins on agriculture. They were very simple, but they were tokens of the service the University would furnish to the farmers of the state. Between bulletins the energetic dean designed and equipped a small laboratory for the experiment station, conferred with the Regents on a curriculum, and selected sites for field stations at Phoenix, Tempe, and Yuma. Somewhere along the way he found the time to direct the sinking of a campus well 100 feet to a plentiful supply of water and the installation of a steam pump that was fired with mesquite wood.

In arranging the curriculum, the Regents ruled that while most of the federal funds were earmarked for the School of Agriculture and the University Experiment Station, the School of Mines deserved full consideration. They further ruled that both schools should have deans who would share equally in standing and responsibilities.

October 1, 1891, was set as the opening day of the University, and with one exception the staff was present and ready for work. Gulley had recommended Dr. Theodore B. Comstock, a graduate of Cornell, as Dean of the School of Mines. C. B. Collingwood, who was to be agricultural chemist, came from Gulley's alma mater. The other faculty members were J. W. Toumey, professor of botany and entomology, V. E. Stollbrand, professor of mathematics and irrigation, and H. J. Hall, instructor in English. Hall arrived late, but he was to outlast them all for he stayed thirteen years, during which time he became the University's first librarian.

One thinks of today's great faculty of nearly 1,000 men and women and wonders how the original six could have been adequate even for a beginning. As a matter of fact, they were more than equal to the task before them, for they were qualified men who would have been welcome in any agricultural or mining college.

These new teachers probably expected that the frontier university building would be primitive and crude, but even so they must have been surprised when they arrived and discovered that the interior had not been completed. Professor Howard J. Hall always remembered with amusement that in the first months the married men of the faculty and their families lived behind cloth partitions tacked on wooden frames. Unmarried men had similar quarters and male students who lived on campus shared a large dormitory on the second floor. Everyone ate in a dining room presided over by a Chinese cook who had been left without a job when Fort Lowell was abandoned.

The Regents apparently accomplished a housing miracle in the main building, for they crowded in classrooms and laboratories for agriculture and mining, an assembly hall and library, offices for the two deans, living quarters for professors and students, a study room, dining room and kitchen, space for a territorial weather bureau, and a darkroom for the development of blueprints. A wooden structure that housed a stamp mill with power machinery to crush, concentrate, and reduce ores stood east of the main building. There were hitching posts for the cow ponies some of the students rode to school in a cloud of dust and, later on, a shelter and corral were built for the horses and buggies used by professors on their field trips.

Twenty-seven years had passed since the First Territorial Legislature had established the University of Arizona with provisions for a Board of Regents and had written a constitution for the university. Six years had gone by since the "Thieving Thirteenth" had failed to give Tucson the capital and had given the city a University it didn't want. Now, on October 1, 1891, the long years of waiting and struggle came to an end as the bell in the east tower of the building rang out its invitation to the youth of Arizona to come to college.

Thirty-two students enrolled for the first semester, but only six of them entered the freshman year of the university course. Twenty-six had to be content with preparatory courses. What else could be expected in a Territory where there were no high schools?

Even though there was no ivy on the outside walls, there was no nonsense inside about the teaching methods, the grades, or the discipline. A student who got 75 passed. One who had 86 passed with credit, and anyone fortunate enough to score 96 was in the honor class.

The failure of a student to do satisfactory work was more than a matter between himself and his teacher. Every such instance was reported to the full faculty at a regular meeting, and records show that the sessions were often devoted entirely to discussion of the work done by individual students. One result was that in three months, nine students were told to repeat work, and three were dropped. This, it must be remembered, was almost one-third of the total enrollment.

Most parents knew nothing about the University requirements and tried to enter so many thirteen-year-olds who should have been in the sixth and seventh grades that the faculty set fourteen years as the minimum age for admission.

In the beginning, the preparatory classwork covered one year. This was extended to two years in 1895, later to three years, and then to four. In 1891, the preparatory students struggled with arithmetic, English, American history, spelling, grammar, and geography. Professor Hall, who became principal of the preparatory school, once declared that he taught everything from "spelling to Cicero and from art to mathematics."

It would probably have been unwise for the Board of Regents to gloss over its difficulties in the annual reports it was obliged to make on the University, the Agricultural Experiment Station, and the College of Agriculture and Mechanic Arts. So the first reports that the Regents and Dr. Comstock, chairman of the faculty, made in December, 1892, present a full picture of trials as well as triumphs.

After reciting the history of the University, the Board said the popular contention that the school was premature was false, since it was not trying to rival Yale or Harvard but "to follow those lines that seem to lead to the best and immediate practical results of greatest value to the entire Territory." The School of Mines, it was pointed out, not only offered opportunities to the student but help to practical miners and to mine owners who wanted information on the most economical treatment of ore.

Of equal importance, the Board said, was the work in the School of Agriculture in testing soil and water, and experimenting with fattening feeds for cattle. Finally, said the Board, if one insisted on considering the University only from the standpoint of the economist, then one should remember that while the University had expended $92,800 of Territorial money, it had also received $113,500 from the federal government and its property value was $13,306 more than the gross expenditure of the Territory.

Dr. Comstock reported on the University and the School of Mines. He said that the departments covered agricultural chemistry, mining and metallurgy, mathematics, biology, civil and hydraulic engineering, English, literature, history, civics, physics, electrical engineering, drawing, modern languages, ancient languages, geology and mineralogy, botany, the arts, and business. Since there were only twenty-nine students at the time the report was written, it is possible that a number of courses were listed but not taught. Nevertheless, Dr. Comstock said in this first report that a beginning should be made on extension courses of value to people of mature years throughout the Territory.

As for the School of Mines, the director said that the demands on the time of his limited staff made it impossible for him to begin a systematic survey of Arizona's mineral resources. He reminded the Governor that, unlike agriculture, the Bureau of Mines got no help from the federal government and depended entirely on limited University funds.

Professor Gulley's report on the experiment station showed that it had not only published six bulletins for free distribution but also had given special attention to early fruits and vegetables at Yuma, and had made a daily analysis of the waters of the Salt and Colorado rivers. Furthermore, almost every irrigation system in the territory had been visited.

All this was in addition to the work in the classrooms where the faculty struggled with young students who had never been taught how to apply themselves or how to reason.

Apparently the main method was to exact strict obedience to all rules and to levy penalties on those who failed to conform.

Each student was permitted 150 demerits and there must have been a long list of offenses falling into the classification commonly called "misconduct," because five or six of these were usually discussed at most faculty meetings. Absence and tardiness were two offenses that always cost at least five points. Running on the balcony cost ten points. One boy who cut a class was not smart enough to leave the building and found that the faculty was not in a mood for fooling. He got fifty demerits. Misconduct during study hours usually drew a penalty of fifteen demerits. There was also a mysterious classification known as "conduct unbecoming a scholar and a gentlemen" which cost the guilty party fifty points. This, however, was easier than the fate met by two boys who were denied permission to attend a circus but slipped away and took a chance. The faculty considered their case very solemnly and handed out seventy-five demerits.

Weekly assemblies were always a source of trouble. They were held each Thursday morning and lasted an hour and a half. The programs alternated between a talk by a professor and a student paper or some class exercise. When 24 per cent of the student body finally cut one assembly, the faculty warned that thereafter all absences would be heavily penalized.

A boy who was scheduled to read a paper at the next assembly tried them out. He failed to appear and was fined thirty demerits. Two weeks later a second boy tried it. He got fifty demerits. The price was going up too fast for comfort, and there is no record that this particular offense was repeated.

There had been an unwritten rule that students who failed to complete assignments could make them up by taking an examination, but eventually the faculty felt it was being imposed on. So it established a fee of one dollar for each test and, since dollars were scarce, this broke up that practice.

Sometimes the faculty seems to have been lacking in a sense of humor, as in the case of a young man who trifled with the honor system. The system was being given a trial and students were asked to sign a pledge written on the blackboard. The pledge read, "I have not given or received any help." This didn't seem emphatic enough for one boy who added, "So help me, God." This so horrified the faculty that they failed him. It took both a written and a personal apology to wipe out the "0."

Yet, though the faculty was stern in enforcing discipline, the revealing records in the minute book show they were extremely kind in many ways. The professors not only gave individual attention to any student who was falling behind in his studies but also talked with the boys and girls about problems outside the classrooms and wrote reassuring letters to parents. When a mother in Jerome wrote, "Please take good care of my little boy," they did just that. If a boy didn't write home regularly and his parents complained, the dean had him in for a lecture. An anxious father who was concerned because his son got a few demerits for whispering during a study period was assured that the boy was merely careless.

Though the faculty was small, it had good teachers whose names were long remembered and whose influence lived on in the lives of their students. Mrs. Mary Walker Adams, who was a member of the first graduating class, never forgot Professor Hall and paid him a high tribute. "He was a fine English instructor," she wrote. "Under his guidance we learned to appreciate the great writers of literature. How glad I am to have had that privilege. We had a very fine faculty. Well prepared for their work and kind and helpful."

Mrs. Clara Fish Roberts still remembers Professor Collingwood with admiration, and there were others who recall Professor Toumey's botany field trips with pleasure.

Brewster Cameron, who began his college career in the preparatory class, was one who realized what superior teaching the beginners received from educators who were not too proud to step down from the college level and teach eighth- and ninth-grade courses. "We preps benefitted," he wrote, "by the largesse heaped upon us."

Physical education was not taught, and, since University life was supposed to be a very serious matter, there was no student activities committee to plan meets and games. Petitions for dances were denied and there were no campus entertainments in the early days. Sometimes groups held picnics on the desert, and Cameron says there was a football team that never lost a game because it never played one. Many years later he wrote:

> What a squad that was. For exercise we'd run through a few plays with the captain or quarterback calling some such signal as '7903.' We had goal posts too and the present team should raise a monument to Stan Kitt and me. We got posts in town and since we didn't have money to hire a dray we hauled them out ourselves, one end on each shoulder and the other ends dragging in the dust of the road.
>
> Our main recreation was chasing jackrabbits and throwing rocks at them.

Cameron doesn't mention it, but someone must have done more than throw rocks at the rabbits, for the faculty minutes of 1892 reveal that the dean asked the Board of Regents to prohibit the use of firearms on the campus.

There were no provisions for athletics for women, and Mrs. Roberts recalls that all she was allowed to do was bat a tennis ball about on a very rocky court while wearing a long white piqué skirt.

Considering the difficulty with studies experienced by students with limited educational backgrounds and the few opportunities allowed for working off youthful spirits, one has to agree that the behaviour pattern was far better than might be expected under similar circumstances today.

According to the old record book, the faculty held its first meeting September 23, 1891 and decided to meet every Friday evening at 6:30. Textbooks were approved at this meeting and professors were assigned to examine incoming students. Not until they had actually given the tests, and discovered what a small number of the students were prepared for university work or even for the advanced preparatory class, could the professors have realized that they must teach the fundamentals. In other words, before they could teach the special subjects for which they had prepared themselves, they must raise their own crops of students. Some might have resigned on the spot had they known it would be seventeen years before university students would outnumber beginners in the preparatory classes and twenty-three years before the preparatory classes would be abolished.

It is not remarkable that twenty-five members of the faculty resigned in the first ten years. What is really remarkable is that there were always good teachers willing to replace them.

The determination of pioneer legislators and Governor Goodwin to establish high standards of education in Arizona was matched in the young University by devoted Regents and professors who actually spoon-fed knowledge to a whole generation. Their determination to turn away no one who could possibly be taught was surely a jewel in the crown of the University of that day.

There is a letter illustrating the point. It was written by the president to a father who was afraid his son could not do the work in the advanced preparatory course. "Bring him to us," the president wrote, "and we will do the very best we can both in oversight and education."

Today's reaction to the University of the Nineties is often a tolerant smile and the remark, "It actually wasn't a University at all; just a rather poor high school."

This was untrue. The fact was that the young University understood the needs of its students and the problems of parents who struggled to give their children opportunities they had never known. How difficult that struggle could be is told in letters like these:

> Dear Mr. President: I cannot pay for my children's board this month but will pay by the middle of next month.
>
> Dear Mr. President: I enclose a money order for \$8.95.1 would have sent it sooner if I had been able to afford it.
>
> Dear Mr. President: I am sending you \$5. Please keep it and give some to Jesse as he needs it.
>
> Dear Mr. President: Inclosed is a check for \$75.00. I wish you would use some of this amount to pay for Willie during the fall term. Also if Willie should need any money for washing or other purposes I wish you would be so kind and let him have it.

The people of the territory of Arizona felt that, when the University took their children, it became a member of the family, and there is no doubt that the University responded by cherishing and cultivating that bond.

The Regents had to cope not only with troubles of parents but also with problems on the faculty. The first line in the minutes of the first faculty meeting said it was "called to order by President Gulley." This continued for five meetings and then the title was changed from "president" to "chairman." Professor Gulley explained in later years that he asked for the change because he felt the title of president was too pretentious for so small a school.

Much has been written and said in an attempt to prove that Gulley actually was the first president of the University, but the report of the Regents to the Governor shows this is not a fact. Gulley was the first professor hired. He recommended the other teachers and knew more about the school than any of these newcomers, so it was natural that he should serve in 1891 as the head of the faculty, but he was never president.

In 1892 Gulley's authority passed to Dr. Comstock, dean of the School of Mines and he, apparently, made a deep impression on the Regents, for on May 15, 1893, they abolished the Council of Deans and made Dr. Comstock sole chairman of the faculty with full responsibility for all departments and buildings except the experiment station. A few days later, the Board changed Dr. Comstock's title to president of the faculty but continued to leave agriculture in Gulley's hands.

When college opened again in the Fall, Professor Gulley revealed his sentiments toward Dr. Comstock by failing to attend the faculty meetings. The clash of personalities continued until the Regents put an end to it at the close of the academic year by creating the office of President of the University, appointing Dr. Comstock to the post, and accepting Professor Gulley's resignation.

The Regents acted after having listened to a report of a special committee, which said that the division of responsibility between the Dean of Mines and the Dean of Agriculture had proved unsatisfactory in practice. The faculty was informed of the change immediately, and the entry in their minutes is amusing. It reports the action of the Board in this language: "Meeting called to order by President Comstock to announce the import of resolutions passed by the Board of Regents. Moved and carried to adjourn."

An effort has been made to show from letters exchanged by Gulley and some of his contemporaries on the faculty that Dr. Comstock conspired with Governor L. C. Hughes to oust Gulley. An unidentified member of the faculty is also quoted as saying that Comstock was a "failure as a pioneer educator in Arizona," and that he "left a trail of bitterness behind him by scheming against those who had performed acceptable and fruitful service."

Interdepartmental quarrels usually leave a residue of charges and countercharges. They often do great damage, but in this instance the action of the Board of Regents mapped a course that helped lead the University to greatness.

The chart the Regents finally drew made the president the executive officer with authority over the School of Agriculture, the experiment station, the School of Mines, and all departments, buildings, and grounds.

Half a century later, Dr. Robert H. Forbes, who had been a member of the faculty under President Comstock, was to say:

> This definite consolidation of the two branches of University activities, which in other states have been divided and scattered, has been of extreme importance to the development of the University of Arizona.
>
> Dr. Comstock's connection with the institution may have been the outstanding service rendered in the consolidated organization and largely responsible for the development of the University among institutions of the Southwest.

CHAPTER 3

1893–1897

THE YEARS between 1885, when the Legislature actually established a university, and 1895, when the first commencement exercises were held, were filled with growing pains in the Territory. The period saw depression, panic, and lawlessness, yet the final total showed progress.

The worst was over in Tombstone, which had earned a reputation as the toughest mining camp on the Pacific slope in the period between 1880 and 1885. Murders, killings, and stage holdups in which U. S. mail was lost became so common there that President Chester A. Arthur finally issued a proclamation declaring a state of rebellion existed against the laws of the United States in the Territory of Arizona and warning the citizens that unless unlawful acts ceased by May 15, 1882, the federal government would send in the army to keep peace.

The warning was aimed principally at Cochise County, and Tombstone did cool off, but men continued to live and die violently there and in other parts of the Territory.

In 1885 in Holbrook two men accused of murder were lynched; the Valenzuela gang, which operated along the Hassayampa River, murdered Barney Martin and his family on the road to Phoenix to get their moneybags, and a year later murdered Joseph Gribble and two Vulture mine guards who were in charge of a bar of gold worth $7,000. The years 1887 and 1888 saw a bloody riot in the Territorial Prison at Yuma, two robberies of Wells Fargo express cars near Vail, and a gun battle on the main street of Florence when Pete Gabriel, a former sheriff, and Joe Ply shot out an argument.

The "Great Wham Robbery," as the papers called it, caused a furor in 1889. A party of masked men trapped and attacked Major J. W. Wham and an army escort on the road to Fort Thomas and got away with a $26,000 army payroll. Eight farmers and cattlemen from Graham County were charged with the holdup and brought to trial in Tucson. There were no convictions, and the public seemed to feel that the clever tricks of the defense attorneys were very funny; but no one laughed about a vicious little war breaking out that year in the Tonto Basin between the Grahams, who were cattlemen, and the sheep-raising Tewksburys. No one laughed because twenty-five Grahams and four Tewksburys were dead when the echo of the last shot died away.

These were also the days of Pearl Hart, widely known as the "Wildcat Bandit." Pearl and one of her friends, who called himself Joe Boot, held up a stage but were caught near Benson. The judge gave Joe thirty-five years in the penitentiary. Pearl got five. She claimed the only reason she looted the stage coach was that she had to have money to get to the bedside of her dear, old, sick mother.

Hangings were not uncommon although no other town equalled the record of Tombstone, where five men were hanged simultaneously on one gallows and a sixth lynched on Allen Street. These events were not exactly public, but sheriffs were always generous with printed invitations to executions. However, Governor N. O. Murphy took exception to a gold-edged bid sent out by Sheriff F. J. Wattron of Holbrook, which read: "The latest improved methods in the art of strangulation will be employed and everything possible will be done to make the surroundings cheerful and the execution a success."

The Governor issued a stay of execution until the cards were withdrawn, and the sheriff sent out a second invitation. This one read:

> I hereby invite you to attend and witness the private and humane execution of a human being. You are expected to deport yourself in a respectful manner and any flippancy or unseemly language or conduct on your part will not be allowed.

In days such as those, it was logical that there would be a hard core of citizens with little learning but vast prejudices who sneered at education and shouted that college was a waste of the taxpayers' money. The Graham County Bulletin represented their views when it said editorially in 1893:

> The Normal School at Tempe is of no earthly benefit to any section of Arizona outside of Maricopa County. Taxes for the maintenance of this institution are levied on many for the benefit of the few. The same applies to the Territorial University at Tucson where there are as many professors as students.

The truth was that the Arizona Territorial Normal School was training needed teachers for the weak public school system, while the University was years ahead of the people in its vision of Arizona's future. Its faculty members were doing far more than teaching a few high-school youngsters. They were carrying on studies and experiments in soils, river waters, plant diseases, insect pests, citrus fruit, date palms, sugar beets, range grasses, and various phases of mining, and, finally, they were constantly preaching the gospel of irrigation and the conservation of the territorial water supply.

Like all pioneers, the people who came to Arizona in its early years had turned their hands to the first occupation that offered steady work and wages, and this was mining. But by 1890 men were no longer tied to a single industry, for cattle and agriculture had made remarkable gains. N. O. Murphy, acting Governor, said January 19, 1891 "The Territory is admittedly richer and more prosperous than ever before, with all of our interests, agricultural, mining, grazing and otherwise of a commercial nature, steadily increasing."

Drought, over-grazing, and panics slowed down the cattle industry in the next few years, but it recovered and grew greater than ever.

Railroads had contributed to growth in population by making the Territory easy to reach from the East and West. One saw few wagons like those in which the early immigrants had made their laborious and dangerous way over the trails, although the hard-riding stagecoach continued to serve many sections for another decade.

Governor L. C. Hughes reported in 1895 that the population was "77,000 exclusive of Indians." There are no records of the white population in 1885, but there are figures for the public schools. These show the enrollment more than doubled between 1885 and 1895, climbing from 6,079 to 12,889, and, although attendance still lagged, it also doubled and rose from 3,507 to 7,641. But, sad to say, the average salaries fell from $78.00 to $68.54 a month, and the school term was shortened by twenty days. This was due to two factors: the depression of the early Nineties and the political situation. The Territory, and therefore the Legislature, was Democratic. The federal government was usually Republican, so the Territorial Governors were members of that party. They appointed Republican superintendents of public instruction who did not always work well with the Legislature.

Actually there was a third reason. The struggling Territory was deeply in debt. It owed $938,720, of which $234,620 was in warrants bearing interest at 10 per cent. Worse yet was the fact that under the founding act the Territory was responsible for debts incurred by cities and counties and these amounted to $1,273,620.

Governors had frequently called the situation deplorable, and in 1895 Governor Hughes finally went into detail. Pointing to annual reports that showed a shrinkage of almost $9,000,000 in property values since the year 1883, he said:

> It is fair to estimate that not more than half of the personal property is assessed and only a small portion is listed at more than half its value, and instead of Arizona's taxable property being placed at a fraction over $27,000,000, it should not be less than $100,000,000. . . . There are those who have their herds of stock assessed at much less than the actual number. In counties where there are thousands of blooded stock there are but few or none on the tax roll. . . . The same can be said of the value of improved real estate and corporation property. . . .
>
> There is a large amount of property and many industrial interests which are now exempt from the tax roll. . . . I would recommend that every interest which receives the protection of the law should be required to pay its just share of the cost of maintaining and enforcing the law.

Under conditions such as these, it could be expected that the public school system would suffer and that the University would not escape its share of hardships. The Legislature in 1892 abandoned a tax of half a mill on which the Board of Regents had depended to meet administrative expenses although it passed an act exempting railroads from taxation. The result was that the Board eventually reduced salaries at the University and dropped four members of the small teaching staff. This meant that scientists who should have been doing research, and whose work had suffered because they had been obliged to teach subjects outside their field, had to take on still more teaching. President Comstock referred to this in his 1894 report:

> We aim to provide for all demands made upon us, which it is possible to meet with our present equipment and faculty. To do this under existing circumstances requires a great deal of devotion and self-sacrifice on the part of the instructors who are often compelled to carry classes in subjects entirely outside of their line of work. . . .
>
> Until June 1, 1894, when the present regime was inaugurated, the position of President of the faculty was very onerous, owing to my inability to secure from every one of the professors a hearty response to such calls as were absolutely necessary for work outside their specialties. Those

> who willingly acceded to these demands, made only after loading myself with the largest proportion of this class of work, were thus more heavily burdened than was proportionately just, and, I regret to say, their ability to make the best showing before the Board in their specialties was thereby seriously impaired. This, I think, was indicated by the reduction of salaries which accompanied the material increase of work required from several, including the President, whose services were retained after the reorganization of the University.
>
> Although this feature did not encourage us in the belief that our previous sacrifices were wholly understood, I am well satisfied that the general plan upon which we are now working is the only practical means of conducting affairs economically and satisfactorily. . . . I desire to emphasize my high regard of the zeal and goodwill shown by every one of my present associates in the performance of duties assigned to them under circumstances which would have made many hesitate to continue. I sincerely hope that their service to the Territory, which can never be adequately compensated, will always be gratefully remembered.

The reorganization Comstock referred to was the abandonment of the original plan under which the dean of agriculture and the dean of mining had controlled the institution, and the appointment of a President who had full authority under the Board. The reference to cuts in salaries was his way of implying that the Regents had dealt unfairly with the faculty.

One of the extra jobs handed to the faculty was the building of an Arizona exhibit at the World Columbian Exposition, which was held in Chicago in 1893. The Legislature had authorized the participation in the belief that a display of "the resources of our great Territory" would interest outside capital, and this was help that Arizona had to have. Many mineral deposits had only been tapped. Arizona's valleys held a sure promise of great production if properly irrigated. Home capital could not finance the costs of such development, so some way had to be found to awaken outside promoters to the opportunities, and a skillfully prepared exhibit at the World's Fair seemed to be the answer.

A commission was therefore appointed and allotted $30,000. Then the tough end of the job of preparing exhibits was turned over in 1892 to the only men in the Territory competent to handle it. They were the young University's experts on mining, geology, irrigation, farming, botany, and animal husbandry. These were the same men who had just taken a pay cut.

President Comstock made arrangements with numerous mining companies for a large collection of gold, silver, and copper ores and shipped it to Chicago. The copper exhibit weighed seven-and-a-half tons and was displayed around a twenty-foot high copper monument, from the Copper Queen mine at Bisbee. Scores of samples of gold-bearing ore, including one weighing a ton, were arranged in cases along with samples of rich silver ore, competing for attention with sections of petrified wood and a seven-foot slab of polished onyx. These were flanked by models of Arizona mines that revealed the shafts, stopes, and drifts of their underground workings. Apache, Cochise, Coconino, Pima, Pinal, Mohave, Graham, and Yavapai counties contributed to the display, showing the wide distribution of the mineral wealth of the territory.

Professor Gulley drew big maps of the Salt River Valley, outlining the water courses and the extent of lands waiting only for irrigation to become productive. The agricultural display, however, failed to equal that of mining, and George F. Coats fair commissioner for Arizona, spoke sharply of the lack of interest shown by Maricopa County. He wrote an article for the *Arizona Gazette* in which he said that the county "had a chance of a lifetime to advertise agricultural sources but it was not taken advantage of."

After that criticism, Maricopa County pulled itself together and shipped canned and fresh oranges, lemons, olives, peaches, dates, plums, and grapes to open the eyes of thousands of people who thought the Territory was useless desert capable of producing nothing but rattlers, Indians, and cacti. The *Gazette* published a twenty-four-page special edition covering the history, riches, and opportunities of Arizona, and 20,000 copies were distributed at the territorial display. University professors contributed to this also, writing articles on soils, water, trees, and irrigation.

Pima County could not equal Maricopa's horticultural display but drew its share of attention with a scale model of the University carrying to prospective immigrants the message that Arizona assured them of an education for their children. The *Gazette*'s special edition paid a short compliment to the University in a single paragraph, which read:

> On the eastern side of the railroad track less than a mile from the depot on a commanding eminence is the University of Arizona; a stately edifice equipped with the most modern and scientific improvements. This institution is the pride of the people of Arizona and it receives their generous

> support. It is also the site of the United States Experimental Agricultural Station and the United States Weather Bureau and is rapidly taking rank with the best institutions of the kind in the country.

It was scarcely true that the University received the generous support of the Territory, and its enrollment of fifty-seven students certainly did not place it in a class with older land-grant colleges; but there was no doubt that the teachers who fashioned the exhibit had rendered great value to Arizona.

Some Eastern newspapers gave handsome publicity to the territorial display, and *Irrigation Age*, which was a magazine devoted to reclamation, filled a complete issue with Arizona features, justifying it with these paragraphs:

> First of all, Arizona appeals now to our interest because she is at the dawn of things. She has waited a long time for her day of development, but it is coming at last, and it now becomes a duty to study her irrigation resources and put them before the world.
>
> The second peculiar element of interest attaches to the fact that the soil and climate of Arizona make it certain that her development will take a different direction from that of other states.
>
> The third point of interest is that Arizona will be the field for projects of the greatest magnitude.

It is interesting to look back today and note that the University Experiment Station had realized immediately that one of its first contributions to the Territory must be made through experiments in irrigation. One of the very first bulletins issued after the University opened its doors was "Irrigation in Arizona," and the introduction carried the announcement that the Regents, "recognizing the vast importance to the territory, agriculturally and horticulturally, of a thorough knowledge of the present and possible development in irrigation resources, have established a chair of Irrigation Engineering."

The bulletin reported on irrigation canals then being supplied by the waters of the Gila and Salt rivers and pointed out sites for dams that would bring thousands of acres of untouched lands under cultivation. The Colorado River was excepted from this survey because it was not being used extensively at the time, but Professor V. E. Stolbrand, who made the survey, predicted:

> As the Territory fills up with people, the necessity for more land will be shown and demanded, and, in answer, Colorado's brown flood will be utilized as easily and completely as the importance of the subject will justify. Let this not be doubted. Far more difficult and costly works have been undertaken and successfully pushed to completion when public weal and hungry capital dictates.

The service the University was both prepared and willing to give in the study and development of irrigation was not overlooked by other scientists, and when the Second Irrigation Congress met in Los Angeles in 1893, Professors Comstock, Gulley, and Boggs were in attendance and Boggs was made vice-president of the National Executive Committee. The early foundations were well laid, for three years later the Irrigation Congress met in Phoenix, and the plans adopted there resulted in the building of Roosevelt Dam.

It must be remembered that the early professors got their knowledge of the resources and needs of Arizona the hard way. They made long journeys on horseback, in buggies, and even on bicycles over the rough desert and mountain trails, often baking under the sun at noon and sleeping under the cold stars at night.

The professors were not as glamorous as the tough-talking mountain men in greasy buckskins who had preceded them. They carried no rifles and drank no whiskey. Yet, while the mountain men left little lasting imprint on the Southwest, the university scientists changed the face of the Territory and raised the cultural and economic life of the people.

President Comstock said in his 1894 report that he frequently heard the University spent $40,000 a year for teachers, whereas it had actually spent $16,916 the previous year and of this amount the Territory had contributed a mere $2,647.49. All the remainder had come from the federal government. Furthermore, he reported, the Territory had paid only $5,390.11 for all university purposes in 1893.

Ruffled by the charges that the University was wasting money on high salaries, Dr. Comstock squared off again and swung some final punches. The salaries of the staff in the School of Mines, he said, were now provided by Congress, but as for the mining bureau: "There is not one dollar available for the work of the bureau itself aside from the meagre sums filched from the general territorial fund, a resource which has been wholly lacking for two years past."

Nor was there any money for traveling expenses. But by using his own horse, the President had covered 3,000 miles on tours of inspection through rough mining country, apparently during school vacation period. In spite of this effort, he said, he was frequently told that "the University was not doing all that could be wished by the mining community for the development of industry." His reply was, "We have done all that has been possible under the circumstances, and I may frankly say, much more than the people have any right to expect."

As he shut the door on the whole matter, he offered the suggestion that it would be a good idea if people investigated before condemning, because if they did they would end up by congratulating themselves.

Having told the critics off, the President noted that since the half-mill tax had been discontinued in 1892, the Regents had found it impossible to build the dormitory needed if students from distant parts of the Territory were to be accommodated. Then he sent his report to the Board of Regents, omitting both the usual, "Respectfully submitted," and his signature.

The Board stood by its president, approved his recommendations, and forwarded the report to Governor Hughes; but in spite of this support Comstock resigned his position in August, 1895, and went to California where he became a successful consulting mining engineer. One of his last official acts was to present diplomas to Charles O. Rouse, Mercedes Ann Shibell, and Mary Flint Walker on May 29, 1895. They were the first graduates of the University of Arizona.

It was a small beginning, but the *Arizona Star*, which reported the commencement in detail, said it was "a successful event in every particular." The School of Mines' auditorium was bright with cut flowers from University gardens, and the room was packed to the last seat by a crowd that listened patiently to a musical program and five speeches. The principal speaker was the Reverend Howard Billman, University Chancellor and Presbyterian clergyman who succeeded Dr. Comstock as president in September. The Reverend Mr. Billman was a native of Ohio, a graduate of Wabash College and Theological Seminary, and a prominent pastor in a Cincinnati pulpit before he came to Tucson for his health in 1888. Soon after his arrival in Arizona, Reverend Billman was appointed superintendent of the Indian School and filled that position for seven years.

The clergyman's only training as an educator and administrator was acquired at the Indian School and in his two years' service as a member of the Board of Regents and Chancellor of the University. But he apparently had no doubt about his own ability and immediately organized the institution on the lines of a church school and a military academy.

Daily morning drill was required of male students with a member of the faculty shouting commands until such time as the United States Army would furnish an officer, and a course in military science and tactics could be added to the curriculum. Women did not escape the new discipline, for while the men drilled, they were obliged to attend classes in physical culture and the rudiments of hospital service.

It was resolved by the faculty "that some measure of military discipline should be prescribed for the government of male students at all times while under the authority of the faculty." As a result, rules were established for conduct during study hour to insure that "proper position and decorum be observed at all times." Students who cut drills had to make up double the lost time, and all students were forbidden to leave the campus without faculty permission. Nine students challenged this rule and went to town without clearing their visit. They were fined ten demerits, suspended for two days, and compelled to put in fourteen hours of extra drill.

This kind if discipline led to trouble with some hard-rock miners who were taking a two-year course in assaying. Nobody was going to tell them they couldn't go to town at night! Eventually the rules had to be relaxed for these adults, and they continued their visits, which it is said, usually included calls at several saloons.

Members of the young cadet corps were given no chance to forget military discipline because they were required to wear smart, dark blue uniforms, and, if the regulations specified in faculty minutes were followed precisely, the corps must have been very handsomely turned out. Officers wore shoulder straps with the letters UA on a sage green background. Non-commissioned officers sported regulation West Point chevrons, and all trousers were adorned with a stripe of lustrous black mohair braid down the outside seams. Military caps were required at drill, and drab campaign hats were worn at all other times.

Many students asked to be excused from drill, claiming practically every known minor disability from catarrh to weak eyes and even "a tendency to suffer from stage fright." But the rules were seldom softened and those who broke them were sure of paying a penalty in demerits and walking a beat for long hours.

President Billman seems to have been deeply concerned over a problem faculty minutes refer to as "the separation of the sexes." The sight of happy boys and girls spending spare time together apparently shocked him, and he had a rule passed keeping men on the second floor and women on the first floor of the main building during the noon intermission. Even this did not seem to bring complete separation, so it was followed by another rule: "In going to and from the University, the sexes shall not intermingle or walk together between the railroad track and the university building." (A mule-drawn street car ran to the Park Avenue entrance.)

There was no graduating class in 1896, but Billman held commencement exercises for students who had completed the preparatory course. Governor Benjamin J. Franklin was the principal speaker, and the *Arizona Star* reported that "the building was thronged with the handsomest men and most beautiful women in Arizona."

Tucson's military band played a concert on the porch before the ceremonies and another in the corridor after the speeches. Parents of students were soon dancing, and their children naturally followed the example. What President Billman thought about this "intermingling of the sexes" is not known, for he took no action. One thing, however, is sure: it was the first time anyone danced at the University of Arizona.

The *Arizona Star* not only reported the ceremonies at length but also carried an editorial praising the progress being made by the school:

> The University of Arizona closes its term today and it can be truly said that it has been the most successful and satisfactory University year the institution has ever enjoyed. More than double the number of students representing the different sections of the Territory were enrolled and the progress made in every department has been most encouraging. The faculty is strong and each particularly fitted for the duties assigned him. Arizona can well feel proud of the University and the work it has accomplished in the past year. The same can be said of the experimental station which has made good progress during the year and gives exceptionally satisfactory results. The Board of Regents, the University faculty and all interested in this institution are to be congratulated on the good showing for the year just closed.

This was brave promotion and made good reading, but not all of it was true. For the size of the school, the faculty was indeed strong, and the experiment station was proving of great service to the Territory. But no student had graduated that year, and there was much criticism outside Tucson over both the immaturity of the students and the low registration. One charge was that Billman "went out and beat the bushes for little boys in knee pants and girls in pigtails." As a matter of fact, he did travel through the Territory and campaign for students, and in this he had the help of some members of the faculty who spent summer vacations as missionaries for the University without pay. Professor J. A. Rockfellow, who was principal of the preparatory school at the time, signed up thirteen students from Cochise County during Billman's first year.

It was not true, as charged by politicians, that "the average age of students befits attendance in a kindergarten," or that the University was nothing more than a "glorified Tucson high school." The president's report to the Board of Regents for the year 1896–97 carried a table showing that out of the 147 students enrolled, eighty lived outside Pima County, and President Billman added that "by actual computation the average age, including all in the preparatory school and excluding several students of mature years who are doing special work in the mining department, is above seventeen years."

The president's averages may have been accurate, but there is a reference in the faculty minutes of September, 1896, to the admission of three students who were less than fourteen years old, and another entry in October said the faculty favored accepting students "who are not quite prepared and allowing them to take work they can do."

There was good reason for the size of the preparatory school; it can be found in the fact that while a quarter of a century had passed since Governor Goodwin laid the foundations for a free public school system, the Legislature had administered school affairs with such ineptitude that there were no uniform courses of study in the grade schools, terms were short, 25 per cent of the children were not enrolled, and compulsory attendance was a joke. As for high schools, there was not one in all Arizona. So parents who hoped that their children might one day be educated men and women turned to the University and the University did its best to handle the job.

None of the buildings had been kept in good repair. A 50,000-gallon water tank and some small buildings, including the $600 wooden shack used as a dormitory for men, had never been touched by a paint brush. The steam boiler was so badly pitted that it could explode at any time, and the water pump was worn out. The Legislature had authorized the building of a stone dormitory but refused to provide funds for an essential addition. Finally, there were certain expenses, such as salaries of some teachers, general administrative needs, and labor which the federal government did not and would not pay. For these needs the Legislature allowed $5,500, of which $3,750 went to pay interest charges and to redeem bonds. This left the institution in such a depressed situation that the low morale of teachers and scientists was reflected in their annual reports. Some department heads made such brief statements that it was evident they were merely going through the motions required of them. Others with more iron in their makeup wrote comprehensive reports and spiked them with poorly concealed resentment.

William L. Devol, professor of agriculture, included comments like these:

> There has been but little addition to the facilities for instruction during the past year. . . . The department is very much hampered in its work because of some very urgent needs which it is not able to supply. . . . The livestock interests of Arizona are too great to be permitted to go longer without better facilities.
>
> The University is founded upon a grant providing for education in agriculture and the mechanic arts and the science appertaining thereto, and the rapid progress being made in the art and science of agriculture throughout the world necessitates the thorough education of the young men and women who are to occupy the farms of the great West in order that they may compete with educated farmers of other parts of the country.

As professor of agriculture, Devol was also director of the experiment station and he spoke out boldly on one of the station's greatest handicaps:

> During the session of the University a part of the time of the director—frequently as much as half of it—was employed in regular University work, as was that of other members of the station staff. During most of this time more than half the time of the irrigation engineer, meterologist, botanist and entomologist as well, was taken up by University work.

Everybody knew that the University was using government funds intended for agricultural research for other purposes, but Devol was the first to let the cat out of the bag in broad daylight. Eventually it cost him his job, because when the U. S. Department of Agriculture reprimanded him for failing to do more experimental work, he sent back word that he had small chance to get his hands on the funds earmarked for his use since the University spent so much of them for running expenses.

Governor Myron H. McCord, a short-term appointee of President McKinley, heard about Devol's answer and ordered him discharged immediately. No one stepped forward to back Devol up, and he was summarily dismissed. Professor Toumey was then appointed acting director of the experiment station, but politics interfered again. President McKinley's advisor, Mark Hanna, gave orders that the appointment should not be given to a member of the faculty, and Washington then sent on one Captain C. S. Parsons.

Miss Estelle Lutrell's manuscript is authority for the story that Parsons was a former livery stable man from Ohio who had served in McKinley's regiment during the Civil War. He served until the Board finally decided he was too ill to perform his duties and let him go.

Professor Devol paid heavily for his frankness, but he was not the only one who spoke up in the 1896 report to the Regents and the Legislature. Charles E. Barnsfeld, assistant professor in charge of the School of Mines, reported rather bitterly on the space and equipment allotted to him:

> This work is of the greatest practical value to the mining engineer, the chemist and the assayer, yet the facilities are very poor. Desk space is limited—only four men can be comfortably accommodated—even then the desks are inconvenient. Much time is spent in traveling from desk to sink and vice versa, often causing me much annoyance in my own work. How are we to accommodate seven at this desk? What provision can we make for possible new applicants? Four advanced students have to be placed at a desk intended for two. The light is poor and early in the afternoon becomes insufficient for weighing.
>
> In the assaying department the same conditions prevail. The furnace room is dark. The furnaces are too small and unhandy for the number of students. A large stationary furnace with good light is needed. In the balance room one can hardly turn around. There is room for but one student beside the instructor.

When it came to summing up, the director fired his last shot with a short fuse. He said, "The needs of the department are a conveniently arranged and properly equipped building."

Probably to Barnsfeld's surprise, the shot paid off a year later when Dr. James Douglas, on behalf of the Copper Queen Company, gave the University

$10,000 with instructions to use the income in the purchase of instruments for scientific research or special equipment necessary for the proper instruction of students in the department of mineralogy and the School of Mines. So far as available records show, this was the first research grant made to the University.

After the Regents' report had time to sink in, the Legislature sent a committee to Tucson to check on the University and see whether the complaints and criticisms of the president and professors were true. They too reported, and what they had to say was a queer mixture of praise, agreement, and fault-finding.

> The buildings were found to be over-crowded and out of repair, and the most pressing need seemed to be for more dormitory room. The best discipline is maintained by the faculty, consisting of 12 members, and there was every evidence of a prosperous educational institution of which the Territory may well feel proud.
>
> The standard for admission to the preparatory course we consider much too low—being reading, writing and arithmetic as far as fractions.
>
> The deplorable financial condition of our Territory demands the most rigid economy in our public institutions. We have no desire to cripple the University in the least degree, neither would we cripple our Territory with lavish appropriations, and to that end we suggest that appropriations for the University should be limited to absolute pressing needs.
>
> We recommend that no appropriation whatever be made by the present Legislature without the following proviso: That no person under 16 years of age be received in the Territorial University who has not completed the eight grades of public school work or its equivalent.

It was not an encouraging report, for while it admitted the difficulties under which the University labored, it was a complete repudiation of President Billman's zealous efforts to overcome the inadequate training provided by the public schools, and he resigned a few months later. First, however, he finished the school year and had the satisfaction of presenting diplomas to three graduates on Memorial Day.

The *Arizona Daily Star* reported that "there was a reasonably good audience" at the commencement ceremonies, and that music was provided by the Mandolin and Guitar Club.

Then the Reverend Mr. Billman stepped out of the picture, leaving his many troubles to Professor Millard Mayhew Parker who succeeded him.

President Parker brought more experience and ability to the school in the desert than either of his predecessors. Like Goodwin, the first territorial governor, Professor Parker was born in Maine. He attended Maine Wesleyan Seminary and was graduated with honors from Wes-leyan University, Middletown, Connecticut. After graduation he was a teacher and principal in eastern high schools for eight years and then went to Pasadena, California. There he founded Pasadena Academy, which was later merged with Throop Polytechnic Institute, which in turn was the forerunner of the California Institute of Technology. He was teaching Latin and Greek and was vice-president of Throop when he accepted the invitation from the University of Arizona in the Fall of 1897.

CHAPTER 4

1897–1905

EARLY PRESIDENTS of the University of Arizona served brief terms and Millard M. Parker remained only from 1897 to 1901. However, the institution completed its first decade of service under his guidance, and his years were marked by the University's increase in enrollment and by its sound academic progress.

The Regents' reports for the years 1897–99 are missing, but reports for 1900 and 1901 are available, and these, with some assistance from faculty minutes, give the sum of the progress made.

The Twentieth Territorial Legislature, which was the last to meet in the nineteenth century, opened a year after Parker took over at the University. Former Governor N. O. Murphy had been reappointed to fill the vacancy left when Governor M. H. McCord resigned to serve as the colonel of the First Arizona Regiment in the Spanish-American War. Murphy was favorably inclined toward higher education and saw to it that state funds were made available for the support and improvement of the University and the Normal School at Tempe. One of his most important moves was a campaign to convert a new building the Legislature had built for a reform school into what is known today as Arizona State College of Flagstaff.

Murphy went along with previous Governors in denouncing the old Arizona system of low valuation and high taxation of property. Land was valued at $1.56 an acre and the tax rate was approximately $3.50. The total taxable property in the Territory was valued at only $31,473,540. This included railroads and mines, a fact which brought a blast from the Governor who said that while it was harsh to accuse an honorable citizen of perjury, any man who made out a false statement of his taxable wealth and then took an oath it was true was guilty of "constructive perjury." Wealthy cattlemen, sheep growers, big corporations, and mine owners came in for the Governor's special attention.

Lawyers also felt the sting of the Governor's temper, for he took time to tell the Legislature that the Territorial Library was in bad condition—mainly because many books, which had been borrowed by attorneys, had never been returned and could be found in their offices from Arizona to Los Angeles. The Pioneer Historical Society, which was one of the favorite projects of the Legislature, was also in a bad financial condition.

President Parker was apparently not a complete stranger to politics, for he made it his business to visit the Legislature with some of his professors. The building program that developed may or may not be attributed to his charm, but he got what he wanted. A new dormitory for men, a manual-training building, and an assay laboratory were authorized, while one of the cottages was ordered remodeled for domestic science. Manual training and domestic science training were new departments. D. H. Holmes, an instructor with practical experience, did so well with the manual-training course that his work was praised in extravagant terms by a legislative committee.

The experiment station was busy as a swarm of bees in a field of blossoming clover. It had bought twenty-eight acres of land adjoining its Tucson farm and established a department of animal husbandry where it carried out experiments of great value to stockmen and dairymen. Three hundred and fifty acres of worn-out range were fenced and sown with native grasses to determine whether such land could be reclaimed. Much work was done on the experimental date farm near Tempe, where 445 young trees from Algiers were set out and nurtured. Efforts were made to establish sugar beets as an important crop, and studies were carried on proving that in some localities winter irrigation of orchards and deep-rooted plants could be followed to advantage.

Important as this work was, it is doubtful if it influenced the people of the State more than the bulletins and the series of leaflets, known as "Timely Hints for Farmers," which the station published. In all, 43,000 pieces of simply-written farm literature were distributed during the 1899–1900 school year alone and made hundreds of friends for the University among the very men who had been unwilling to believe that a college could put money in their pockets.

The School of Mines, which had been somewhat neglected, now began to furnish a dramatic type of service to other hundreds of taxpayers. It should be kept in mind that while agriculture had been getting much help from the federal government through grants supplied to the University, mining continued to be the greatest producer of wealth in the Territory, and many people spent all or part of their time searching for minerals. Sometimes their finds were worthless, but again they showed gold, silver, or copper. The difficulty was that few prospectors could tell rich ore from poor ore and therefore went to an assayer, who charged a high price for his service.

In its new assay laboratory the School of Mines took this service over at prices barely covering the cost of fuel and fluxes.

For $1.00 the school would test a sample for one metal and for $2.00 it would test for four metals. Fourteen hundred tests were made in one year, and while the University made no profit, it did have the satisfaction of performing an important service. The only drawback was the stamp mill, which made such a racket that teachers and students growled, and there was always a demand that it be moved miles away.

President Parker set up higher requirements for admission to the short course in assaying, mineralogy, and metallurgy. Students were required to be at least eighteen years of age and have sufficient knowledge of English, mathematics, and science to enable them to do the work to their own advantage. A higher standard was also set for preparatory students, who were now asked for twelve instead of nine credits when they applied for admittance. Finally, four-year courses of study leading to the degrees of bachelor of science and bachelor of philosophy were introduced, and these were capped by the master's degree in science and arts.

Athletics had been slow in developing on the campus. Outdoor basketball was introduced in the fall of 1896, and croquet was played in front of the girl's dormitory. There was an intramural tennis tourney during commencement week of 1897, and on January 27, 1898, the *Arizona Star* reported that a baseball team had been organized and was waiting a challenge. A Tucson team accommodated the students and, according to the *Star*:

> The U students were out in force and color to inspire their players but the town boys were too good and won by a score of something like 4 to 1. That is in that proportion for the scorer didn't have room to record all the tallies.

The two teams met again on Thanksgiving Day and this time the University made a better showing, but the contest must have been a wild one. The score was 13–13 in seven innings.

President Parker gave athletics a helping hand in his report to the Board of Regents. In it he said:

> Physical training is conducted at a great disadvantage owing to the fact that the institution has no gymnasium facilities.
>
> Athletic sports have become so important a part of college life that the absence of adequate facilities for physical training is a serious drawback to the symmetrical development of modern educational institutions.

> A building and equipment adequate for present needs might well be provided as soon as funds are available.

According to old timers, the first football was played on the ground now occupied by the auditorium and museum. The second field was about where the library and humanities buildings stand, and this was the athletic field until 1912. Then, there was a third field east of the College of Agriculture where the teams played until the present field was opened in 1929. There was no grass on any field until 1917 and team spirit must have been high to keep the boys playing on the hard and often stony vacant lots.

George M. Parker, the president's son, was captain, in 1899, of the first eleven to schedule games with outside opponents. It was not much of a team, for it lost to Tempe Normal 2–11, lost to Phoenix Indian School 0–11, nipped a town team 5–0 and finally beat a team of boys from the Tucson Indian Training School 22–5.

President Parker had the true executive's ability to select and surround himself with good men. Some of the members of his faculty remained with the University for many years and gave such outstanding service to the institution, and to Arizona, that their names are carved deep in the history of the Commonwealth. Among his appointees were G. E. P. Smith, professor of civil engineering and physics, Frank Nelson Guild, professor of mineralogy, and J. J. Thornber, professor of botany.

Dr. Smith, who joined the faculty in 1900, was transferred to the Agricultural Experiment Station in 1907, where he was placed in charge of irrigation engineering. The University library lists thirty publications bearing Dr. Smith's name, and there is no way of determining how many speeches he delivered or how many times he was called on for expert opinions on the use and conservation of Arizona's water supply. Among his many publications is an old bulletin entitled *The Colorado River and Arizona's Interest in its Development*. In it, Dr. Smith presented a panoramic view of the geographic, economic, and political problems that confronted the people in the fight to capture the water necessary for the irrigation of their arid acres. He closed his survey with a paragraph that shows how wide his vision was:

> Arizona's future is, to a high degree, wrapped up in the development of the Colorado. The highest statesmanship is demanded at this time that the latent wealth of this great natural resource may be wisely and speedily secured and that this great Commonwealth may share its benefits in the largest practicable measure.

Professor Guild, joined the faculty in 1897, and for 42 years exemplified in the university community the able and dedicated teacher and research worker of the basic physical sciences.

His first title was that of Professor of Mineralogy. Later he served both as professor of Optical Mineralogy and Professor and Head of the Department of Chemistry and, still leader from 1923 on, gave full time to his special field of Optical Mineralogy.

He did much to develop work at the University of Arizona in mineralogy and in chemistry, and to lay a firm foundation for later developments in these fields.

Professor Thornber was brought to Arizona in Dr. Parker's last year, and time would show how wise had been the selection of this deceptively quiet man. A botanist, first and last, for half a century he helped educate generations of farmers and cattlemen. Among his valuable publications are his work on the 375 species of plants and grasses of Arizona, and the bulletin on seventy-five poisonous plants dangerous to cattle.

Thornber rode the ranges of Arizona in a buggy during his earlier years. The student newspaper sometimes spoke of his return from a journey of several hundred miles. It was not unusual for him to wear a derby hat on these expeditions, and while they may have smiled at his headgear, the tough cowmen and farmers respected his knowledge and advice.

Reminiscing about his experiences with the people he met on his travels, Thornber said he was always treated with courtesy wherever he went. "On the whole," he said, "they really wanted to learn and appreciated any help I could give. The remembrance of their warm hospitality has stayed with me."

The professor was probably as well known for what he called his "skunk boat" as he was for his derby hat. The "boat" was a canvas box without a cover, the sides of which were pulled up as high as they would stretch and tied to the buggy and convenient trees. Thornber frequently slept on the range under the stars, and since skunks were what they are today, only far more numerous, he took no chances but spent the night in the "boat," leaving the animals to prowl around outside.

Professor Thornber was director of the Agricultural Experiment Station from 1921 to 1928 and Dean of the College of Agriculture from 1922 to 1929. Many agricultural bulletins issued over a period of forty years bear his name. There are no southwestern libraries and probably few farm or ranchhouse book shelves that do not have some of his writings.

All this would seem to have been enough for one man to accomplish, but Thornber made one other contribution that changed the scenery of the Southwest and provided comfort as well as beauty when he fathered the introduction of the tamarisk tree from Africa.

As Thornber remembers it:

> I saw an article which a French scientist in Africa wrote about these trees. I sent him a letter asking if he would send me a dozen cuttings. He did and all but two of the cuttings lived after they were set out in the introduction garden on the campus. When we found them to be a sturdy, fast growing tree which provided much shade and needed little care, we gave away cuttings to all who wanted them and so our experimental trees became the ancestors of thousands of trees one now sees in Arizona.

It was President Parker who discovered Dr. Robert H. Forbes, now Dean Emeritus of the College of Agriculture and invaluable friend of Arizona and the University. Forbes was busy at work as a chemist for the experiment station; but Parker realized that he had a man who needed a wider field, and made him director of the station, a position he held with distinction for eighteen years. A later president would name him Dean of the College of Agriculture in the year 1915–16. It was an honor long overdue, for Dr. Forbes had actually been in charge of all agricultural work since 1899. He held the deanship until the British government called him as an expert consultant on agricultural work in Egypt in 1918. After that came a tour of duty in the French Sudan. Dr. Forbes' interest in the University and the state he helped to build did not end with his tours of duty in Africa. Rather, he returned to Tucson and served in the State Legislature for fourteen years, until 1952. His gifts to the University, which honored him with the title of Dean Emeritus of the College of Agriculture, have been numerous and important. Probably the most important and certainly one which added to the beauty and development of the campus was his gift of the Olive Road property on which the new Fine Arts Center stands.

Miss Estelle Lutrell, a librarian who joined the University in President Parker's time, was, therefore, a contemporary of Dr. Forbes. She left this evaluation of him:

> His keen interest in the problems of the Southwest, his will to do and his inexhaustible energy combined with both

> scientific and executive ability made his service to the state one of rare value. Dr. Forbes was ever a gifted speaker, a splendid host and a vigorous organizer. For a man of his manifold gifts to take root and grow with the pioneer state was a piece of good fortune, possibly not comprehended at the time that the service was rendered. His departure to take up agricultural work in Egypt and later in the French Sudan, though a loss to Arizona, gave him a wider and more adventurous field of endeavor.

Answering an interviewer who asked him what he considered the University's chief contribution to the state had been, Dr. Forbes dictated this reply:

> You have to take into consideration the thousands of graduates who have gone out into society and contributed to not only the development of our own Southwest but our whole country.
>
> So far as agriculture is concerned, it began in a very primitive way before this became an organized Territory. But these beginnings were first studied by those of us who came first into the Territory because we couldn't teach agriculture without first knowing something about it.
>
> You will find on the front of the agriculture building this legend—Research—Education—Extension. That's the logical order in which we worked for the benefit of agriculture here. Research to find out about this strange new country into which we had come. Then education, passing on what we had begun to know to primitive classes organized within the institution and also without the building itself, in the shape of farmers' short courses which were attended by farmers from all over the State, in an effort to convince them we knew something about agriculture here. Then after this primitive beginning the necessity of reaching out to the people, who could not afford the time or the money to come to the institution, with extension work which you know is now highly organized and an important branch of the work, so that our development is very well expressed by that legend—Research—Education—Extension.

> It has taken important and unexpected directions. For instance, in 1910 cotton was not grown in this part of the country at all. It is now our most important crop. Varieties were discovered which were suited to our climate and soil, and irrigation conditions. Various other crops and horticultural plants and trees were successfully tested until now agriculture actually makes a greater return in money than mining. So that shows an illustration of the old saying that seeds may develop into great trees. This has been the history of agriculture in Arizona. It is interesting, of course, to know this development can only continue as we are assured of water with which to continue it.

It was President Parker who sensed the full capabilities of Professor Howard Hall, principal of the preparatory school, instructor in English, and director without pay of the University's little library. Hall was in his early twenties when he joined the faculty in 1891. He had been selected by Dean Gulley, and like Gulley, Collingwood, and Toumey, he was a graduate of Michigan State Agricultural College. Although he left the campus long ago, there are graduates living who remember him as a fine teacher, and Mary Walker Adams speaks of "the quiet, gracious manner in which he rebuked immature pranks."

From his earliest months with the University, Hall quietly dedicated himself to the task of building a library. To start with he had a few scientific books on agriculture; these were kept on a shelf in Dean Gulley's office. Then, as he added books and documents, he moved into the southeast corner of the main building where he used shelving, a desk, and a gate that had been returned from the Arizona exhibit at the Columbian Exposition.

By 1900 these quarters were a disgrace to an institution that called itself a university. Hall had accumulated 10,000 bound and unbound books, bulletins, and government reports—as well as valuable files of magazines. They were filed on rude wooden stacks and could be reached only by way of sixteen-inch aisles which presented a problem to some. The best that could be done in the way of a reading room was a space about twenty feet square, and, since the library was now supplying 220 books a month, some of the students must have done their reading standing up.

Hall took his problem to President Parker, who told him to write a complete report for the Board of Regents and the Legislature and, while he was about it, to get preliminary plans and estimates on the cost of a new building and equipment. Hall's report was polite but definite. He warned that the books acquired so painfully over a period of nine years, and now an absolute necessity in every department, were worth $9,000. If the guardian angel of the library ever took a holiday all this could easily go up in smoke. Hall said mildly,

> The risk of the library from fire is not lessened as the years go by. The main University building which houses the library is constructed of inflammable material and is exposed to such menacing conditions as are constantly present in the chemical laboratories, in the heating of the building by 18 stoves, and in the use of kerosene lamps and imperfect wiring of the electric light system.

Both Parker and Hall wanted $30,000 but knew it would be preposterous to expect the Legislature to approve such an amount for a library building and equipment. That figure was what the main building had cost only a few years before, and a proposal that an equal amount be spent on a building for books would set the politicians working overtime sharpening their hatchets. But the President and the professor were equal to the challenge. They had the plans drawn to include space for the Territorial Museum, the President's office, and some classrooms.

With friends of the University stressing the economy of housing books, museum, classrooms, and the President's office under one roof, the Legislature authorized $25,000 for the building. Delays held up construction, and the library was not opened until 1905. By that time a new President was in office; but the credit for the long forward step will belong always to Parker and Hall.

To be honest about it, the Legislature made less fuss about spending the $25,000 than the faculty did over the location of the building. *The University of Arizona Monthly*, the student paper, found that the faculty thought the library—the old College of Law building—would be squarely in the center of the campus and would cut off a view of the city from Cottage Number One, North Hall, the mechanics building, and the dining hall. They said, "It would forever destroy the symmetry so characteristic of our grounds." To this the editor added his personal comment and wrote, "Protests, not loud but deep, have arisen from students, townspeople and faculty alike. It is hoped that such a mistake will not occur."

The Territory had built, and the Legislature dedicated, a new capitol building at Phoenix on February 24, 1901, while the University was arguing for a library. Naturally, it was a gala event. Special trains puffed into Phoenix bringing delegations of exuberant citizens from all parts of the Territory. At least they were exuberant before they went home, as evidenced by a newspaper man of that day in the following report:

> Today all hands and the cook are engaged in dedicating the new capitol and this evening the structure will be 'dampened' in the most approved style. There will be a punch bowl in the Governor's office, another in the office of the secretary, a third under Charlie Shannon's especial protection in the Council Chamber and still another with official backing in the Assembly Hall. If that will not lay far over the best cocktail route ever travelled in the Southwest I miss my guess.

The history of the Twenty-first Legislature and of the Territory during the tenth anniversary year of the University produced a great many pieces of news more important than reports of cocktail parties. Governor N. O. Murphy dealt with some of them in a long inaugural address that revealed the Territory was making a phenomenal growth. The census taken the previous year showed that the population of Arizona was 122,212; an increase of 100 per cent in a decade. The assessed valuation of taxable property had increased $1,200,000 in twelve months. The Governor estimated the production of 1,280 mines at $40,000,000 a year and charged that while these mines were worth $100,000,000 they were paying taxes on a valuation of less than $2,000,000. Agriculture, horticulture, and cattle raising had suffered from a severe drought in 1900, and Murphy urged the Legislature to take radical steps to conserve the water supply and support the building of storage reservoirs. "It is clear," the Governor said, "that there can be but little enlargement of the irrigated area without the storage of the flood waters of the streams."

A committee to examine conditions at the University that year made an encouraging report to the Legislature. It said the students were being as well-fed for $15.00 a month as the charge would allow and recommended a new dining room and kitchen. The new manual-training school, which was now housed in a brick building, was praised with enthusiasm. The University ran out of money in setting up the school, but the Copper Queen Mine contributed $3,000, and the Morrill fund gave another $10,000 for equipment.

The committee spoke well of the plans for the new library and museum building, which, it said, "would meet the needs of the institution for all time to come." It also dwelt gravely on the constant danger of fire in the main building.

Best of all, the committee recommended that the territorial appropriation be raised from two-fifths to three-fifths of a mill, praised the teachers for their methods, commended the Board of Regents for its management, and reported that sweet harmony reigned among Board, faculty, and students.

As so many governors had done ever since Richard C. McCormick had urged Arizona's right to statehood in 1872, Murphy made a strong plea for the Legislature again to memorialize Congress on the subject. There was a particularly good reason for breathing life into the proposal in 1901, for President William H. McKinley was planning a tour of the nation by special train. He was scheduled to stop in May at Phoenix, where he would view fertile fields, visit a gold mine, and make a speech.

The Republican Party had pledged itself to support statehood for Arizona, New Mexico, and Oklahoma; newspapers spread the hope that the President would speak out firmly when he visited Arizona. The *Tucson Citizen* did not expect this much from McKinley and grumbled that he would spend a day in Phoenix but only five minutes in Tucson. *The Citizen* said with sarcasm that while the President would probably enjoy seeing a town that was merely a winter health resort, he would do better to spend more time in Tucson, "the home of all that is best and most characteristic of the Southwest." Nowhere else, it said, could he get as good an impression of the "life, spirit, dash, and enterprise" of the people.

The Legislature drew up a memorial and particularly emphasized the point that since the Territory now had a University, two normal schools, and a grade school system serving 15,000 children, it was in a position to offer superior educational advantages to all. It appeared that education was at last recognized as an asset deserving to be mentioned along with mines, farmlands, cattle, and climate.

As *The Citizen* had feared, the memorial failed to move President McKinley, who evaded the big question in one paragraph of his Phoenix speech:

> I congratulate you on the splendid type and character of your people and I leave with you my best wishes for their happiness and progress and that they may soon be able to show the Congress of the United States that they have builded well and strongly and wisely in this great Territory and are prepared to be admitted to the Union of States.

This, *The Citizen* said, was "nothing more than a polite expression of goodwill and hope that under the circumstances could not have been well avoided."

The five-minute stop in Tucson was a great disappointment. Three thousand people, including the University cadets, went down to the railroad station at night to pay their respects to the President, but the train crew snarled up its signals, and McKinley's coach was halted so far down the track that only a few citizens got more than a glimpse of a portly form and a plug hat. There was no speech and *The Citizen* dismissed the whole affair with the remark:

> The Republican President has just passed through New Mexico and Arizona and not a word did he utter to indicate that he favored the maintenance of his party's pledge.

Even if McKinley was not impressed by the growth of Arizona, there were others who were not so blind. One of them was Henry L. West, a correspondent for *The Forum*, who wrote:

> There can be no more convincing example of the faith and industry of the American people—the same sublime courage which enabled the Puritan and the Cavalier to carve an empire out of the wilderness of the Atlantic coast—than the oases where the desert lands of the United States have been transformed by irrigation. . . . The time will come when the arid domain of the West will maintain many millions of souls.

The University had 225 students and nineteen faculty members when it held the commencement marking its tenth year. These figures represented progress when measured against the thirty-two students and six faculty members listed in 1891, and the Board of Regents was so pleased with President Parker's work that it not only reappointed him for four years at its June meeting but increased his salary $400 a year.

Then, with a suddenness that amazed and shocked friends of the University, Chancellor William Herring wrote to the President on July 12, 1901, and asked for his resignation because the Board considered his manner of speech in the presence of faculty members including female instructors, "made his future service undesirable."

President Parker refused to resign. He was bewildered by the Board's action. In a letter to Chancellor Herring, he referred to his reappointment at an increased salary only a few weeks before and said:

> Your action said, "we have watched your work for four years; we have considered that work in all its relations; to the youth, to the community, to the cause of education, and to the institution which we hope shall become great as the coming years shall add to the superstructure that shall rise upon the foundation you have laid so well; and we believe those interests will be best served by your continuing to administer the affairs of the institution for another four years" . . . the alleged charges are of a nature which I know and you know and everyone who knows anything about me knows are false and contrary to my nature and every act of my whole life.

Apparently informed of the correspondence between the Board and President Parker, but hesitating to make the dispute public, *The Star* nevertheless came to the defense of the President in an editorial on August 27.

Praising the University for its rapid development in the last four years, *The Star* said:

> To President M. M. Parker is largely due this remarkable growth. It has been remarked many times by citizens familiar with the institution since its establishment that with the installation of M. M. Parker as President the University has experienced a new birth. And this was true for the whole policy was gradually changed, discipline established, improvements in every department introduced with marked results. The faculty was pruned and strengthened and made more effective.
>
> All this was to be expected from President Parker for he was and is admirably adapted and qualified to the gratification of all friends of education.
>
> The Board of Regents showed its appreciation of the services and character of President Parker when at the close of the University year in June, it re-employed him for another term of four more years with an increase in salary of $400 per annum.

President Parker insisted that he be permitted to present a defense to the Board before final action was taken and appeared before the Regents with his attorney on September 5. The Board permitted them to take seats while it transacted routine business. Then it adjourned to another room where it went into executive session and discharged the President without hearing him or his attorney.

The Arizona Daily Citizen made a bitter attack on the President and approved of the action of the Board in an editorial on September 9 in which it said:

> In view of the approaching scholastic term at the University it becomes the duty of the Board of Regents to act with firmness and expedition in the present emergency.
>
> The Regents are endowed with the duty of governing and managing the University. . . . Parker was a hireling and had no more interest in the University than the extent of salary. The Regents were too kind to the weak and infatuated man. . . . He alone was responsible for his dismissal. He has been a failure and a mistake.

Neither *The Star* nor *The Citizen* printed an explanation of the basis for the charges made by the Regents, so far as is known. Unfortunately, the September and October issues of *The Star* are missing, and there may have been some comment on the Board's conduct following the meeting of September 5.

The unwillingness of the Tucson press to speak plainly on the Parker affair was remarked upon by the *Bisbee Review*, which said:

> The false modesty that restrains the press of Tucson in discussing the question in its true light keeps the distant reader in a quandary as to just what were the charges against the President.

After looking back at the record, it is impossible to agree that President Parker was a weak man or a failure. His policies were sound and his vision was clear, even on the question of establishing a student press. It was under President Parker that a monthly journal called Sage Green and Silver appeared. The name, format, and policy changed often during the years. It became successively the *University of Arizona Monthly Magazine*, November 1, 1900 to May 1, 1908; *University Life*, a bi-monthly newspaper, October, 1908, to May, 1910; *Arizona Life*, a monthly magazine, November, 1910, to May, 1911; *Arizona Weekly Life*, a newspaper, November, 1911, to May, 1912. There were other titles, but on October 13, 1915, the students finally settled on *Arizona Wildcat* at the insistence of Editor Orville McPherson.

The Board of Regents chose to appoint Frank Yale Adams, who was then teaching history and pedagogy and serving as military commandant of cadets, to the post of acting president in September, and in May, 1902, the appointment was made permanent. Adams was a successful commandant, knew something about the affairs of the University, and was so popular with the students there is a possibility that the Regents were influenced by the attitude of the student body. At least that is what the students thought, and what was published in the *University of Arizona Monthly*:

> At a special meeting of the Board of Regents upon May 3, Acting-President Adams was appointed President of the University of Arizona. There were many applicants for the Presidency before the Board, but when the vote was taken President Adams was unanimously chosen. The mind of the Board upon this question had been singularly secret up to the time of the meeting and as a consequence the student body felt that it must make every effort in its power towards securing its own choice—Professor Adams—as President. So it presented a petition to the Board of Regents, previously circulated among the students and signed to a man by everyone, stating its choice and its reasons therefor. It is the source of decided happiness amongst the students that Professor Adams is to continue in the capacity of President.

Adams had been educated at St. Lawrence University, Canton, New York, and held a master's degree in history. Before coming to Arizona, he served as principal in New York high schools and taught in a West Point preparatory school. He had no previous university experience as teacher or administrator.

The term of this fourth president was a short one. He remained two years, resigning in 1903, and the period was not marked by outstanding development. The Legislature did approve the expenditure of $25,000 for the new library and museum building but, as has been said, this was due to the work of President Parker and Professor Hall. President James Douglas of the Copper Queen Mining Company sent a gift of $5,000 for a gymnasium while Adams was in office, but this also was due to President Parker's plea and to the influence of Chancellor William Herring.

The Legislature made no new appropriations to provide for university growth, and Adams' annual report to the Regents is general rather than specific.

He said he felt that courses had been strengthened, teaching had been more effective, and the attitude of the student body had been commendable. The reports of the departments show only that they continued to work with their usual vigor. In summing up, Adams said, "The internal administration and discipline has been without friction, everything showing a quiet and steady growth."

Miss Estelle Lutrell, instructor in English during Adams' term, presents a different picture in her historical manuscript:

> The leading members of the faculty, desirous of having the organization expand with a broader idea of University education in view, considered that under the circumstances but little advancement was likely to be made. . . . The faculty made a direct appeal to the Governor, asking that an educator of recognized standing be appointed, and that some security in tenure of office should be assured him. The appeal had its effect. Governor A. O. Brodie who came in at this time adopted a different attitude from that of his predecessors in office, saying to the University authorities, in his somewhat burly fashion, 'You men have got to go ahead there and make your own institution.' With this change of front the Regents set about the task of securing a man with the requisite qualifications. Upon authorization of the Board, S. M. Franklin, a graduate of the University of California, wrote President Wheeler of his alma mater, asking him to make a recommendation. Dr. Kendric Charles Babcock, whom he suggested for the post, was the unanimous choice of the Board over other candidates.

Dr. Babcock, a native of New York and a graduate of the public schools of South Brookfield who went west for his college work, graduated from the University of Minnesota in 1899. He taught history at Minnesota, first as a fellow and then as an instructor, after which he entered Harvard, where he received both his A.M. and Ph.D. Then he turned west again and joined the faculty of the University of California, where he became an assistant professor of history and political science. He held that post and rank when the University of Arizona called him in 1903.

The appointment was hailed as a significant step forward into a new and finer educational era and Dr. Babcock's inauguration was celebrated with public ceremonies at the Tucson Opera House on November 4, 1903. Governor A. O. Brodie and his staff, the Board of Regents, pastors of Tucson churches, members of the Legislature, and county school officials filled the seats of honor on the stage while the general public packed the house in anticipation of meeting the new president and hearing Benjamin Ide Wheeler, president of the University of California, deliver the principal address.

The *Arizona Daily Star* of November 5 gave the event the heaviest publicity it had ever accorded the University, with a two-column story under a double-column head on page one and an interview with President Wheeler on an inside page. After referring to "the most brilliant assemblage ever gathered together in Arizona," *The Star* said:

> A spirit of cordiality and confidence pervaded the meeting. All who were able to hear and take part in the ceremony were inspired with new hope for educational facilities and stimulated with a renewed energy and determination to see the University of Arizona one of the greatest institutions of its kind in the United States.

Governor Brodie spoke for the Territory and said, "The hearts of all Arizonians should swell with pride in being able to secure such an able educator."

In a long and eloquent address, President Wheeler warned against making the University "the football of shifty popular moods or of party politics, or worse, of factional strife." In his summing up he reached oratorical heights that had not been touched since C. C. Stephens helped turn the first sod in 1887:

> Long as your mountains stand, here stands the University of Arizona; in teaching, influence and example, cleansing and pure as the sunshine that purges your hills; in sympathy with the various works of men, generous and free as the ranges of your plains; in hold upon the eternal truths deep-seated as the ways by which the Colorado seeks the sea. Here let it stand, highest embodiment of society's ideal purpose, guide to those who seek, helper to those who toil, fostering mother of good citizens of the State.

The following day the *Star* commented editorially on the importance of the occasion to the Territory and Tucson:

> Yesterday morning thousands of the daily papers of the United States through the Associated Press published the proceedings of the ceremony and more than a column of President Wheeler's admirable address. This informed the people of the country at large that Arizona had a University, that it was located at Tucson, that it was of sufficient importance to secure one of the renowned college presidents to aid in the ceremony of installing Dr. Babcock.

President Wheeler revealed also that Dr. Babcock had been of great service to statewide education in California because of his ability to help high schools improve their curricula and teaching. This was something in which the University of Arizona's Board of Regents and faculty were deeply interested, since they hoped to be able to turn the preparatory students over to city high schools in the near future. What they could not foresee was that the preparatory school would stay with the University for twelve more years, and what they were too impatient to accept was that many young colleges in pioneer states found it necessary to offer high school courses first if they were to get any students who were prepared to do college work.

Deep as Dr. Babcock's interest was in this field, he had more immediate problems. His first move was to discontinue the frequent faculty meetings so that the teachers and researchers could go about their work without weekly and sometimes semi-weekly interruption. Then he turned to the curriculum, where he added a course in irrigation and a new course in metallurgy, ordered that each student in subcollegiate work must qualify in reading and penmanship or take the subject without credit, and that no student could enter business courses who had not taken two years of English with a passing grade.

All was going smoothly until what may be called "the Great Rebellion" broke out, and even then the faculty minutes contained only the announcement that the President had called a meeting to consider matters of discipline.

Matters of discipline indeed! The campus was afire with revolt against Dr. Babcock.

It should be noted that the students had been given no part in the big civic welcome accorded the new president. Practically everybody was on the program except representatives of the student body, and the long reports the *Daily Star* gave of the event do not mention that students even attended the ceremony.

It was said afterwards that President Babcock felt deeply hurt by the rebellion, and perhaps he did. It would be a normal reaction. But he had not yet learned to understand young people brought up in border homes where every man thought himself the equal of any other, especially if the other man wore a plug hat as Dr. Babcock did from time to time. Nor is it strange that the students failed to appreciate a president whom they knew only by his tailored perfection and formal dignity, or that they reserved judgment until time brought an opportunity to apply a measuring stick.

St. Patrick's Day furnished the opportunity and the students asked for a full holiday only to be turned down by Dr. Babcock who wrote in green ink on the petition: "I may be 'green' but not so 'green' as this."

A story has come down through the years that the students were infuriated because holidays on St. Patrick's Day were customary. A search of the faculty minutes, however, fails to show that the University ever shut up shop to honor St. Patrick. It is true that the student body did ask for holidays on the slightest excuse, such as the arrival of a circus, but the requests were never granted and the worst that happened was that three or four boys cut classes.

Perhaps the students felt the President had laughed at them. Again, they may have intended no more than a jocular attempt to try out Bab-cock's authority, but whatever the reason, the fun suddenly got out of hand. The student body paraded downtown and took the holiday that had been refused. When the leaders were disciplined for this there were further acts of insubordination. Babcock was hanged in effigy on the campus after he had suspended the leaders, and a movement sprang up to call a sympathetic strike but this was voted down.

The story was carried in the daily press of the Territory, and there was a general uproar that didn't make for calmness on the campus or anywhere else. Even Governor Brodie got into the act and, being an old army warhorse, he pranced and snorted about student refusal to obey orders, telling the Regents and the President to maintain their position if they had to dismiss every student at the University to do it. Ringleaders were punished with extra drill and some, including two who later became prominent Tucson businessmen, Harold Steinfeld and Monte Mansfield, were put to work laying bricks.

In time, of course, high feelings simmered down, but they had attracted so much attention that Dr. Babcock had to mention the event in his annual report:

> A serious student disturbance, arising out of a few real and many imaginary grievances, occurred in April, 1904. A number of older students who had been registered at the University for several years, as well as some of the younger students, were involved. The faculty committee on

> discipline made a long and thorough investigation. Before quiet was restored one student was expelled (and for refusal to leave the dormitory was arrested, tried and fined $30), one suspended indefinitely and five sent home. One instructor was dismissed for cause.

After that, President Babcock ignored the whole affair. Short and slender though he was, there was case-hardened steel in his backbone, and nothing moved him from what he considered his duty. He was the best trained and best educated administrator who had set foot on the campus and he knew it. Further, he expected respect and got it, even when the price was a lack of affection on the part of both faculty and student body.

The new president's first interest was in lifting the educational standards by raising entrance requirements and broadening the curriculum. To accomplish this he strove against great difficulties to enlarge the faculty, to cut the teaching loads, and to bring in new specialists.

Like President Parker, who had preceded him, Dr. Babcock was a good judge of men, and nothing hurt him more than to lose them. But he showed that he was a realist when he dwelt on this in a report he made to the Board of Regents:

> The University of Arizona is still small, new and remote from the older and greater universities; it is unable to pay high salaries. It must expect, therefore, that as long as it has excellent men, it will be looted from time to time by stronger competitors. It must accept one of two conditions; it must either continue to seek out the best men, and trust to being able to enjoy the fruit of their labors for a few years, certain that sooner or later they will be called away; or it must be content to get along with mediocre men. The safety and progress of the University rests on the first plan, even at the cost of continued inconvenience and perplexity.

One of his outstanding selections was Dr. Andrew Ellicott Douglass, who came in 1906 to teach physics and geography, stayed to become a world-famous scientist, and after fifty-four years [1960] is still giving distinguished service.

Dr. Douglass founded the Department of Astronomy and supervised the building of Steward Observatory and the installation of its thirty-six-inch telescope. Then, establishing tree-ring research, he led the way in the development of the science of dendrochronology. The Board of Regents established a research laboratory in 1937 to perpetuate his collections, his program, and the records of his research.

An able administrator, as well as a scientist, Dr. Douglass was secretary of the faculty for many years and served as acting president of the University between Dr. Babcock's departure in December, 1910, and the arrival of President Arthur H. Wilde in May, 1911.

In Dr. Babcock's first report to the Board, in which he covered the years 1903–04, he began with the grounds and the condition of the buildings, commenting particularly that there was a marked betterment in the appearance of the institution. Roads had been improved and many palm, olive, and cottonwood trees had been planted under the direction of the experiment station. He had one fault to find with a new gateway soon to be built of brick, concrete, and timber at the main entrance to the campus. He said it would emphasize the shabbiness of the original barbed wire fence that enclosed the University grounds.

By sinking the University well an additional forty feet and installing a new pump, the water supply had been increased 40 per cent. The old steam plant had been converted to electricity and students and teachers had been finally freed of the intolerable racket of the stamp mill which had been relocated on a new site northeast of Old Main. These seem like minor details today, but they were of great importance in the year 1904.

Dr. Babcock reported that the new library and museum building had been accepted in November, 1904, although one stack room, a work room, and three classrooms had only packed earth for floors. When the time came to dedicate the building in February, 1905, the dirt floors were ignored by the local press, which wrote pridefully of the newest addition to the campus. The *Tucson Citizen* saw it this way:

> The dedicatory exercises of the new Library and Museum building belonging to the University which were held last night in Herring Hall, otherwise the gymnasium, were attended by an audience representing the very *creme de la creme* of Tucson's upper world.
>
> Being a frontier town there were not as many dress suits in evidence as there might have been had the scene occurred at Harvard, Yale or Princeton, but nevertheless the gowns worn by some of the ladies, while probably not creations of

> Felix or Worth, were yet sufficiently handsome to elicit the admiration of even a male reporter and as for the gentlemen, they were gentlemen and garbed as such. But this is not a society report.
>
> The reading room on the second floor is equipped with countless electric lights with the approved green shades, looking for all the world like the local room of a big modern newspaper and in the other apartment are to be seen rows and rows of books.

President Babcock delivered an address in which he praised Professor H. J. Hall as the man who had planned the building. He added that when Hall began to create a library twenty years before there had been only a handful of books, while today it was farther along than Harvard had been when it was 100 years old. The principal speaker was Chancellor William Herring, who was awarded the honorary degree of LL.D.

East and south of the new library rose the white portico columns of the gymnasium, which had been made possible by the gift from the Copper Queen Company. A basketball team played there that winter, and the gymnasium's usefulness was reported by President Babcock to be growing each month. He added that "courses in physical training and healthful exercise have unquestionably improved the general temper and tone of the students."

The President had both good and bad news about the faculty. The good news was that the staff had been enlarged. There was now a new professor of metallurgy, another of physical training, and a trained librarian, as well as additional instructors in physics, physical geography, and mathematics. Still needed was a professor of irrigation engineering and practice, but this problem would not be too difficult to solve since the U. S. Department of Agriculture had provided $1500 toward the salary of such a man if the Territory would match the amount.

The bad news was that twenty-one teachers had left the faculty. Stanford, Iowa, and the U. S. Department of Agriculture had taken several of the top teachers and researchers. This was a blow, but one for which the President and the Board of Regents were prepared.

Discipline, Dr. Babcock said honestly, was not as good as it might be. Most of the troubles, he said, were caused by students in the preparatory school. He expressed hope that, since a few high schools were being established throughout the Territory, it might not be too long before the University would be relieved of at least the burden of first-year preparatory students. After that, it could concentrate more efforts and funds on advanced work.

The dining hall, the report said, had continued to feed students for $15.00 a month, a feat that was possible because it was paying eight cents a pound for beef roast. Unfortunately, however, President Babcock had found a shortage of $800 in the mess fund, caused by someone's failure to make students pay their board bills. Since the dining hall had been expected to be self-supporting, the President saw no way out except to reduce the quality of the food—which probably meant using more stewing beef at four cents a pound—and to require cash in advance and raise the price of meals to $17.00 a month. None of the expedients was popular, for he reported:

> As the board at best is very simple and at times monotonous, though always wholesome, such retrenchment meant necessarily dissatisfaction and criticism. Since the establishment of the cash-in-advance rule there has been no accumulation of unpaid bills. . . . The policy of advance cash payments for board and for the customary fees in chemistry, physics, etc., was not inaugurated without considerable friction and complaint on the part of the students, but a method so obviously fair and businesslike has finally approved itself to all.

As for improvements, Dr. Babcock said it would be fine if the Legislature would approve funds to finish the library, improve fire protection methods on the campus, fill up the old cesspools, and install modern sewer lines connected with the Tucson system. He estimated the total needs would cost $20,500.

Apparently both the Legislature and the Board of Regents had complete faith in the President, for he got everything he wanted. The library and museum building was completed, the fire protection system was rebuilt—though not before the dining hall burned—and two companies of students were organized to handle hose that could throw 500 gallons of water a minute. A system of sewers was constructed, the new gate was built, and the old barb-wire fence was finally replaced with wood posts and iron pipe railings. The Board also authorized the President to have a gallery built at the west end of Herring Hall and gave him permission to buy a horse, buggy, and harness for university use if he could do it for $600.

Faculty and curriculum had not been overlooked. Dr. G. E. P. Smith was transferred to the experiment station and appointed to the newly authorized post of irrigation engineer. A department of music was approved, and new classes were added in modern languages. The University was now teaching

Spanish, Latin, French, and German and giving the master's degree in mining and agriculture. The noted William Phipps Blake, who was retiring with the title of professor of geology (emeritus), was succeeded by Professor Cyrus F. Tolman, a graduate of the University of Chicago with several years' experience in the Southwest.

Football was growing in importance. Arizona's eleven played its first games outside the State in the fall of 1905, meeting Pomona and St. Vincent. Unfortunately, it lost both contests but the *Los Angeles Herald* paid this tribute to the courage the Arizona visitors showed in the Pomona contest:

> Many games have been played in Los Angeles during past years and many gallant stands have been made but nothing in the history of western football can compare with the quiet, desperate courage with which the Territory lads faced their first overwhelming defeat of the season yesterday afternoon. They faced it with the grace of a hero and the desperation of a fiend and played football for its true worth down to the last minute. The final score was Pomona 41, University of Arizona 5.

St. Vincent was tougher than Pomona and slaughtered Arizona. Its team had been recruited from the St. Louis University eleven that had played during the World's Fair, and it was far too good for the boys from the desert, who had to leave the field in the second half because they ran out of players. The score was 55 to 0 when the officials stopped counting and the only feature that deserves to be remembered is that the game was the first contest ever played under lights.

More important than sport was the action of the Board of Regents on April 10, 1905, in adopting Dr. Babcock's suggestion that no more students below the second grade in the preparatory school be accepted from cities of 5,000 inhabitants after September, 1906. As a result, Tucson organized a high school and enrolled fifty students in its first class. This caused a slight drop in university registration figures, but President Babcock was able to report a total enrollment of 210.

Financially, the University was in excellent condition. In addition to the $25,000 received annually from the Morrill fund and $15,000 from the Hatch fund, a new grant for agricultural extension work had provided $7,000, and this would be increased $2,000 a year until it reached $30,000. A territorial tax of three-fifths of a mill was producing increasing revenue, and as a result of this prosperity, President Babcock did something unprecedented. He said he was going to let one session of the Legislature pass without making a number of small requests, and he did just that.

CHAPTER 5

1905–1914

THE DECADE from 1900 to 1910 was one of the greatest in Arizona history, for in that period the pioneers were at work on projects of tremendous economic and political importance. These pages of territorial and state history belong in a history of the University since University and Commonwealth shared the struggles and the victory.

One must go back for just a moment to a time hundreds of years before the dawning hours of the 20th century when the Indians who peopled the Salt River Valley raised their food by watering the thirsty desert soil with an irrigation system of ditches and canals. These builders vanished and were lost in the shadows of the past, but traces of their handiwork outlasted the attacks of sun, wind, and water.

The white man who followed them centuries later saw the signs of the work done by the ancient people and was not slow to read the message, for as early as 1867 these newcomers began building their own irrigation system. Yard by yard they dug ditches with shovels or horse-drawn scoops and carried the waters of the Salt River to distant fields. Then, as the land responded and lush green acres stretched out farther and farther, new settlers streamed into the valley in such numbers that it seemed as if there would never be room for all of them. But so eager were the people for homes and farms and so determined were they to master the desert that by 1897 they were tending almost 200,000 acres of irrigated land.

Then nature turned on them and brought a drought that lasted three years. The Salt and Gila rivers dwindled to creeks. Farms blew away in clouds of dust and Phoenix withered like a mining camp when the ore gives out. There was a great spring flood in 1900 and the rivers rose, but now there was too much water. It swept out little dams made of soil, rocks, and brush, ate away the banks of the canals and roared down the Salt and Gila to the Rio Colorado. Again the sun took over, and again there were searing winds that swept the dry topsoil away.

The people would not give up. They began to use the magic word "reclamation" and to dream of building a giant dam behind which the waters of the river could be stored, and measured out when needed into canals and ditches.

There was a canyon in the Tonto Basin that was a natural spot for such a project. It was eighty-five miles from the valley and sixty miles by a primitive road from a railhead, but the site was so ideal for a dam that nature seemed to have designed it for that purpose. The big obstacle was the cost, which would be so great that neither the people nor the Territory could finance it. Therefore, as they had often done during the years of struggle that had gone into the development of the Territory, the people turned to the federal government.

It took an Act of Congress and the influence of President Theodore Roosevelt to bring success, but when the fight was won the reclamation of arid lands became a national policy that was to change the economy, not only of Arizona, but of the entire West.

Strong individualists though they were, the farmers of the Salt River Valley subordinated their personal rights for the benefit of all the people in 1903 and pooled 200,000 acres of land in a Water Users Association which guaranteed to repay the government for its investment.

Work began on April 8, 1905, the first water was released May 15, 1907, and the dam was dedicated March 16, 1911, by Theodore Roosevelt, whose name it bore. The task had taken six years to accomplish, but when it was finished Roosevelt Dam was welded to the mountains, rising 284 feet above bedrock and stretching 1,000 feet across the canyon. The 17,800-acre reservoir behind it would hold nearly 1,500,000 acre feet of water that would irrigate 246,000 acres of land. The total cost exceeded $5,500,000.

Even the small, cold type in the report of the U. S. Agricultural Census for 1910 becomes exciting when one follows it and discovers that in the single decade since 1900, the value of all Arizona farm property increased by 150.5 per cent, the acreage of improved lands increased 37.6 per cent, and their value soared by 271 per cent. Farm property values in Maricopa County jumped from $8,214,000 to $33,879,280, and the value of the crops raised in the Territory rose from $2,472,348 to $5,496,872, which was a gain of 122.3 per cent. As for population, it went from 122,931 to 204,354.

It was all called a miracle and in a sense this was true. But it was brought to pass by hundreds of men with drive, ability, and imagination—and high on the list were the scientists of the young University of Arizona, who had been contributing and guiding factors in the development of agriculture, cattle raising, and irrigation. The shelves of the university library hold many records of the work done through the Agricultural Experiment Station by Professor E. M. Boggs, Dean Robert H. Forbes, Dean J. J. Thornber, Professor G. E. P. Smith, and others. After extensive surveys from saddle and buckboard, Professor Boggs had written a classic called *Notes on Irrigation* when the University was three years old, and when he summed up his findings he all but painted a picture of the great dams that would someday be built. This is what he wrote:

> It is worthy of note that the causes which have made irrigation a necessity in Arizona have also provided the means for its easy accomplishment. Here is found the perfect combination of high mountain ranges which influence rainfall: the valleys of gentle slope which may be formed into vast storage reservoirs by dams in the narrow canyons at their outlets, and below all lie the broad and fertile plains which need only the life-giving water to awaken into activity their latent forces and cause them to yield the most bountiful harvests. Upon viewing for the first time these plains, so common to Arizona, the beholder is amazed at their wonderful extent and perfect fitness for irrigation.

There is much more to the story, for progress did not stop with 1910. A diversionary dam was built at Yuma and four dams were added on the Verde and the Salt, but even these could not provide for the cotton-growing acres around Coolidge, Casa Grande, Eloy, and Florence; therefore Coolidge Dam went up in 1930 at a cost of $8,500,000. Including the Laguna and Granite Reef diversionary dams, eight dams were built at a total cost of approximately $32,000,000. The results were that the population of the state climbed to 435,573, cotton replaced the dairy industry in importance, citrus groves flourished, and alfalfa became commercially important.

The decade in which man began to reclaim the desert was also the period in which Arizona fought for statehood; and while the University could not take an active part in that battle, it shared the hopes of the people, and its interests were bound up in theirs.

The campaign for statehood had been opened as far back as 1872 when Richard C. McCormick, the second territorial governor, was elected delegate to Congress. He carried the subject to the floor of the House, and while he accomplished nothing, he did as well as succeeding Legislatures that vainly petitioned Congress to admit Arizona to the Union.

Two efforts were made by the Legislature to write a state constitution and thus move Congress to action, but these failed to impress the national lawmakers. Finally an enabling act admitting Arizona did pass the House in 1894, only to die in the Senate. This happened three times, and the hopes of the people rose and fell until 1900 when the Republican Party went on record as favoring statehood for Arizona, New Mexico, and Oklahoma. The future seemed bright that year but it was merely a mirage. Nothing of moment happened until 1904 when a bill was introduced in Congress to admit Arizona and New Mexico as a single state. Practically all of Arizona joined in opposing the proposal, and the Territorial Legislature passed a concurrent resolution in 1905 denouncing joint statehood in this ringing paragraph:

> We insist that such is without precedent in American history. It threatens to fasten upon us a government that would be neither of, by, nor for the people of Arizona. It would be a government without the consent of the governed. It humiliates our pride, violates our tradition and would subject us to the domination of another commonwealth of different traditions, customs and aspirations. With the most kindly feelings towards the people of New Mexico, we must protest against this proposed union and would rather remain forever a Territory than to accept statehood under such conditions.

Another year passed, and in 1906 Senator Joseph B. Foraker of Ohio offered an amendment to the joint statehood bill which provided that both Territories should vote on the issue. If one rejected it, then jointure would be considered a dead issue.

The campaign in Arizona was now as hot as a forest fire in a high gale. M. G. Cunniff, a magazine writer for *World's Work*, toured both Territories to test the opinions of their citizens and one paragraph in his article, "The Last of the Territories," sums up what he learned:

> New Mexico was lukewarm. Many said, "No!" More said "We want single statehood. A half loaf is better than no bread."
>
> There was no such wavering in Arizona. Asking that question was like touching a match to a cannon cracker. Men did not merely say, "We don't want joint statehood." They made speeches. They told parables. Lawyers overwhelmed me with arguments, doctors analyzed the situation, storekeepers detained me to tell me all about it, conductors hung over rear seats of cars to discuss it, mining men,

> business men, teachers, editors, Democrats, Republicans, Prohibitionists were all in the same mood. Sheriff Jim Lowry of Yavapai county said to me in Prescott, "Sir I'd like to see Arizona a State. But half a State with New Mexico as the other half? Well I'd rather see it a Territory till I die." That was the gist of what they said.

The votes were cast in November, 1906. When they were counted, New Mexico had voted for joint statehood, but Arizona had defeated it by a roaring five-to-one majority. It was a great victory for Arizona, even if it did leave her where she had been ever since Governor Goodwin proclaimed her a Territory in 1864.

Two more years went by and again hopes rose when President Theodore Roosevelt urged that the territories be admitted, and both the Democratic and Republican parties in their campaign platforms pledged favorable action. Congress, however, refused to move until after William Howard Taft had been elected President. Then it passed the enabling act, and the President signed it on June 20, 1910. Three months later, Arizona held a constitutional convention, and the people voted overwhelmingly to accept the constitution written at that meeting. The convention had been a repetition in miniature of the national political struggle between progressives and conservatives. Even the slogans were the same. "Initiative, referendum, and recall," was one phrase that stirred men to high feelings. It was natural that Arizona should favor a liberal constitution. This was border country where every man was jealous of his rights, and at the moment labor was in a strong position under the leadership of G. W. P. Hunt. President Taft had warned that if a provision for recall of judges by popular vote was included in the constitution it would be vetoed. But Arizona wrote it in and the President kept his word.

This meant another delay and a second vote in 1911, at which time the people agreed to omit the offending clause. Only then did Taft accept the constitution, and when he finally signed the proclamation making the Territory a state, all Arizona erupted in one pyrotechnical spree. Seven months later the state would amend the constitution and restore the recall of judges, but on February 14, 1912, it had no thought except for a celebration.

Phoenix was the scene of the principal jubilee because statehood meant the inauguration of G. W. P. Hunt as the first state governor. A 48-gun salute touched off the program, and ten anvils rang the march step for a mile-long procession of bands, guardsmen, school children, and members of civic and fraternal organizations. The inaugural ball was held outdoors so everyone could dance in the streets, and thousands of citizens who packed the business section from curb to curb cheered for hours.

In Tucson they tied down the siren on the waterworks. Whistles on Southern Pacific locomotives, mills, and factories screamed; church and school bells went wild, and firecrackers exploded in bunches. A holiday was declared at the University, and exercises were held during which the cadets staged a full-dress review and saluted a new flag with forty-eight stars.

Bisbee shook its hills by firing off forty-eight sticks of dynamite on Copper Queen Mountain, and Wickenburg celebrated for three days without resting.

Emotional orators rose to supreme heights, and in the heat of the moment were sometimes slightly ridiculous but nobody cared, not even when Senator John T. Hughes spoke of "deliverance from almost a half-century of territorial bondage."

Throughout these years of turmoil President Kendric C. Babcock had held to the belief that the University did not belong in the political forum and would perform its greatest service by continuing to assist in the development of agriculture. He pointed out that the experiment station was doing invaluable work, and in this he was on firm ground, for the station was increasing the scope of its activities. At the same time the emphasis remained on the development of crops that were commercially profitable. This, the President said, meant a great deal to taxpayers.

Farmers' institutes were carrying the University far beyond the limits of its home campus. Wherever men were willing to listen they were met by a specialist who talked their language. He might find only six men gathered under a watertank at Wellton, and again he might find 300 farmers and cattlemen waiting for him in the Academy of the Latter Day Saints at Thatcher. One thing was sure: the subject would be one the farmer understood—the result of Professor Thornber's studies on methods of improving grazing lands, Dr. Forbes' years of research in date culture, the growing of alfalfa, potato culture, the efficient use of irrigation waters, or new methods of fighting plant pests and diseases. All this went on throughout the state, while back on its home grounds the University added a two-year course in agriculture in 1908, and in 1909 bought eighty acres on the Rillito River near Tucson where it planned to build a model dairy for the coordination of instruction and research.

The need for a new science building had been great, and this was met in 1909 with a $40,000 structure. That left the first floor of Old Main empty, and the experiment station took it over but kept its heart set on a new building for agriculture. President Babcock also reported to the Board of Regents that plans must be considered for an auditorium to meet the needs of the students.

To the satisfaction of everyone the President was able in 1908 to present an encouraging summary of the growth of high schools. He said:

> Five years ago Phoenix was the only town in Arizona which had a fully equipped and regular four-year high school and in only two or three other towns was there any stirring towards the formation of high schools by carrying a ninth grade and perhaps a tenth. In Prescott and Mesa some progress was made but Tucson, Tempe, Douglas, Yuma, Flagstaff and the rest either depended wholly on Territorial institutions or went without high school instruction. At the present time 12 towns have high schools; Phoenix, Prescott, Bisbee, Douglas, Clifton, Morenci and Mesa have graduated classes from the four-year course approved by the University; Tucson has about 100 pupils in its three classes and will graduate its first four-year class next year; Globe, Yuma, Tombstone and Tempe are regularly organized and are progressing towards a four-year status as fast as the course of school events and months will permit them.

This was great progress, but it had not come easily and would not have been made without the unflagging help of Dr. Babcock and the University. President Wheeler of the University of California had told the Territory in 1903 that their new university president would be of great value in building up secondary schools, and Dr. Babcock justified the recommendation. He knew that full university status would never be achieved until the preparatory school could be discontinued. This, in turn, would be possible only when high schools were opened. If there was to be action on this soon, he was the man who had to encourage the school boards. During his first three years he gave much of his time to this work, driving the long, rough roads between settlements that had no railroads. He spoke wherever a county institute would invite him, and counseled in person and by correspondence with school officials and teachers.

Looking back on this work when he left the University, Dr. Babcock said, "I count it as one of the most valuable things I have been able to do here that I could aid in the development of the secondary schools."

It was obvious in June 1910 that the University, like the Territory, had reached new peaks, and Dr. Babcock felt it was time to present his resignation. The United States Bureau of Education had offered him an important post that held a fresh challenge, and he accepted it. In marking the end of his service, the Regents spread a resolution on the minutes in which they said:

> In accepting the resignation of Dr. Kendric C. Babcock as President of the University of Arizona, the Board of Regents desires to give expression to its sincere regret that he is severing his relationship with the institution to the upbuilding of which his intelligent administration has contributed so largely.

A second tribute to Dr. Babcock appeared the following year. This one came from his successor, Dr. Arthur H. Wilde, who had been in office long enough to appreciate the extent of his predecessor's achievements and who opened his first annual report with the following paragraph:

> Dr. Babcock's administration was a real epoch in the history of the University. He called to the institution most of the present able faculty, and supported them in maintaining high standards of work. He built up among the students a greater respect for good order and for the University. Science Hall and other buildings were erected. The agricultural department and its demonstration farm were established. The personality and work of Dr. Babcock won many friends for the University in the state and the recognition of the stronger universities of the country. In brief, Dr. Babcock made the institution.

Dr. Babcock's assignment in the U. S. Bureau of Education was to make "a classification of universities and colleges with reference to bachelor's degrees" and great was the disappointment at the University of Arizona when he rated it "Class II" (Engineering). This meant that only the engineering graduates were fit candidates for a master's degree in a good graduate school, and even they might have to put in an extra year of study. Protests brought no results, and it was 1924 before the classification was amended and Arizona was accepted by the Association of American Universities as a "Class A institution, without reservation." Only then could Arizona graduates and transfers enter all other universities without losing credits or doing extra work.

When President Babcock resigned, the indefatigable Dr. Andrew E. Douglass, professor of physics and astronomy, was appointed president pro tem, at an advance in salary of fifty dollars a month. He held the office until Dr. Arthur Herbert Wilde, sixth president of the University, arrived five months later.

Born in Massachusetts, Dr. Wilde left New England in 1901 with a Ph.D. degree in medieval history from Harvard to become a member of the faculty of Northwestern University. There he advanced rapidly to such posts as registrar, assistant to the President, and principal of Northwestern University Academy. His administrative ability made such an impression on the Board of Trustees that they created a new office for him where he used his talents in helping direct the policies of all Northwestern's schools.

Arizona's Board of Regents felt this was the type of man needed to pick up Dr. Babcock's work. They were particularly interested in Dr. Wilde's success in increasing registration at Northwestern, because it was high time that something of the kind was done in Arizona.

There were only 195 students at the University when Dr. Babcock left. This was less than one student for every 1,000 persons in the Territory. Governor Richard E. Sloan made a report in 1910 in which he touched on the point and said:

> In efficiency and in facilities afforded for the higher education of our youths the University of Arizona ranks with the most advanced institutions in the country. It is prepared in addition to the ordinary academic courses to furnish those leading to a degree in mining, engineering, metallurgy and civil engineering. The faculty is composed of teachers of the highest standing in educational work. The equipment is of the best and is ample for the requirements of advanced work in all departments of science. . . . With the extension of the high school system in the Territory the University is becoming more and more a recognized part of our system of public education and a larger percentage of high school graduates are entering the University than formerly. This justifies the hope that the attendance of students from the Territory will soon be commensurate with the cost of its maintenance.

This was one of the situations that President Wilde faced when he came from the settled and conservative circles of the midwest to a Territory that had not yet shaken off the thinking of a frontier land. He was accustomed to heavily endowed institutions of learning. The University over which he now presided had no such support. It depended on government grants and territorial taxes.

The new President, however, soon proved that he could adapt himself to change, and concentrated on the task of establishing closer and warmer relations between the people and their University. He said that the school must follow the example of the experiment station, whose members had given 210 lectures at 176 meetings in various counties that year. Following his own advice, the President in his first move put Tucson and the campus behind him for a summer at Prescott and Flagstaff, where he met a welcome that warmed his heart. The Prescott Chamber of Commerce gave him a handsome set of wrought iron gates for the University, and there were dinners at which he had an opportunity to tell the story of the school. When he returned, however, it was with the belief that while there was a kindly feeling towards the University, there was also considerable ignorance of the work it was doing for all the people. This disturbed him, as one discovers in reading his first report to the Board of Regents in 1911:

> The University is too often identified with the City of Tucson only—indeed it is frequently called the University of Tucson. It is the duty of the University and all its friends to make its service broad in content and area, appealing to every section of the State, that it may be in fact the University of Arizona.

This certainly was not a new policy. President Babcock had followed it with great success in his campaign for high schools, but Dr. Wilde wanted to extend and increase the outside work and intended to lose no time. His initial report to the Regents reminds the reader of a man with a new broom. He announced that the first year of preparatory classes would be dropped in 1912 and the second year in 1913. After that the remaining two years would be discontinued.

The President was contemptuous of the department of music which had been established in 1906 and said:

> For several years the University has endeavored to give to the students some helpful discipline in music, but the results have, in my estimation, been too meagre to compensate for the effort. I believe either more or less should be done with this work: either the University should give the

> subject in a dignified way with credit in the curriculum or it should be dropped altogether until this can be done.

Dr. Wilde felt that domestic economy was another subject that needed to be vitalized. The course had been given by one teacher who also taught botany, and this didn't satisfy him at all. He said a thorough college course was needed "at the earliest possible moment," because few high schools taught even elementary work in the subject, and because it was needed to attract young women. Up to this time, he told the Board, the University emphasis had been on lines of interest to men only.

Other suggestions were that law, which was taught at night, should be expanded to a full, one-year course, and that second and third years should be added as soon as possible. Bacteriology, he said, needed a laboratory and a special instructor who would make tests for physicians at a very small charge. Recommended also was the creation of a traveling library system for smaller towns and villages. This suggestion had originally been made by Professor Hall in 1902.

The President noted the four-year courses in agronomy, horticulture, and animal husbandry and the two-year course in agriculture but recommended the addition of a short course in agriculture "for the benefit of farmers who cannot undertake a longer course of study."

One gets another picture of a man in a hurry from the requests for new buildings with which the President closed his report. Dr. Wilde wanted the following structures within four years: an auditorium, a museum, a building for the agricultural department and the experiment station, a mining engineering and metallurgy building, a new shop, and a clubhouse for university men. Incidentally, the President noted that he had exceeded his budget by $3,500 because he had felt it necessary to improve and increase accommodations for an anticipated growth in enrollment. He was dissatisfied with the small rooms in North Hall, each of which housed two students, and he had added a sleeping porch. At his suggestion a similar addition had also been built above one of the wings of South Hall. (Note: North Hall was razed in the Fall of 1957 to make way for a geology building, and South Hall was razed in 1958 to make way for a new home economics building.)

President Wilde's expectations of an increased enrollment were soon justified. His report for 1912–1913 showed a record enrollment of 254 students. This was an increase of thirty per cent in two years and was accomplished in the face of the fact that there now were only seventy-four students in the preparatory school. The total enrollment would have been higher if the President had been willing to include seventy-seven adults taking the farmers' short course. But he was satisfied with solid figures, and he could say:

> With a diminution of the number of preparatory students there is an added sense in the faculty and student body that the University is really a University and the students college students.

The President mentioned with pleasure the significant fact that since he had taken office in 1910, the freshman class had grown from twenty-seven to eighty students and the sophomore class from twenty-two to thirty-five. This, of course, would lead to larger graduating classes.

A milestone in public relations had been reached in April, 1911, when the University was host at its first high-school week. Seventy school officials and members of four track teams participated that year, and the number grew annually. Scholarship contests and athletic events soon called the best students and athletes in state high schools to the campus. They saw the growing University in action and carried the news of their welcome back home. One of the most popular features was the final contest between debating teams. This was the high point of the year in a league of high school teams holding elimination contests that awakened local pride.

Agile pole vaulters, muscled shotputters, speedy shorthand experts, and talented students in English, mathematics, physics, and home economics mingled on a friendly basis and kept their enthusiastic cheers echoing across the campus.

Governor Hunt took note of the way the University was reaching out in Arizona and wrote a special article for *University Life* in which he said:

> The University is making a state or helping to shape its affairs upon that broad base of intelligence which begets moral and mental courage. This is the highest duty, stated in general terms, towards the public and the individual.

Actually the University was doing more than keeping pace with the growing enrollment, for it was planning for the future. The curriculum was re-studied, and mining courses were revised after a conference with the heads of major mines.

Law was dropped temporarily in 1913, but the loss was offset by many gains. The President reported:

> A beginning of a more compact organization of the University has been made in the constitution of the Agricultural College of the University to include all agricultural instruction, research (in the experiment station), and the work of the farm.

A Department of Home Economics with a four-year course was organized, another four-year course leading to a bachelor's degree in science of commerce was established, and so was a course in bacteriology. These were all of great importance because they would lead to the College of Business and Public Administration, the School of Home Economics, and the Department of Bacteriology and Medical Technology.

It must be noted that these advances were made possible by liberal appropriations from the Legislature. The total appropriation for all University work in 1910–1911 had been $47,800. In 1911–1912 the aid was increased to $87,670 and in 1912–1913 it went to $90,000. Then it soared. President Wilde got the agricultural building he wanted, and the appropriation for two years was $436,300, or $218,150 a year.

It was magnificent support from the people of the youngest state in the nation. They faced the fact that federal funds had reached their limit of $80,000 a year, and they took the burden of higher education on their own shoulders.

No recital of the progress made under President Wilde would be complete without devoting attention to the formation of an extension division which gave fifty-six lectures in twenty-one towns in 1912, crisscrossing the state from Flagstaff to Douglas and from Yuma to Hol-brook. The figures look small today, but the time, the seed, and the soil were right, and from the small beginning have come annual harvests of tremendous importance to Arizona and the University.

The first work, done in 1912, was largely experimental and consisted in part of lectures, public discussions, and debates. This type of service gave way in 1916 to correspondence courses on both a formal and an informal basis. The informal courses proved unsatisfactory and were discontinued when formal courses began to attract increasing enrollment.

Dr. E. J. Brown was chairman of the University Extension Committee, and Dr. H. B. Leonard served as head of the Correspondence Committee from 1912 to 1916. Dr. Francis C. Lockwood was made Director of General Extension in 1918. In 1919 the committees were merged and the schedule of services was broadened to include correspondence courses, extension classes, extension lectures and lecture courses, visual education, a loan service to libraries, and the Arizona high-school debating league. Dr. Alva O. Neal, Registrar, succeeded Dr. Lockwood as Director in 1923, and in 1927 Mr. Max P. Vosskuhler, who had served as assistant under both Neal and Lockwood, became Director.

A map, published in 1922 by the *Arizona Daily Star*, showed that the University was giving instruction that year in seventy-three localities. Thirty-five years later correspondence courses were being given in 108 Arizona localities, forty-three states, and fourteen foreign countries, while extension courses were taught to students from fifty-nine cities, towns, and villages.

Extension work was given originally to help fight the old claim that the University was a Tucson institution, but it became of much more significance as the years passed, because it carried education to adults while the University proper was concerned primarily with young people.

Short courses were found inadequate because, in the words of Correspondence Director Vosskuhler, "short courses mean short cuts." As a result, every effort is made today to make the standards in extension courses the equal of standards on campus. Papers are prepared and examinations are given and corrected by University teachers.

The extension program was well summarized in a report on the growth of the University since World War II which was written in 1957 by Dr. Robert L. Nugent, Executive Vice-President, for the January-February issue of the *Arizona Alumnus*.

> Probably the best brief description of the overall extension program is the statement that it includes all areas of public service other than the program of resident instruction and the program of research.
>
> Under the heading of *extension classes* come chiefly evening classes both on and off campus, arranged primarily for adults. During a typical recent year 1,958 individuals were enrolled for 126 extension classes; including 80 in Tucson; 22 in Phoenix; four each in Fort Huachuca and Yuma; two each in Bisbee, Clifton, Douglas and Show Low; and one each in Ajo, Casa Grande, Coolidge, Eloy, Mammoth, Morenci, Safford and Thatcher.
>
> During this same year 1,500 individuals were enrolled for 2,116 *correspondence courses*.
>
> Between 1940–1941 and 1955–1956 the number of extension class students increased from 193 to 2,281, or

nearly 12-fold, and the number of correspondence students from 674 to 1,723.

An extremely important development in the extension program has been the establishment and operation entirely in the Phoenix area of programs leading respectively to the degrees of Master of Electrical Engineering and Master of Mechanical Engineering.

Apart from extension and correspondence study the general extension division reports the following figures as typical of recent years:

One hundred twelve members of the general faculty delivered 693 public lectures to an estimated total audience of 84,061 and faculty members made 102 radio and TV appearances. Nine hundred and twenty-seven broadcasts and 62 telecasts were made by the Radio-TV Bureau with the radio programs being heard regularly over 13 of the 16 radio stations of the State and 1,695 University motion picture films were shown a total of 9,025 times, including showings in 70 Arizona communities.

The Agricultural Extension Service, financed chiefly through federal funds, has a total staff of about 70, with central offices on the campus, a branch in each of 13 of the 14 counties of Arizona and a field program in each of the 14.

Statistics for a typical recent year include: 12,274 farm and home visits; 15,678 office calls; 16,871 telephone calls; 1,664 news articles or stories prepared for the papers of the State; 2,298 meetings of adults with a total attendance of about 110,000; 4,076 meetings of 4-H boys and girls with a total attendance of about 90,000.

Special programs of the College of Fine Arts included 61 appearances in Arizona communities before an estimated total audience of 26,000 and 41 appearances in Tucson.

The publication of the Bureau of Business Research, entitled *Arizona Business and Economic Review* goes out each month to a mailing list of 4,000.

When these figures are totalled they show that extension services make more than 370,000 contacts a year in Arizona, and even this does not include the broadcasts and telecasts that reach many areas of the state or the thousands of copies of helpful bulletins distributed annually.

While Dr. Wilde, no doubt, had an educator's interest in extending University teaching, there were influences in the state that contributed to the emphasis he placed on the need for closer relations between the school and the state. Maricopa County wanted the College of Agriculture moved to Tempe and in 1911–1912 carried the subject to the state Legislature in a circular headed, "A Proposition to Create a State Agricultural and Normal College for the State of Arizona to be Located at Tempe." Two principal points were raised. One was that the school should be in or near the largest agricultural area in the state. The second was that the presence of such a school aided the development of a town and it was argued that as many towns as possible should have state institutions.

The University answered with a special supplement in the annual record in which it asked the question, "Shall the University of Arizona be Dismembered?" Then it set up its rebuttal in which it said:

> No agricultural school needs a great mass of agricultural land at its doors. The school can as truly and thoroughly illustrate the teaching of agriculture on smaller and typical areas as on greater. The principles are the same; the difference is only in the extent of application. In some ways the smaller area is better, requiring intensive study and culture. The school's farm is, for illustration, not for intensive tillage and profit. Successful teaching in engineering does not require railroads, highways and bridges on the campus; nor the principles of mining a shaft on the college grounds; metallurgy is thoroughly taught in good laboratories and frequent visits to smelters. So with agriculture: a farm of moderate size, easily accessible, serves the purpose.

As for the argument that state institutions should be distributed among as many communities as possible, the University replied that the common good was more important than local benefits. It argued that even if Tempe donated the land for a College of Agriculture the annual operation would certainly cost the state an additional $20,000 to $30,000 a year. The experiences of other states were quoted, and a list of those that had chosen to build one strong University was compared with a list of states that divided their support.

So far as services to Arizona were concerned, the University said, rather pointedly, that it was the business of the experiment station to serve the whole state and that this could best be accomplished by studying the complete range of agricultural problems including the pumping of underground water and irrigation by canals.

The bulletin then reminded the state that the agricultural experiment station was merely an office and that the work was done in eight substations which were named:

> At Yuma, for dates and intensive agriculture, at Phoenix for sheep breeding and horticulture, at Tempe for date culture on alkali soil, at Prescott, Snowflake and Sulphur Springs Valley for dry farming, on the Helvetia mesa for range improvement and on a five-acre tract at Tucson for general improvement.

Finally the University drove in this nail: it was studying or cultivating 360 farm acres throughout the state—exclusive of the forty-nine square miles of the Helvetia range—against five acres of land near Tucson. The clinching blow was supplied by a letter from James Wilson, United States Secretary of Agriculture, which read:

> The Department of Agriculture has taken the stand that after a state has established its higher educational institution, erected buildings and provided equipment, it is unwise to make very radical changes, such as would be involved in separating the College of Agriculture from the University, after it has been maintained for a considerable time.
>
> The question of expense is also to be considered—the expense not only of erecting buildings and providing equipment, but the expense of maintenance which would be in your case largely a duplication of the more general courses of the University.

Since the University was getting $80,000 a year from the government and there was no assurance that this money would be transferred to a new school at Tempe, the prospect of higher taxes discouraged legislators from counties outside Maricopa, and the agricultural courses and experiment station remained where they were.

President Wilde approved of student body self-government and noted with pleasure in his report for 1913–1914 that the students had adopted a constitution. But he apparently had little understanding of the need for an athletic program and failed to mention the subject until he made his final report. Even then there was a hint of disapproval in his remarks. Noting that there was no other college team within 500 miles and that the Arizona squad had lost money on a trip to California, he felt there was no hope for a good football schedule and no profit in a poor one. He said:

> Our University has been compelled to play high schools and other local teams or else be without a schedule. It is the belief that playing games with high schools does not help the University nor promote the best spirit between the University and the high schools.

After this survey the President mentioned briefly that J. F. McKale, coach at Tucson High School, had been appointed athletic director for the coming year and would have the cordial support of the students and townspeople. There was no reference to support from the administration, and there was a reason for the omission.

The university coaches had usually been men who knew little about coaching and even less about handling the men who came out for the teams. The post of athletic director had been established in 1912 with faculty status, but the student newspaper only dared to hope for better days and a release from what it called "the tramp coach system." The first director resigned and the students asked McKale to apply for the position. He agreed and called on President Wilde but was told by letter that the position had been filled.

This failed to satisfy the students, who appealed to the Board of Regents. The Board went over Dr. Wilde's head and McKale received a second letter notifying him that the appointment had been given him at a salary of $1,700 a year. The result was a series of seasons in which teams often brought glory to their alma mater.

President Wilde was deeply interested in comfortable dormitories and in student academic achievements. One of his first acts had been to improve the men's dormitories. He was responsible for the building of Arizona Hall, and it was he who replaced the old stoves in the women's dormitory with a central heating system. The student body organization and the Associated Women Students were launched with his blessing. It was also under Dr. Wilde that University honors were established, and he presided over the assembly in which they were first presented in May, 1912. The Merrill P. Freeman medal, which is still a cherished award, was given at that assembly for the first time.

Dr. Freeman, who was a Regent, gave the medal originally for military proficiency. Later he agreed to a change in the requirements and presented two medals, one for men and another for women, as rewards for scholarship, character, and qualities of leadership. His will provided for continuing the awards.

There were many problems of administration which must have taxed the time and patience of President Wilde. One of these was caused by the state law which said that if as many as five deaf, mute, or blind students applied for enrollment, the University must accept and teach them. Until 1912, deaf and blind students had been sent to California institutions, but at that time, private citizens who were interested in these handicapped children persuaded the Legislature to appropriate $5,000 for a school at the University. This was a meagre sum, especially in view of the fact that all blind students would continue to attend school in California and their board and tuition would be paid from the appropriation.

One year proved that the plan was not feasible, and the Board of Regents appealed to the Legislature in 1913 to provide a separate school for the deaf and mute; but the Legislature turned them down on the basis of economy, and the university school opened its second year with twenty pupils. Boys were taught handicraft, and girls took a course in domestic economy. There were also classes in lip-reading and in written and manually-spelled English. Henry C. White, the principal, reported at the end of the year that considerable progress had been made but that more support was an absolute necessity. The Legislature then raised the appropriation to $15,000. Blind children, however, were cared for in California until 1919.

Trouble soon arose over teaching methods, since there were two schools of thought and each insisted it was right. There was difficulty over classrooms. Houses just off the campus were used but were inadequate in every way. Finally the School for the Deaf and Blind was moved to Speedway and Grande Avenue, but it was not until 1928 that the Legislature divorced the school and the University.

Still another cross that President Wilde had to bear was an attack leveled at his office and the Board of Regents in 1914 by State Senator A. A. Worsley of Pima County. The Senator criticized the way the school for the deaf was being conducted, charged that the Board deceived the Legislature to win larger appropriations, repeated the old criticism that there were too many teachers, blasted the conduct of students, objected to the practice of sabbatical leaves introduced by President Babcock, and said, finally, that the University was infringing on the eight-hour law. It was impossible to draft an immediate reply because Governor Hunt had failed to appoint the required number of Regents and there were not enough Board members in the state to make a quorum. Eventually the charges were answered by Dr. Wilde, who said they were false and had aroused resentment among the faculty.

There is an interesting sidelight on this incident in an article in the *Arizona Star* written by Dr. W. V. Whitmore, who served for several years on the Board.

> Although the first State Legislature had provided an increase in the Board of Regents from four to eight, and for both political parties to be represented, yet Governor Hunt did not appoint these additional Regents for two years. In the fall of 1913 Chancellor Waters moved to California. The result was that for several months no meeting of the Board of Regents could be held because of a lack of a quorum. Finally the Chancellor made a special trip here from Los Angeles in order that a meeting might be held. The business of several months was transacted, but in a few months more the situation was as bad as before. Chancellor Hereford and Treasurer Wheatley notified Governor Hunt, so I am informed, that unless some additional Regents were appointed so the affairs of the University could be properly administered, they would resign. The result was that on April 14, several of us were appointed. I am thoroughly convinced that, had not Providence come to our rescue, some of us Republicans would never have been appointed.

One constant annoyance was the inadequacy of the financial administration of the University. The institution had grown in Dr. Wilde's time from a school with a state appropriation of $47,800 to one with an appropriation of $218,150 plus $80,000 contributed by the federal government. Yet President Wilde and a typist-bookkeeper were expected to handle the books, pay bills, take discounts, and watch the cash. Finally a registrar was appointed in 1913 to deal with student records, while general business operation was entrusted to a professor of mathematics who took over the books. This was not successful.

It is probable that President Wilde felt he could not cope with political attacks plus financial confusion and still do justice to his broad duties, for in May, 1914 he said farewell to students and faculty and went to Boston University. There he built the department of education into a school in four years and served as dean until his retirement twenty-one years later.

His final message to the Board of Regents presented a plan for a reorganization of the University. He said that in his judgment the school was now ready for a College of Science, Literature, and Arts (known today as the College of Liberal Arts) and a College of Mines and Engineering. These, with the College of Agriculture, would give it three colleges. It was his belief that:

> Every instructor and every student in the University would and should have a primary connection with one or another of these colleges; the faculty of each college would meet frequently for discussion of its work and with other faculties for general University interests. The President of the University or, in his absence, the dean or director, would preside over the meetings of each faculty. Every student would be under the direction and discipline of his proper faculty and a minimum of disciplinary duty would come to the President of the University, thus relieving him of one of his most uncongenial tasks and giving this to a group of men who know the student intimately in his daily class work.

President Wilde also revised his views of the need for more emphasis on mining instruction. He had said once that the principal emphasis should be on agriculture, but he now felt that because of the economic importance of the mines and the fine opportunities for instruction the work should be expanded. Proper work, he warned, could not be accomplished unless there was money for "more instructors, more room, and more equipment."

He closed his services with a word of thanks to the Board of Regents and said the reasons for his resignation had become more convincing with time. In a final address to the students he begged that they cherish the University and left them this thought:

> A University is not a business, it is not a mill. It is a spirit, a personality, a composite personality. The good that you do becomes a moral possession of the University. The ill that you do becomes a drug on its spiritual energy. The justice you cherish becomes a part of the justice of the University.

CHAPTER 6

1914–1922

ON AUGUST 7, 1914, the Board of Regents gave the presidency of the University of Arizona to Rufus Bernhard von KleinSmid—making two errors in the spelling of his name—at a salary of $4,500 a year plus a home and utilities.

The seventh president was a native of Illinois and a professor of psychology and philosophy with an M.A. degree from Northwestern. He had done research in criminology in an Indiana penal institution and had taught at Northwestern and DePauw. His name was apparently unknown on the Arizona campus but he soon took care of that. The day after he had addressed his first assembly, the students were his devoted admirers and in a few months all Arizona was talking about him.

The Southwest loved orators, but it never before had seen or heard the equal of this handsome, magnetic, and eloquent man whose commanding voice carried conviction in every syllable.

He had only one theme—*Greater Arizona*—and he made it a flaming torch that set the campus ablaze with enthusiasm and aroused the State to a new appreciation of its institution of higher learning. Dr. Howard A. Hubbard, professor of history, who came to the University in 1912, remembered:

> Wherever von KleinSmid found an audience, on the campus, in the town and throughout the state, he talked about 'Greater Arizona' and repeated one phrase—'I am proud of the young men and women of this state!'—Soon the faculty, student body and citizens accepted his spirit as their own. He had sold them the idea.

One of President von KleinSmid's first acts was to establish frequent student assemblies which he addressed as president, instructor, fellow student, and friend. These proved so popular that short daily assemblies were held which, Dr. Hubbard said, attracted faculty as well as students.

Arizona Life covered the new President's speeches and announcements at great length and quoted parts of his first speech in which he said:

> Don't think you are preparing for a future life. You are forming your character now. The kind of person you are now is the kind you will be when you finish college.
>
> Your first obligation to this school is good scholarship. I do not mean phenomenal scholarship. That is best in books. . . . The encouragement should be for the student who can go from September to May, doing high grade honest classwork . . .
>
> Find at least 20 minutes a day for your look ahead. It will inspire you for the things you need to do.

The paper also reported:

> Prexy seemed especially impressed with the fact that in the short time he had been at the University he had met several people who apologized for various things about the University. He said he was tired of hearing people apologize for Arizona because he did not think there was any reason for such apologies. He did not think we need to apologize for our future outlook. We are getting things done just as every university gets them done. He compared the UA with Harvard in its early days and said we had a much better start than it did and that Harvard had nothing to apologize for. He complimented students for their spirit and yells and said there certainly was nothing to apologize for along those lines. He said he could not think of a single reason for Arizona not getting everything it wanted.

The President said that the future depended on three factors: a faculty that could merit respect for scholarly attainment, an efficient physical plant, and a school spirit that would show such pride in the University that it would build goodwill throughout all Arizona. *Arizona Life* answered him in an editorial outlining the advances which, it said, were the goal of the student body:

> The scope of our idea for a 'Greater Arizona' should extend into the future to a time when our College of Mines has increased to many times its present size and we are

> equipped with good means of properly housing it; to the time when we are equipped with a new observatory and a handsome new armory; we should look forward to the time when we have a complete graduate school on our campus; when our separate departments—especially law and philosophy—have been enlarged, and to the development of our department of psychology.

It seemed like a vain hope for a University with only 203 regularly enrolled students, but one by one all the objectives except the armory were reached.

Although he was not a strong supporter of college sports at the time, Dr. von KleinSmid knew how to capitalize on student enthusiasm, and when Coach McKale's eleven beat New Mexico 10–0 and defeated Pomona 7–6 in a game that upset all Pacific Coast predictions, the President conducted the largest assembly ever held and told the crowd that the victory was a promise of that "Greater Arizona" they had been talking about. This was what the students wanted to hear from a president, and an editorial in the campus paper reveals their spirit. The editor wrote:

> The greatest football season in the history of Arizona has closed. The team has passed through its most successful season, losing but one game, that to Occidental, 14 to 0. The Wildcat now calmly sits on top of the ladder. The blue and red banner flings to the breeze and to the Southwestern country the news that Arizona is placed on the map to stay. The winning of the Pomona game has meant more to the University than any other event in its history.

The formal inauguration of Dr. von KleinSmid was held January 11–12, 1915, and the daily press gave it columns of space. The *Star* opened its coverage with a six-column story under a black and breathless headline:

> FROM MAINE TO CALIFORNIA SCHOLARS COME TO ATTEND DR. KLEINSMID'S INAUGURATION
>
> Ninety-one Institutions of Learning Honor Arizona's University and its New President by Sending Delegations to Greatest Gathering of Educators ever held in the Southwest; Student Contests and an Arizona Pageant Mark the First Day's Program with Varied Forms of Entertainment, Formal

> and Informal, for Visiting Scholars; Inaugural Service Following Procession is Climax of the Inauguration.

Mentioning that formal academic occasions were rare in the West, *The Star* paid grave attention to the traditions involved in the ceremonies. Then it went into the order in which the procession moved, naming each group and explaining the significance of the colors and designs on the gowns, hoods, and mortarboards.

The program on the first day included a military review, receptions, dinners, a basketball game, and, on the football field under the stars, an elaborate pageant which told the story of Arizona from the days of Father Kino to the coming of statehood. Miss Estelle Lutrell, wrote the four acts and designed the scenery. *The Star* said it was a "gorgeous pageant," and even today a reading of the script shows it was no mean production. Students built the sets and played all the parts. The cast was big, one scene calling for forty actors.

The stage was on the site of the present library. There was no lighting system, but students took care of that problem. Bonfires were built at various spots, and in the light of their leaping flames, Indians, priests, settlers, soldiers, and miners unfolded the history of the state.

As the pageant opened, a native chant sounded from the shadows and Indians came out of the darkness to build a council fire. The ceremonies were interrupted by a messenger who brought news of the coming of the great "Black Robe." Kino appeared with a group of missionaries and a band of Spanish soldiers who carried a huge cross. As the missionaries chanted, some of the Indians knelt while others brought gifts of fruit and flowers. Then the cast faded into the shadows again and the firelight found only the ancient symbol that had been planted in a new land.

Reverent silence was finally broken by the voices of white men who came with cattle and a plough. They made preparations to turn a furrow but were attacked and slain by Apaches. More settlers appeared, and these, too, were attacked; but this time American dragoons drove the Apaches away and stood guard over the wagons.

Then came the railroad, depicted by a station scene in which miners, school teachers, farmers, peddlers, cowboys, and rangers alighted from a passenger car. Last of all was Geronimo, in chains. The scene signified the end of the Indian wars and the coming of education and commerce.

There followed an interlude during which students piled fresh wood on the fires, and then the red and yellow flames revealed the figure of Columbia seated on a dais under an arch. A priest, a soldier, and a miner appeared, carrying a large valentine. Placed at Columbia's feet, the valentine opened and a small boy in cowboy costume stepped out and pinned a new star on an American flag. As Columbia accepted the banner, hidden electric lights on the arch above her head flashed forth and spelled out "1885—U. of A.—1915." Cast and audience sang, *Alma Mater*, and the pageant closed.

Mrs. C. Z. Lesher and Mrs. Orville McPherson played the parts of Indian maidens. "It was really very effective," according to Mrs. Lesher. "Practically everybody in Tucson was there and not only filled the bleacher seats but sat on the hard ground of the playing field."

The formal inauguration of President von KleinSmid at the National Guard Armory followed an academic procession that was two blocks long. The ceremony could not have been more dignified or elaborate had it been held at Harvard, which, *The Star* pointed out, was the father of such affairs. Noted educators, students, alumni, and members of the Board of Regents welcomed the new president and praised him without reservation.

Bishop Edwin Holt Hughes, who had been president of DePauw University when Dr. von KleinSmid was a member of the faculty, spoke with sincere feeling of his former professor's regard for young people, and told the audience that their new leader had been the most popular man on the Depauw campus. He added:

> Deal kindly with your President. He is a good, clean, and strong man. There will be no night so dark that he will not get out of bed and walk mile after mile with any of you students to advise and help you gain the right track.

Dr. Abram Winegardner Harris, president of Northwestern University, was equally complimentary. He said that with the coming of Dr. von KleinSmid, Arizona students need look no longer to the great educational institutions of the East for training, but should give their loyalty to their own state university.

Dr. William V. Whitmore, who had been one of the Regents to extend the invitation to Dr. von KleinSmid, spoke of the satisfaction the Board felt over its choice. "No one has to tell the Board what a treasure it has," he declared. "We realize he has brought more favorable publicity to the University in five months than it has received in five years."

Not the least of the tributes came from Frank Culin, Jr., student president, who said:

> The student body have reason to be proud of Arizona

> as it is. We have a splendid faculty. Our new President has taken part in all our affairs. He has made changes and is liked all the better for them. He has convinced students that whatever he does is for the betterment of the University. He has won the entire support of the student body.

The Daily Citizen presented its views in an editorial:

> In the acquisition of Dr. von KleinSmid for the Presidency, the University of Arizona has made a real find. The new President has fitted in with the temperament and spirit of the community and has given the University and the students a new inspiration and a new impetus. The power of his personality is already being felt in all departments and abroad he is constantly making new friends for the University and bringing home to the people of the state the importance of fostering their chief institution of learning.

Dr. von KleinSmid's response to the honors paid him was a warning that the University was and would continue to be more than a teaching school. He said in part:

> I would not have the atmosphere of the University exclusively scholastic. I do want students to go out and demonstrate to the people of the state that it has been worth while to spend thousands of dollars on the education of our young men and women, but it is not fair to judge a University by its per capita expense.
>
> The University also serves the state in a general way by its extension work, thus trying to place its facilities within reach of every citizen of the state. Through its departments of research it holds out sure lines of procedure. Who can estimate the per capita cost of works of this character?
>
> The education of students represents scarcely one-third of the endeavor of your state institution.

As a final honor, the Board of Regents conferred on Dr. von KleinSmid the degree of Doctor of Science and gave him the new seal of the University.

As might be expected, a few students showed up eventually who mistook the President's spirit of camaraderie for weakness and experimented with his good will. The *Arizona Wildcat* reported that a number of college men had seized the little streetcar that made the last night-run from the city, lifted it off the tracks, and left it on the campus. Dr. von KleinSmid brought the subject up in assembly the next morning. He was calm but there was no hint of laughter in his voice when he announced that the guilty students would leave the room and put the car back where they had found it. It was back in ten minutes but the student athletic fund was charged $60.00 for damages done to the car, and the student fund did not come by $60.00 easily in those days.

The year 1915–1916 was a busy one, alive with important developments for students who reflected the fresh spirit by changing the name of their newspaper from *Arizona Life* to *The Arizona Wildcat* and then began building the giant "A" on Sentinel Peak, which is now known as "A" Mountain. Fourteen Saturdays were spent digging trenches and filling them with rocks, and when the final day arrived President von KleinSmid cancelled all classes so that every student might join the work crew and help complete the task. According to *The Wildcat*, men passed an endless chain of buckets filled with cement up the steep slope and poured the contents around the stones. Women students arrived at noon bringing lunches and coffee for the workers. Before night, whitewash was applied to the stones and the job was finished.

The Wildcat said the letter could be seen for twenty to thirty miles on principal roads and added an editorial which commented:

> In years to come when your children attend the University of Arizona you will tell them of the fact that you helped to build the Big A, and they will point to it with pride and tell their friends and classmates that you helped put it there.

Arizona's debating team defeated a law school team from the University of Southern California this same year, and when USC defeated Columbia University for the college debating championship of the United States, Arizona claimed the national title. The campus was crackling with activities, and the 1916 issue of *The Desert* describes eight formal dances given by fraternities, sororities, and clubs. The junior class produced *Trelawney of the Wells* and the class in Elizabethan drama marked Shakespeare's anniversary with scenes from *Henry V* and Shaw's *Dark Lady of the Sonnets*. Both were played on the lawn of the West Cottage. At the same time the class in oratory had what *The Desert* called a most successful season, closing the year with a debate on the question: "Resolved: That the Military Forces of the United States Should Be Substantially Increased." The U. of A. team won a unanimous decision and first prize went to Grady Gammage who later became President of Arizona State College at Flagstaff and Arizona State University at Tempe.

Delta Phi, Sigma Phi Beta, Sigma Pi Alpha, Gamma Phi Sigma, and Gamma Delta held initiations and dinners while a new organization known as the "A" Club was formed. Members were required to be of sophomore standing and to have won two varsity letters.

Other organizations active that year, when the institution became a University in fact as well as in name, were a women's glee club, the Aggie Club, Society of Civil Engineers, Mechanical-Electrical Engineering Society, a girls' debating society known as "The Wranglers," Young Men's Christian Association, Associated Students, the Women's League, and the West Cottage Boosters. Military activities reached a new high with the formation of a provisional regiment of two battalions composed of four companies, and the holding of a military ball that drew the largest crowd ever to attend a university dance.

All this evidence of a healthy student spirit was accompanied by significant progress in academic and administrative policies. President Wilde's last report had recommended the reorganization of the University into three colleges, and, on Dr. von KleinSmid's approval, the Board of Regents put the plan into effect. The College of Agriculture had been established at the end of Dr. Wilde's term. To this were added the College of Letters, Arts, and Sciences and the College of Mines and Engineering. Three deans were then appointed. Dr. Robert H. Forbes was made Dean of the College of Agriculture as well as Director of the Agricultural Experiment Station, Dr. Andrew E. Douglass became Dean of the College of Letters, Arts, and Sciences, and Dr. Gurdon Montague Butler was appointed Dean of the College of Mines and Engineering.

Dr. Howard Hubbard recalled in later years that the reorganization had upset a few professors. He said:

> Some members of the faculty had always gone to the President with their problems and objected to going to a dean whom they considered one of their equals. I remember hearing of a department head who went to von KleinSmid and said, "I came here to have a fight." von KleinSmid said, "Good! There's nothing I like better than a fight. But remember, I'm holding the handle of the whip."
>
> I don't remember that we had any trouble in the College

> of Letters, Arts, and Sciences. We could appreciate the fact that the President was making a University out of a school and we accepted the change.

Two other important changes marked this important year in university history. The first was the discontinuation of the preparatory school. High schools were now so well established that it was unnecessary to educate preparatory school students. Another advance that contributed to the reputation of the University was the establishment of a department of law. In four years this became a school and in ten years was made a college by an act of the Legislature.

Harry C. Westover, judge of the U. S. District Court for the Southern District of California, wrote a letter on his days as a law student at the University of Arizona in which he said:

> My brother [W. H. Westover, who is now practicing law in Yuma] and I were the first two students enrolled. Dr. Samuel Fegtly who had practiced law in Chicago was imported by the University. I remember him as a tall, lean sort of man with a large head on which perched a mop of bushy hair. I also remember there was a professor from Yale who stayed a year or two. I believe there were several lawyers from downtown who gave courses.
>
> Many of our classes were held in Old Main which, even at that time, was an old building which had been condemned more or less, and there was considerable discussion about tearing it down and erecting a new building.
>
> I can remember Dr. Fegtly telling us on more than one occasion that he didn't care about the correctness of answers; that he did care about our reasoning and would give us a grade if our answers were incorrect but well reasoned—perhaps better than the grade we would receive if our answers were correct but not well reasoned. In other words, he was trying to get us to formulate theories of law rather than memorize cases and give remembered answers. I know of no one who could have received better instruction in the study of law than my brother and I during the three years we were in law school.
>
> World War I intervened and as a result many of the

> students joined the armed forces. My brother and I left in 1918 for our armed service duty. Our departure was sometime prior to graduation. Nevertheless, we were allowed to take the bar examination and were admitted to practice law by the supreme court. Our diplomas were given to our representatives at commencement exercises.

Dr. von KleinSmid was fortunate enough to make a firm supporter of Governor George W. P. Hunt, who served seven terms as chief executive. It was an unusual alliance. Dr. von KleinSmid was a cultured scholar and successful administrator who was prominent in academic circles. Hunt was a man with a very limited formal education. But Hunt was devoted to the task of bettering the lot of the common man, and to achieve his goal he became a champion of labor and a battler for liberal legislation. A seasoned politician and leader of the last Territorial Legislature in 1909, he was the natural head of the convention that wrote the constitution of the new state. It was equally natural that the basic law of this constitution would be representative of what Hunt's enemies called his radical philosophy.

It was a foregone conclusion that once the constitution was accepted, the people would make Hunt their governor; this they did, giving him a margin of 11,123 votes over his Republican opponent. The voters of Arizona knew what to expect of him and were not surprised when his first message urged that the mandates laid down in the new constitution be written into laws immediately. Among the mandates were the eight-hour day law, a child labor law, an employer's liability law, an arbitration board for labor disputes, adequate mine inspection, a corporation commission, a rigid anti-usury law, workingman's compulsory compensation, and the initiative, referendum, and recall.

As is not unusual with self-educated men who have come up the hard way, Hunt was a strong supporter of public schools and institutions of higher education. Samuel L. Pattee wrote an article on the Governor in the April, 1935, edition of *Arizona Historical Review*. Here he said Hunt was "determined that the children and youth of the new state should have the opportunity that had been denied him to obtain an education and, if possible, a higher education." Pattee wrote:

> He realized that not everyone could become highly educated, but held to the belief that everyone would be better off for whatever education he could assimilate and that it was the business of the state to see he had the opportunity to do

the best he could.

Hunt's first message favored free textbooks, the teaching of agriculture and, possibly, mining in the high schools. He followed this with what he called, "A comprehensive plan for the University." This plan showed true vision and went far beyond anything presented to the Legislature since Governor Goodwin had called for the building of a University in 1864. Hunt told the Legislature:

> I deplore the policy which has heretofore been pursued of building the state's greatest educational institution on a crazy quilt patchwork scheme. From year to year or from period to period, as the requirements of the University dictated, and as the necessary appropriations could be secured, buildings—generally of a cheap and unsubstantial character—have been added to the plant, apparently with no definite idea for the future. I realize the impossibility which has existed and which now exists, of erecting at one time all, or even a considerable portion of the buildings which will be required from the institution fifty years hence; but I recommend that before any more recommendations are made for improvements, a comprehensive and elaborate plan for a University not only beautiful but adequate for the needs of a century, be adopted. With a goal to work to thus established, buildings may be added from time to time, unit by unit, so placed as to fit appropriately into the finished scheme, so designed as to harmonize architecturally with those surrounding it and to come after, so constructed as to endure for ages. This is the modern method of systematic growth by which the world's greatest institutions of learning are being developed. Whether viewed from the standpoint of economy, efficiency, or architectural superiority, it is the proper plan.

In addressing the Second Legislature in 1915, the Governor again took up the cause of the University and said:

> In the scheme of modern government, the state university is becoming an institution fraught with great possibilities. Encouragement of higher education among the young

> men and women of a state is one of the worthiest objects to which we can bend our energies. Arizona especially, because of her vast mining industry, has an exceptional opportunity for the upbuilding of a superb school of mines in connection with the state university. . . . The Board of Regents and faculty of the University are, I believe, entitled to legislative co-operation in developing the mining department to such an extent as to quickly assist the institution in acquiring a nationwide reputation for excellence and efficiency. To facilitate the growth of the University in other directions, the strengthening of its industrial arts and vocational pursuits curriculum is almost equally desirable. The extension work which the agricultural department of the University is already carrying on in such a way as to afford invaluable instruction and experimentation in the rural districts of the state may be applied to equal advantage by other divisional units of the University.
>
> In this connection I urgently recommend that a suitable appropriation be made for the purpose of enabling the University to increase its facilities for extension work.

Governor Hunt got quick action on his appeal for the College of Mines. The Legislature passed an appropriation carrying $75,000 for a mines and engineering building, with the proviso that the sum must be matched by private gifts.

When President von KleinSmid heard about it, he packed his bag and headed for New York where he interviewed executives of Arizona mining companies and talked so eloquently that they gave him $100,-000. The contributors were: Calumet and Arizona Mining Company, Inspiration Consolidated Copper Company, Miami Copper Company, Old Dominion Copper Mining and Smelting Company, Phelps Dodge Corporation, and Ray Consolidated Copper Company.

When Dr. von KleinSmid took over at the University, extension services consisted of public lectures, discussions, and the distribution of publications. The best men of the faculty were contributing their time and efforts to giving free lecture courses throughout the State. Records show such names as Andrew E. Douglass, G. E. P. Smith, G. M. Butler, Byron Cummings, E. J. Brown, Frank C. Lockwood, Howard A. Hubbard, and Ida Whittington Douglass. These teachers were not digging old lectures out of the files and repeating them to adult audiences; they were trying hard to present popular as well as informative talks. Among subjects listed were: High Mountain Climbing in Peru and Mexico, Irrigation in Italy, Wonders of the Mineral World, The Cliff Dwellers, Longfellow—the Servant of American Culture, and concert lectures on Chopin and Schubert. A number of the lectures were illustrated.

When Governor Hunt recommended that this extension work be stepped up, the University found an opportunity to introduce correspondence courses and to teach night classes on the campus. All this was more than a temporary burst of activity. It was an indication of the regular pace at which the institution would move forward under its new president.

The College of Agriculture building was completed and occupied in 1915, and the second year of Dr. von KleinSmid's administration brought a gift from Mrs. Lavinia Steward of $60,000 for an observatory as a memorial to her late husband. President von KleinSmid and Mrs. Fred C. Roberts (Clara Fish Roberts) were responsible for convincing Mrs. Steward, who had a deep interest in astronomy, that she could not endow a finer memorial. The University then matched the Steward gift and was able to purchase a magnificent thirty-six-inch reflecting telescope.

Visits to famous observatories, the search for a site, plans for the building and the choice of a telescope devolved on Dr. Douglass, who served as director from 1918 to 1938 and is now (1960) Director Emeritus. World War I interfered with construction, and the observatory was not dedicated until April, 1923; but much credit for obtaining the initial gift must go to President von KleinSmid.

Governor Hunt had told the Second State Legislature that the University needed more dormitories for students from the state at large, and the Legislature provided for two such structures. These added to Dr. von KleinSmid's fame as the "building President," but it is probably true that he could not have made such progress without Governor Hunt's faith in education and his approval of the capabilities of the Board of Regents and the President. This faith was demonstrated on one occasion when the Commission of State Institutions clashed with the Regents over recommendations. Hunt stepped in, ordered the Commission to accept the Regents' plans, and later saw to it that the commission was abolished. He said at the time that no institution could be operated by two governing bodies.

One of the three deans appointed by the President was new to the campus. He was Dr. Gurdon M. Butler, who loves to tell the circumstances under which he was hired. In an interview given in the summer of 1957 he said:

I taught for 10 years at Colorado School of Mines and then went to a tiny little school which is now Oregon State College. They had about 32 students and I told the President that the place could never amount to much until they got more than that. I suggested that he send me out into the state to recruit students and he agreed. The result was that we doubled the registration my first year and doubled it again in my second year.

von KleinSmid heard about this and one day when I was out in the wilds of Southern Oregon an Indian came in with an offer of a job as Dean of the Arizona School of Mines. I didn't even know how to pronounce Tucson, but I walked for three days to a telegraph station where I could accept by wire.

von KleinSmid did a good job for Arizona. When he got here it was known as 'Tucson University' but when he left the people thought and spoke of it as the 'University of Arizona.'

While I went to Arizona only as Dean of Mines and Engineering, the Regents' added the title and work of Director of the Bureau of Mines so I have reason to know that some really splendid things were done for the state.

One of our outstanding men was George Fansett. His bulletin on field tests for common minerals went through many editions. Fansett made great use of it. He went out every year and instructed prospectors on methods of determining the presence of metals and identifying their nature. Actually these were little extension schools and they were often held in mining camps. His bulletin was the textbook. Individuals and the industry as a whole got a great deal out of it. Nobody we have ever had at the University has made so many friends for us as George Fansett. I admire him tremendously for the splendid job he did.

William Jennings Bryan, Secretary of State, was promoting closer unity among the nations of the Western Hemisphere in 1915, and through his influence the University was invited to send delegates to the Second Pan-American Scientific Congress that met in Washington during the 1915–16 holiday season. The Board of Regents sent President von KleinSmid, who addressed the representatives of twenty-one nations and made such an impression that he was invited to visit the University of Mexico. This was expected to open the way for an exchange of students, and, since Arizona and Mexico had many common ties, it was hoped they would share mutual benefits. The invitation was accepted, and, though war interrupted the negotiations, in 1919 the President finally visited the National University in Mexico City, where he met with President Carranza and his cabinet and received an honorary degree.

Dr. José N. Macias, Rector of the University of Mexico, repaid the visit that same year and received Arizona's honorary LL.D. degree at the time of the twenty-fourth commencement. Tomas Montana, professor of English, who accompanied the Mexican visitors, gave an interview to the press during which he said:

> The relations between the University of Arizona and the University of Mexico have been forever cemented by the visit of your president to our country and our national institution. He has exemplified a spirit of national co-operation and friendship which no amount of misrepresentation by fomenters of trouble, such as are always with us, will be able in the future to eradicate.

This effort lead to unofficial visits by Dr. and Mrs. von KleinSmid to Panama, Ecuador, Peru, and Chile in 1920. The Latin American countries proved gracious hosts. Ecuador and Chile admitted the President to honorary membership in the faculties of their universities, and the University of Peru granted him the degree of "Doctor en Filosofia y Letras." Under a grant made by the Carnegie Foundation, since that time, the program of scholastic relations between the University of Arizona and the University of Sonora at Hermosillo has grown immeasurably and strengthened the bond between the United States and its neighboring republic Mexico.

The attention Dr. von KleinSmid had given to promoting public relations in the state was now beginning to pay off. Undergraduate and graduate enrollment increased by 107 in 1917, while the total registration moved from 633 to 780. These figures included short-course students in farming, mining, home economics, and correspondence.

This was the biggest gain the University had made in a single year, and there was great hope that the rate would increase. But the shadow of war darkened the campus in the spring of 1916 when General John J. Pershing led a punitive expedition into Mexico on the trail of Pancho Villa, the guerrilla chief who had invaded the United States and killed seventeen persons in Columbus, New Mexico.

Congress created an officers' reserve training corps in June, and the Board of Regents asked that an infantry unit of the corps be established at the University. The request was granted, two retired army officers being detailed to direct all military work on the campus. June 18 saw the national guard ordered to the border, and southern Arizona was in an uproar over the possibility that Villa might invade Arizona as he had invaded New Mexico.

A home guard was organized in Tucson. Business and professional men kept rifles behind their office doors and Colt revolvers in the drawers of their desks. Private automobiles were listed and owners were required to keep them ready to transport the guard to any battlefront that might develop. Mexicans who fled into Arizona from Nogales, Sonora, spread the rumor that 3,000 Yaquis were plotting to run a train loaded with dynamite through that town and explode it at the international border. Then, when all was confusion, the story ran, the Yaquis intended to take the road to Tucson.

Ranchers at Sasabe, Ajo, and Arivaca sent their women and children to Tucson, which was living in a state of high agitation and sleeping with one ear open for the sound of an alarm. The situation was not much calmer at the University than it was downtown. The summer vacation was on, but faculty members formed a military company to protect their families and to guard the campus.

The new agricultural building was declared to be a fort and faculty families were required to stock it with a week's supply of food. All male professors and staff members were armed. Those who owned no rifles were supplied from the cadet stores. A partial list of these guards can be found in the library. It carries such names as G. E. P. Smith, W. E. Bryan, J. J. Thornber, W. S. Cunningham, and Howard A. Hubbard. Professor Thornber, who was elected captain, took his company into the mountains once a week for target practice. Dr. Hubbard said the drills under the hot summer sun were no fun, but added:

> We used to take time out and get into long arguments over whether we would march down the Nogales road and meet the Yaquis outside the town, or stay on the campus in our fort and fight a defensive battle. The question was never settled and Sergeant Frederick Dickie who was our drill master got a little tired of it.

Dread of a Yaqui invasion passed, but was replaced by a greater fear that the nation might be forced to abandon its policy of neutrality and enter the war against Germany. National leaders were talking about preparedness and President Wilson led a "preparedness march" down Pennsylvania Avenue in Washington in June, 1916. A month later a similar parade in San Francisco was marked by the explosion of a bomb that killed six people. Two radical union leaders were arrested, convicted, and sentenced to life imprisonment. Congress passed Army and Navy appropriation acts and created a Council of National Defense with power "to coordinate industries and resources for national defense and welfare."

The dawn of 1917 was dark with the clouds of war. American ships were being sunk by German submarines, and President Wilson issued an executive order to arm American merchant ships. Members of the Cabinet agreed that war could not be avoided, and on April 2 Wilson went before a joint session of Congress to ask that war be declared against Germany to "make the world safe for democracy."

Like most educational institutions, the University responded immediately. On April 5, the day before Wilson signed the declaration of war, Dr. von KleinSmid was authorized by the Board of Regents to inform Governor Thomas E. Campbell that the campus and all buildings and laboratories were at the service of the nation. The Council of National Defense accepted "the generous and patriotic act," and told the school to stand by for orders. Commencement exercises were advanced to May 1, to permit men in the senior class to enter officers' training camps as soon as possible, and the graduating class received diplomas after hearing William Jennings Bryan deliver an address on "Our relation to Our Government, to Society and to God."

Presidents and directors of experimental stations in all land-grant colleges in Pacific Coast states were now summoned to a conference in Berkeley, California, to plan on mobilizing efforts to step up industry and increase the production of food. Dr. von KleinSmid and Dr. Robert H. Forbes represented Arizona. Later in the year, the League of the Southwest was organized with Arizona, California, Colorado, New Mexico, and Wyoming as members. Under the leadership of Dr. von KleinSmid, it concerned itself at first with meeting government needs in agriculture and industry. Later it was to turn its attention to the water problem.

The University opened on schedule in the Fall, and Dr. von KleinSmid talked at length to the students on the part the institution was taking in the war. He was especially happy to be able to report that 80 per cent of the University of Arizona men who had entered officers' training school had won commissions, a figure 30 per cent above the national average.

The Wildcat editors noted with pride and regret that large numbers of students were leaving campus for the armed services and announced that copies of the paper would be mailed to all students in uniform.

The Agricultural College planted and cultivated a war garden and gave the dining hall first option on the produce. Captain Angus R. Smith, USA Ret., organized 160 men students into three infantry companies. A chapter of the American Red Cross was formed, and every woman student was asked to sign up for knitting needles and yarn. The quota was 900 units and included sweaters, helmet liners, and wristlets.

University girls dressed as Red Cross nurses ushered at a football game between the faculty and the University Club. Some of the girls sold peanuts while others had the pleasant duty of giving a heroic player first aid whenever he felt he needed it. *The Wildcat* said it was surprising how many players were knocked out and how often the ambulance had to be rushed on the field. Students and faculty contributed $1,031 to the student Friendship War Fund campaign conducted by the YMCA and YWCA. Commencement was advanced to December 21, 1917, and graduating seniors went into service immediately. Twenty men were admitted to the third officers' training school.

Important as the University's contributions to military training on the campus were soon to be, they could not exceed in importance the work that the College of Agriculture carried on through the experiment station, extension division and the department of home economics in 1917–1918. It would take a separate book to cover the success with which the college adapted itself to the war needs of the state and the nation as county agents, home demonstration specialists, and boys' and girls' clubs spread out into the counties.

Although Dr. Forbes was sent to Egypt at the request of the British government in February, 1917, and President von KleinSmid was made acting Dean of the College of Agriculture, the organization Dr. Forbes had left behind him carried on with great efficiency. Every activity, including the distribution of thousands of helpful leaflets, was geared to increasing the production of food. During the year 1917 a total of 6,700 calls were made at individual farms and 622 group meetings were held with total attendance of 29,720. Thousands of home gardens were planted before the war closed and many families ate home-grown vegetables for the first time.

Preservation as well as production of food was stressed and this meant teaching methods of canning, drying, and storage. Home demonstration agents held fifty-four large canning schools that were attended by hundreds of women, and eight teams of five girls each held scores of smaller schools, while farm boys carried out projects in growing cotton, corn, grain sorghum, pigs, and potatoes. Two hundred and fifty purebred sires were brought in to improve herds and flocks. "Sheep on every farm" was the slogan of a campaign that increased production in Apache and Navajo counties. County agents demonstrated the use of tractors in Maricopa County before as many as 1,000 farmers and taught dairymen how to build and use silos. The record for 1918 was 1,285 demonstrations attended by a total of 29,000 persons, and 5,407 visits to farms.

The University of Arizona home economics women matched the record of the men that year, for the reports show they travelled 31,526 miles to carry their messages and demonstrate their methods to Arizona housewives.

While these specialists spread throughout the state, the campus was changing. The government had asked the University to provide vocational training and practical work in the mining trades to meet a call from General Pershing for specialists in mechanic arts and crafts.

Plans for preparing quarters for the army were assigned to Dean Gurdon M. Butler. He directed the construction of barracks, shops, and mess hall, and provided equipment and instructors for courses in rough carpentry, blacksmithing, and electricity and motor mechanics.

Advanced military classes swung picks and shovels in constructing model trenches east of the athletic field. These were built on a scale of one inch to a foot and had fire trenches, barbwire entanglements, flares, and bells.

September, 1918, saw a second government contract signed, under which a Students' Army Training Corps was organized for technical training of enlisted men, and by the time the school year opened in October, the academic students were practically lost in the shuffle. How true this was can be learned from Dr. von KleinSmid's statement that "curriculum and traditions have been literally pulled to pieces." If a more detailed picture is wanted, one need only turn to *The Wildcat*'s description of the campus as it was in October, 1918:

> Those who returned to the campus found all they could do was to float around until final adjustments were made.
>
> Civilians and soldiers by the hundreds were hurrying to and fro in the business of intensive army training. Great army trucks were busy unloading supplies into rooms which were formerly used for classes or recreation. Huge machine shops, storage yards and large cantonment buildings are now situated where four months ago there had been gardens. On the athletic field where the Wildcat teams formerly met worthy opponents in football or other athletic contests may

now be seen hundreds of soldiers in military drill most any hour between daylight and dark. The old mess hall where the students used to eat in true family style and enjoy a social half-hour at each meal has been converted into an army mess where 200 soldiers march in and sit at a command. They sit at long tables and dive into the chow, gobble it up in 10 minutes and go out to halls which used to be homes for men on campus but are now converted into barracks for the regular army and are equipped accordingly. At the head of each soldier's bed stands his rifle, side arms, full equipment and his luggage. Doors are to be taken off the sleeping rooms which will then accommodate more sleeping space. Even the old gymnasium and the Women's League rooms are being used as temporary barracks for the new men who are continually pouring in from every part of the West.

At the first sound of reville [*sic*] in the morning, the soldiers' quarters on the campus immediately come into action and the clash of sidearms and of soldiers jumping into their clothes may be heard from every direction in the dark. At 6:15 after a little lively exercise they march to breakfast. At the voice of the bugle, which sounds many times a day, the campus comes alive with hurrying soldiers coming from every direction. During the call to the colors at retreat the entire campus stands at attention or salutes as the case may be. After taps at 10 p.m., the campus is dark and silent and any straggler venturing near is confronted by a stern, armed sentinel who demands an adequate explanation.

Nearly all the girls have returned and brought about 100 new girls with them. North Hall and East and West cottages are filled with girls and many who are properly chaperoned are staying in town. The parlor in North Hall has been converted into a dining hall where all campus girls eat. They live in a little world all by themselves. The War Department does not even allow men and women in the same classes.

The girls are taking special war courses which will fit them to fill all kinds of technical and clerical positions in order that more men may be released for the front. Not only are the girls doing this but they are taking over all student body and semi-academic student activities which the men

> have given up in pursuit of the intensive war training program. Together with these things, Red Cross work, YWCA, the girls are performing a very important function on our campus as well as in the war program. They deserve and are receiving great praise for so capably responding to the needs of the great cause.
>
> Now about the social life of the college community; we don't know. Ask the War Department. Fraternities lose their individuality in the army. All fraternity men and student army training corps must dispense with fraternity life and move into the campus barracks. The civilian students who do not live on the campus will form at least one club and take over at least one fraternity house as their own. The other fraternity houses will be taken over by the University and will be used to house a few regular University students. It is possible the soldiers may be granted one afternoon a week off, and possibly a few hours on Sunday, but of course, nobody knows.
>
> In all probability, there will not be many social events except possibly a few that may be held off campus. The regular assembly will be held in the auditorium every Sunday afternoon, and everyone is invited.

The influenza epidemic that swept the nation in the Fall and Winter of 1918 hit the University in October, and both college and army officials took quick steps to put the campus under quarantine. The following notice was posted:

> On account of the prevalence of Spanish Influenza in many sections, as a preventative measure this campus is under absolute quarantine beginning at six o'clock, Thursday, Oct. 2, and continuing until further notice. Admission to the campus is on quarantine pass only. Students who live on campus must move off before the quarantine is established, prepared to remain for the period of the quarantine. Faculty members and employes are admitted on pass but must avoid association with all persons outside their own home while off campus. Particularly must they remain away from all public assemblies such as picture shows, church services and public lectures.

There were reasons for alarm because the nation-wide epidemic was taking thousands of lives, and army camps, where men lived in congested quarters, were hit especially hard. The University, however, came through with a fine record. Four hospital wards were set up in Old Main and on the top floor of the agricultural building. A ten-room house east of the campus, which the Regents had purchased and equipped as an infirmary in June, 1918, was of great value. Dr. von KleinSmid, in his annual report, spoke of its acquisition as "providential."

All classes were suspended, and the University community, greatly aided by physicians, nurses, and Red Cross workers from Tucson took over the care of the sick. Supplies of bed sox, pneumonia jackets, night shirts, and sweaters, as well as quantities of delicacies, were furnished without charge. Faculty members worked as nurses, staffed a diet kitchen, and fumigated quarters. Some carried hot coffee to sentries who patrolled the campus at night.

The final score was two deaths among the soldiers, no cases among women students, and very few among the men. The figures spoke eloquently of the skill with which the challenge was met.

The worst of the epidemic was over when war ended in November, but it was not until January, 1919, that classes were resumed and the campus was back to normal. *The Wildcat* said:

> Perhaps the most interesting change on our campus has been the sudden transition, in less than a month, from a very efficient military training camp boasting 600 men, to a regular, thriving, University such as has never been known before in the history of the Southwest. The only remaining evidences of the training camp of war time are the temporary wooden structures which have been respectively the barracks, cook house, auto shop, hospital and Y-hut. With the exception of the Y-hut, which is being used as a social center for men students, all these buildings are standing idle.
>
> The brass buttons on the khaki-clad fighting mechanics corps will be seen no more on the campus and there is a corresponding cheerfulness on the faces of the male populace.

Government war contracts with the University expired early in December, 1918, when Washington gave the order for the demobilization of troops, and the "fighting mechanics," as they were known, faded from the campus.

In the following year, the Board of Regents signed an agreement to participate in the education of disabled veterans, and 194 of these men were registered. Many, however, had not completed high-school work, so the University set up courses in trades and industrial education for them. A second group, known as Federal Board of Education students, all of whom were honorably discharged service men with high school diplomas, was admitted to regular courses in 1920–21 and fifty received degrees.

The University emerged from the war far stronger than when it went in. Not only did it win friends in the state, but it also was accepted as a member of the Association of American Colleges in 1919. There was a notable increase in enrollment. This was true also in other universities, for the war created a "Go-to-College" spirit. But not all universities saw the enrollment triple between 1915–1920 as did the University of Arizona.

Naturally, as the number of students grew, so did the size of the faculty. There had been thirty-one full professors, associates, assistants and instructors at the close of 1914. In 1920, there were fifty-five faculty members, including four deans.

Miss Estelle Lutrell wrote with a touch of nostalgia of the social life that bloomed after the close of the war. She said:

> The President's house was enlivened as never before by a continuous round of student and faculty functions. The personality of the President, ably supplemented by the social gifts of Mrs. von KleinSmid, exerted a unifying influence throughout the University. Those of diversified interests were brought into better understanding with each other and differences of opinion were softened by the gracious hospitality which prevailed. Legislators, regents, friends from town, students, parents, faculty and the administration staff were entertained at large receptions as well as in small groups. No opportunity was neglected to promote friendly relationships.

Winter programs were never complete without climbs to "The Window" in the Catalinas to "Bat Cave." Week-ends and holidays were frequently spent riding the desert or exploring the mountains. Hundreds of winter tourists, however, got an appreciation of the desert the easy way. They wandered through the campus cactus garden in front of Old Main and marvelled at the 600 species of desert growth.

College opened on October 8 in 1919, and Dr. von KleinSmid delivered an address that the student paper called "inspiring." Under his guidance, the University recovered rapidly from war's interruption. Summer school, which had been inaugurated in 1918, was continued. The Board of Regents appointed Professor D. W. Working of the United States Department of Agriculture as Dean of the College of Agriculture, and that same year saw Dr. von KleinSmid introduce intelligence tests for male students and recommend a College of Education. He had been responsible for setting up a school of education in 1915, but had always felt it should become a college.

Women students, who had been shifted from one cottage to another, moved into a fine college home of their own when the doors of Maricopa Hall were opened in the fall of 1920.

The War Department gave the University 100 horses and provided equipment and forage, whereupon the Regents built stables for an R.O.T.C. cavalry squadron in which 250 men registered. Out of this came a polo team and many cavalry officers who eventually served in mechanized divisions during World War II.

Intense efforts to aid programs in the state and nation naturally slowed down after demobilization, but not all the momentum was lost. The staff of the College of Agriculture spent weeks giving special courses in range-stock production, and students made a long tour to large ranches in most of the counties. Experts also went out when communities appealed for aid in fighting typhoid fever and carried on clean-up campaigns.

Athletics reached a high point when the Wildcats defeated Occidental's eleven 27 to 0 in 1919. Louis Slonaker, later Dean of Men, was a famous athlete in those days, and starred in this game. The team elected him captain, and the whole school celebrated with a special assembly and an all-day holiday.

It is interesting to note that the highest possible degree of loyalty to the University of Arizona marked *The Wildcat* in those days. Its pages boasted continually of the growth of the school and the excellence of the faculty. Intercollegiate debates got great attention on page one and so did news of the annual farmers' and homekeepers' week. Sport sometimes suffered, as it did in one issue when the basketball schedule received less than half a column while agriculture got five columns and the Sock and Buskin club's production, "*Mice and Men*" got one.

The university debating team, composed of Fred Fickett, Jr. and Hess Seaman, defeated the University of Southern California team and won a unanimous vote of the judges as well as an eight-column banner line and a two-column story in *The Wildcat*. The University had previously beaten Texas and now sent its team to the coast where it defeated both Occidental and Redlands.

About the only University feature that seemed to draw no enthusiastic response from the student body was a large and handsome aviary which was originally located inside the main gates. It was the gift of Mrs. Lavinia Steward, donor of Steward Observatory, who hoped that a collection of Arizona birds would be a campus attraction. The cage was the largest and finest in the Southwest, but *The Wildcat* said editorially that the collection was too small and that too many of the birds were not indigenous to the Southwest. Even the ducks, it was contended were not true Arizonans.

The cage was moved to a site between what is now the Student Union and the Women's Building. However, that space was eventually needed for other purposes and the aviary was moved again, to a location on Highland Avenue and Fourth Street. This time it was the Tucson public which had no use for the birds and feelings mounted until legal action was threatened, on the ground that the cage constituted a public nuisance because the birds awakened citizens too early in the morning.

Dr. Homer L. Shantz, who was then President, met with a group of citizens and told them, with a genteel sting in his words, that he felt a university "should be built in the country and no one allowed to live within five miles." "Everything the University does," he said, "seems to cut in on someone." He reminded them that they had complained about the location of the cavalry stables, and now they didn't like the birds. "Two years ago," he added, "citizens living south of the University said the barking of laboratory dogs kept them awake. The dogs were moved to the north side of the campus and people on the north complained. When the dogs' vocal cords were cut so they couldn't bark, the humane society jumped on us for our cruelty."

It was finally decided that the citizens would withdraw objections to the cage if the University would dispose of an eagle, some cockatoos, and a macaw, all of which were prime offenders. After that, the cage seems to have vanished.

Another event in which the student paper was deeply interested was the possible formation of a Southwest Intercollegiate Conference, which it felt would mean better football games and more of them. This might have been the biggest news of 1921, except for the bomb exploded by the *Star* when it carried a telegraph story on October 8 revealing that the University of Southern California had offered the post of President to Dr. von KleinSmid and that he would probably accept.

Although the *Star* buried the story inside its morning edition, *The Citizen* gave it a nine-column banner line on page one the next afternoon. It said the loss of Dr. von KleinSmid would halt the building and expansion of the University. *The Citizen* followed this the next day with a two-column editorial on the front page, warning that ninety-nine per cent of the people would look upon the resignation as a calamity.

The Citizen used no names but it spoke of "marplots" who had made "a waspish and unjustifiable attack on the University" at a time when the President was considering offers from the University of Denver, American University in Washington, D. C., and the University of Southern California, but had not fully determined to leave Arizona. Said *The Citizen*:

> We have witnessed the astounding spectacle, at a time when the University was at the zenith of its fame, of men, themselves benefited by an extraordinary education in most instances, deliberately setting out for reasons which can only be characterized as sordid, to destroy the enlargement possibilities of the institution, to attack the administration, criticize the President and to minimize and criticize a University executive whose standing is so high that other schools are bidding against each other for his services.

"Destroying the enlargement possibilities" could only mean there were interests that thought Dr. von KleinSmid was spending too much money and that appropriations should be cut. In the opinion of the editor of *The Citizen*, President von KleinSmid had learned that a "political campaign was about to be worked up against his administration for financial reasons and that he chose to leave the decision to the people."

This was the reward, *The Citizen* said, of one who had "found a small college and built a great University." It closed its comments with this sentence, "The history of the institution must always be written with a considered realization that he gave it its impetus towards greatness."

At no time did the retiring President show even a trace of animosity. His letter to the Regents expressed warm thanks for what he called their never-varying support and loyalty. As was his custom, the President went before the students, and *The Wildcat* preserved his remarks in a long article reviewing his success at the University. The article said:

> Whatever differences have held sway in the past, they fade to nothing in the calm realization of what he has done for the student body, the institution, the State of Arizona and the cause of education.

It is possible that there is a true picture of Dr. von KleinSmid's motives in a second *Citizen* editorial in which the editor said that the President had told him he loved the kind of work he had done in Arizona and preferred to go where he could continue to be a builder.

President von KleinSmid left the University in December, 1921, to assume the presidency of the University of Southern California, following a banquet given him by the faculty at Maricopa Hall and a tribute published by *The Wildcat*, which remembered that he had personally greeted each member of the student body every September.

The faculty remembered him for many reasons but particularly because he had established the colleges and approved of the establishment of a faculty constitution. This first Plan of Administration was adopted by the faculty on October 1, 1920, subject to the approval of the Board of Regents. On May 2, 1921, the faculty formally adopted the plan as revised by the Regents.

CHAPTER 7

1922–1928

IRRIGATION and World War I created an era of rich expansion in Arizona before the eighth president of the University arrived.

Cotton was white gold and 100,000 acres were devoted to its cultivation. Prices shot up for copper and cattle; there had been a heavy sale of horses and mules to the army. Agricultural acreage had increased almost 400 per cent between 1910 and 1920 and this demanded new dams below the Roosevelt reservoir. Fully 100,000 head of cattle grazed in the state in 1920. Mining towns boomed as the copper companies produced almost 600,000,000 pounds of the red metal. The University's experiments with dates and citrus were paying rich returns and its extension specialists were in demand everywhere.

In 1910 the population of Arizona was 122,931. By 1920 it had boomed to 334,162, and Phoenix passed Tucson as the state's largest city. Meanwhile, the University had more than kept pace with the growth of the state. From an enrollment of 161 in 1900, which represented one student for every 765 inhabitants, in 1920 it reached an enrollment of 1,369, or one for every 224.5 inhabitants. This growth and the contributions the institution made to the Commonwealth in mining, agriculture, and cultural progress won praise in 1922 from the U. S. Department of Education in a report of a survey it made that year. It said:

> The people of Arizona must realize that their institution is no longer a high school of early years, nor even the simple college of 20 years ago, but that it is a real state university, comparing favorably in scope with the higher educational systems of most of the other states of the Union. . . . In one thing particularly is Arizona to be congratulated, namely, in her steadfast adherence to the plan of building up a single state university in one place. . . .
>
> In scope of work and efficiency of instruction the committee believes that the College of Letters, Arts, and

Sciences compares favorably with other standard colleges of the same type throughout the United States. . . .

The School of Education of the University stands alone in the state in the type of work which it is giving and does not duplicate the field of the state normal schools at Tempe and Flagstaff. . . . The committee believes that a College of Education is not only justified but vital in its importance to the state and its influence upon education in Arizona. . . .

For 17 years the Agricultural Experiment Station represented the sole efforts of the University in the field of agriculture. The station has sponsored much of the legislation passed by the State Legislature bearing on range improvement. . . . It has contributed largely not only to profitable farming in the State, but also to general knowledge of effective methods of livestock production. . . . The fact that the area of farm land in the State has increased more than four fold during the decade 1910–1920 has without question been due in part to the experimental work of the University through its Agricultural College and Experiment Station. . . .

During the last five years the College of Mines and Engineering has made remarkable progress. An excellent building has been erected in part by state funds and in part by private subscription. . . . The college's facilities for training in mining engineering are excellent and in some particulars of the very highest rank. . . .

The archaeological work of the State Museum has been noteworthy and the recent completion of the Steward observatory with its 36-inch reflecting telescope will permit a program of astronomical research for which the climate of Arizona is particularly adapted. The committee wishes to indorse heartily the progressive spirit which has led the people of Arizona to devote considerable funds to the development of that research and experimentation which should be so vital a part of the work of a state university. . . .

"The committee is impressed with the earnest spirit in the School of Law and with the excellent training and experience of its faculty members. . . . The amount and quality of the work now required for the LL.B degree undoubtedly compare favorably with the requirements of many standard law schools of the country.

> It is the opinion of the committee, after personal contact with the faculty of the University of Arizona, that those in charge of the University have succeeded in attracting to its service an unusually capable and well-prepared group of teachers and investigators. The loyalty of the faculty to the University is marked, and the *esprit de corps* is excellent.

The minutes of the meetings show that the Board of Regents hoped to find a new president in an eastern college. Regent Dwight B. Heard tried to locate a suitable man but had no success. Chancellor John H. Campbell and Regent Louis D. Ricketts were then sent east with full power to select an executive and hire him on the spot. They too failed and Deans Frank C. Lockwood, Gurdon M. Butler, and D. M. Working were appointed to serve as a committee of administration. Winter and Spring passed before the committee was relieved of its duties and Dean Lockwood was made acting president. Summer passed and newspapers began to murmur that the University was merely drifting and marking time. This was not true, because the Regents' hands were full.

Prosperity had faded in 1920 when the effect of the primary postwar depression which had been plaguing the nation reached Arizona. Production indexes showed losses and prices fell. General business was slow until the middle of 1921 when industry and commerce began to recover.

During this period the Regents wrestled with serious financial problems. They ordered the deans of the colleges to make a total cut of $16,000 in their budgets and recommended to the Governor that, in view of existing conditions, a previously provided increase in the tax levy be deferred.

Despite this check, the University continued to make progress. Resident enrollment increased by 250 students. A department of French was established under Professor A. H. Otis, and a board of athletic control was created with a full-time graduate manager and representatives from the student body and faculty. Louis Slonaker was appointed graduate manager and alumni secretary.

The organization was scarcely completed when Orville McPherson and Kirk Moore were on the doorstep with a suggestion that a stadium be erected. They were a trifle early, but the seed they planted lived to produce today's stadium.

The search for a president produced no results until the 1922–1923 University year was about to open and a man from the west appeared before the Regents. He was Dr. Cloyd H. Marvin, dean and assistant director of the University of California at Los Angeles; and on September 1, 1922, the Regents announced his appointment. The title of professor of economics went with the post.

The new president was thirty-three years of age and the newspapers made much of the story that he was the youngest man to fill such a position in the United States. Born in Ohio, he had attended Leland Stanford University and then had transferred to UCLA where he had taken both his B.A. and his M.A. During the first world war he had been a captain in the air corps. At the close of the war, he entered Harvard where he received his Ph.D. He then returned to UCLA where he was appointed associate professor of commerce, assistant director and dean, and business advisor.

President Marvin met his student body for the first time at the opening assembly, September 27, 1922, in the patio of the agriculture building, and *The Wildcat* remarked, "He looked more like excellent material for Coach McKale's football squad than a college president." Then the paper said editorially:

> After an extended period of watchful waiting it is with a cheer of joyful relief and contentment that we, the students of the University of Arizona, welcome Dr. Marvin as our president. Relief because we are released from the tension with which we more or less consciously waited the choice of the new executive and contentment because of the seeming success of the quest. We welcome you, Prexy, and we need you. There are many things to be done; a new gym, an athletic field, a library, auditorium, and science building.

President Marvin's inauguration was combined with the dedication of the Steward Observatory in April, 1923. Dr. Ernest Carroll Moore, director of the University of California at Los Angeles, delivered the principal address. Honorary degrees of Doctor of Science were conferred on Dr. V. M. Slipher, director of Lowell Observatory, and Dr. G. Aitken, director of Lick Observatory. The program closed with a formal reception at Masonic temple which *The Star* called one of the most brilliant occasions Tucson had seen.

The Star was much impressed with President Marvin's business background and felt that hopes for his success lay in his efficiency. Editorial opinion looked forward to the day when the University would become one of the leading educational institutions of the United States, and it added that this would be brought about by applying President Marvin's policy of "blending the collegiate atmosphere in the clear air of business efficiency."

A month after he had been established at the University, Dr. Marvin made two proposals which angered some of the faculty. He said he felt that the new faculty constitution was "inadequate" and that a special committee would be appointed to investigate it. He also requested that the Board of Regents approve the reduction of departments from forty-nine to twenty-eight, questioned the reappointment of some dozen members of the faculty, and accept six new men who he felt were educators of distinction.

The committees appointed to amend the constitution accomplished little, and finally the Board issued a special administrative bulletin in the Fall of 1926 that contained what were called "Ordinances of the Board of Regents." The reduction of the number of departments was another matter, though some lost nothing but their names. Ten departments were reduced to one by listing them under "College of Agriculture" without further designation. Greek and Italian language courses became the classical language department. Mining, engineering, metallurgy, and ore-dressing were all grouped under mining. All social science was included in the Department of Economics and the School of Home Economics became a department in the College of Agriculture.

President Marvin gave newspapers five reasons why these changes were necessary. They were: "First, to make for more efficient administrative channels; second, to avoid duplication of work; third, to strengthen the morale of the personnel of the departments; fourth, to create a better academic standing; fifth, to make for a better promotion scheme." The Board of Regents voted for the changes, and President Marvin told the Wildcat that the adoption of his policy had moved the school forward twenty years. In the minds of some, however, it seemed possible that the clock might have been turned back rather than ahead.

This feeling notwithstanding, President Marvin's administration was marked by notable accomplishments. The first library, which had been expected "to last for all time," had become inadequate. The Regents debated the possibility of an addition, but gave up the idea and asked the Legislature for a new building. They got $190,000 and ground was broken January 17, 1924, by Dean J. J. Thornber of the College of Agriculture, who ploughed a furrow that marked the foundation line. Students began to use the building in September, 1925, and threaded their way among workmen, under scaffolding, and over piles of materials until the structure was completed on May 27, 1927. It had cost, by that time $450,000 and was then, as it is now, one of the handsomest public buildings in Arizona.

A new men's gymnasium was also built during these years. It cost $166,207 and was completed July, 1926. The basement was designed for the School of Military Science and Tactics. Nor was this all the building that was done. A new power plant went up, Herring Hall was rebuilt as a women's gymnasium, and Apache Hall, which had been a men's dormitory, was rebuilt for the School of Music. Streets were paved, ornamental lighting was installed, and underground conduits were constructed for power lines, water and heating pipes.

Despite their family troubles, the Regents knew the University was sound and that its progress merited an advance in rank, so they appealed to the Association of American Universities to send a representative to re-appraise the institution. The association sent Dean David Robertson in 1924. He made a careful survey and on October 31 wired congratulations on the admission of Arizona to the list of accredited institutions. President Marvin declared a holiday when the news arrived and the students celebrated at Herring Hall with a punch bowl and a dance that lasted all day and into the night.

Credits earned at the University of Arizona were now accepted by the best schools in the nation, and graduate students from the department of education commanded secondary school certificates in California.

The University soon formalized an interest in methods of mass communication by introducing a three-unit course in journalism under Dr. G. D. Sanders, a practical newspaper man from the east. Dr. Sanders made *The Wildcat* a laboratory and only journalism students were permitted to fill the editors' chairs. This wise policy has never been changed and has resulted in the building of one of the finest college newspapers in the country. Some interest was also shown in radio. Towers were erected on the roof of the mines and engineering building, and Dr. Paul Cloke, head of the department of electrical engineering, entertained hopes of establishing a broadcasting station. But the necessary equipment would have cost $25,000 and the money was not available. Today that sum would be only a drop in the bucket.

It was not until 1939 when Harry Behn was made director of the radio bureau, that the University was able to broadcast programs throughout the state by tying its equipment to two Tucson stations.

It must be said, however, that President Marvin's administration did not pass untroubled. During much of the four and one-half years of his administration the Board of Regents, the faculty, and even some churches were split by factional fights aired throughout the state by the press, and finally made the subject of legislative investigation.

Some members of the faculty attacked President Marvin and his policies with great bitterness while others became his violent supporters. But soon the anti-Marvin bloc in the faculty called on the American Association of University Professors to send a committee to investigate the treatment of teachers, and the association complied.

When the report was released, it proved to be about the only calm appraisal made. The committee said it felt too much emphasis had been placed on the introduction of business methods into the academic field and that a lack of consideration had been shown for certain members of the faculty. But, the committee said there had also been worthwhile accomplishments, and it named the raising of the salary scale, the granting of sabbatical leave without loss of salary increases, and the employment of some new professors of high repute.

This investigation was mild compared to the one demanded simultaneously by Tucson citizens under the leadership of the Reverend E. C. Tuthill, president of the Tucson Ministerial Association. The Board of Regents agreed to conduct further investigations and met daily with Governor Hunt and a court stenographer in attendance. The *Tucson Daily Independent*, a short-lived newspaper that appeared during this period, carried the testimony in front-page stories from early August to late September, 1926.

The Board finally voted not to accept the charges made by the ministerial association. Governor Hunt then proposed that Dr. Marvin and six discharged members of the faculty be continued in their positions "if they agree to sink their differences and work for the welfare of the University." Dr. Marvin and three of the six teachers agreed, but the other three refused.

The controversy went on during the fall months while the Board waited for Governor Hunt to make the next move. Meanwhile, the newspapers of the state were loud in their support of Marvin. There are huge volumes of scrapbooks covering the period in the University's special collections and the clippings show that the editorial comment was unanimously pro-Marvin. From the *Verde Copper News* and the *Miami Silver Belt News* to Bisbee and Douglas, the press was united.

The *Tucson Daily Citizen* which was wholeheartedly for Marvin interjected its own view which was that a faculty member whom it called "the Mad Dean" was at the bottom of the whole affair. *The Citizen* said, "During the long continued agitation the shadow of the 'Mad Dean' has lurked in the background, sinister and brooding."

E. E. Ellinwood of the Regents, however, a political foe of Hunt, said the Governor was trying to plunge the University into politics and promised that if his own campaign for the Democratic nomination for governor succeeded he would immediately re-appoint Marvin president of the University.

Still trying for a compromise, the Board then voted to retain Dr. Marvin and the six discharged teachers, but to abrogate the faculty constitution and to take over the sole right to discharge the president or any teacher whom the Regents thought unsatisfactory. President Marvin and four Regents, including

E. E. Ellinwood, president of the Board, resigned immediately, and Ellinwood wrote Governor Hunt a letter on January 19, 1927, in which he said, "The discord and dissension which exists among some members of the Board are real and unreconcila-ble." Regents who resigned with Ellinwood were Cleve W. Van Dyke, John J. Corrigan, and John H. Campbell.

At this point the Legislature debated whether President Marvin should receive a vote of thanks and whether the Governor should discharge all Regents, a question which missed passing by only two votes. The House did manage to pass a demand for a complete investigation of the financial and administrative affairs at the University.

State newspapers unfavorable to Governor Hunt assailed him on a charge of having made the University a political football. In the heat of the controversy, one paper referred to the students as "pawns of controversy." *The Arizona Daily Star* insisted that President Marvin had done well and that the University was now "a storm-torn ship at sea minus a pilot."

It is interesting to note that *The Wildcat*, usually so voluble, made no comments on the warfare involving the president, the Regents, the town, the Legislature, and many newspapers in the state. When President Marvin resigned, *The Wildcat* mentioned it very briefly.

Dr. Marvin moved on to the presidency of George Washington University in Washington, D. C.,—a position he filled with distinction until 1958, when he was made president emeritus.

The Regents began the search for a new president of the University of Arizona. It was not long before they appointed Dr. Byron Cummings acting president, with an advisory committee consisting of Dr. C. T. Vorhies of the College of Agriculture and Dr. E. P. Mathewson of the College of Mines. C. Zaner Lesher, who had been assistant registrar since 1922, was named to fill the position of registrar. The committee served until September when Dr. Cummings was formally named president.

As president, Dr. Cummings seems to have had a peaceful administration. Campus life went on at its usual pace. A *Desert* queen was elected, there were dances and polo games, beanies were burned, elections were held, the band gave concerts, and the debating team met Southern California, New Mexico, Denver, Colorado, Utah, Idaho, and Oregon, while the university cavalry troop won the highest rating the U. S. Army gave any western university or college.

A special edition of *The Wildcat*, issued in honor of high-school day, closed the college year of 1926–27 and buried all the troubles under a burst of publicity for the progress made. The issue featured the campus buildings and their cost. The largest, of course, was the new library, built for

$450,000. Cochise Hall had cost $250,000 while Maricopa had been completed for $190,500. The unfinished gymnasium called for $150,000, and the agriculture, and mines and engineering buildings were listed as in excess of $175,000 each. Fine engravings of campus scenes and imposing structures filled the pages of the paper, which was distributed to students in all high schools of the state.

The Regents opened the academic year of 1927–28 with the announcement that they had selected Dr. Homer LeRoy Shantz as president, but that he would not take office until July, 1928, and that Dr. Cummings would continue to fill the post until then.

Dr. Shantz was professor of botany at the University of Illinois and had a national reputation in his field. Born in Michigan, he attended high school in Colorado and took his B.A. degree in botany at Colorado College. His doctor's degree was conferred on him at the University of Nebraska where he taught for a time before going to the faculty of the University of Louisiana. While attending college, he spent his summer months studying the alkali and drought structure of the Great Plains states for the Department of Agriculture and in doing work for the Land Commission that took him over practically all sections of the United States.

When he went to Illinois in 1926 as professor of botany and head of the department, Dr. Shantz was known for many articles on vegetation in Africa and the western United States. His deep interest in the agricultural problems of the southwestern deserts was well established and made his appointment as president of the area's greatest University seem an excellent choice.

Faculty and students settled down to wait the coming of the new president. As *The Wildcat* said, "The smoke of the trouble of the last two years has lifted and the University is still in the same location and going on its upward trend." *The Wildcat* perspicaciously pointed up at that time what a third of a century later is perfectly clear: That during a stormy period, the institution had by no means marked time, rather it had gone foreward, developing the physical plant in critical respects, and intensifying the policy of bringing to the university faculty people of undeniable reputation. Finally it was of great importance that during this period the goal of recognition by the Association of American Universities was successfully achieved.

Workmen finally completed the new library, and dedication ceremonies were held on October 23, 1927, with former President von KleinSmid as guest speaker. Students were extremely proud of the beautiful building, but they were miffed at the librarian who erected a sign on the lawn of the outdoor study-patio forbidding them to smoke there.

Bad feelings also broke out between the student body and the City of Tucson. *The Wildcat* was bitter about the alacrity with which city police arrested students, and it reprimanded a judge for being unnecessarily tough on them. It added that Tucson citizens were quick to call students "noisy ruffians" but slow to support athletic events and noted that the best football game played on the campus had drawn only 3,200 Tuc-sonans while an ordinary Phoenix high-school game had drawn 10,000 Phoenicians.

The rift could not have been very serious, however, for Tucson alumni were working hard for a stadium. The Regents had finally approved designs for such a structure, but they had no way of financing it and handed the big problem over to the alumni who opened a campaign for funds in December, 1927.

Faculty and students met their next president for the first time in January, 1928, when he paid a short visit to the campus for a conference with Dr. Cummings. Speaking to an audience that packed the last foot of standing room, Dr. Shantz modestly refused to outline future plans and paid high compliments to Dr. Cummings and the faculty for the work done and the progress made while the institution awaited his coming.

The drive to raise funds for a stadium swung into high gear that winter under the leadership of Louis Slonaker, alumni secretary and graduate manager, who toured the state and addressed gatherings of alumni in almost every city. In fact, the Winter and Spring of 1928 seem to have been a busy period. The Regents discussed the possibility of purchasing land fronting on Olive road. *The Wildcat* launched the first of a long series of campaigns for the opening of the library on Sunday; Dr. Douglass was worrying for fear the increasing illumination of Tucson and Tucson Airport, plus dust resulting from the growth of the city, would make it necessary to move the Steward Observatory to the mountains or the cactus forest; pay for unskilled labor on the campus was raised to the unheard-of sum of forty cents an hour; Professor Cable announced that a speech major offering twenty-four credits would be added in September; and *The Wildcat*, which had been given perfect liberty by President Cummings to criticize both the city and the University, acknowledged its freedom in the following laudatory editorial:

> Before his term comes to an end we want to pay a tribute to the man who has been at the head of the University for more than a year. Falling heir to the most difficult job that has ever been given to a man at the University of Arizona, he has fulfilled it with great credit to the people of the State,

the University and himself. His problem was to pacify two groups that had chosen up sides and were causing all kinds of trouble; two groups that were at swords' points.

There is always a little discontent; it would not be human if there were not. But today we believe the scene is more serene, the faculty and students more content than they have been in years. Everybody is going about tending his own business and doing his work. For this situation the credit must go to Dr. Cummings. He has done an almost superhuman job.

CHAPTER 8

1928–1937

PROMPTLY on July 1, 1928, Dr. Homer LeRoy Shantz moved into the president's office, then located in the College of Agriculture building, and Dr. Cummings returned to his duties as director of the State Museum and head of the Department of Archaeology.

The desert school held a great attraction for Dr. Shantz. His interest lay in the types of growth found in both grasslands and semi-arid country and in their economic significance. Not only did he range the plains and deserts of the United States, but twice in his lifetime he crossed Africa, studying and photographing its plants. The second safari took him over his first trail for the purpose of determining what changes had occurred during the years.

So well was Dr. Shantz known for his work and his scientific papers when he came to Arizona that scientists thought of him first as a botanist and only secondarily as a university president.

A sure sign that Dr. Shantz did not plan to devote all his time to administrative duties, but intended to continue his research, could be found in the fact that he frequently lectured to groups of students in the Department of Botany and in 1931 became a member of the teaching staff and in 1935 head of the department. He turned the room adjoining his private office into a library for his books, maps, photos, and notes. Botany students were always welcome there.

Professor J. J. Thornber had asked to be relieved of his duties as Dean of the College of Agriculture and director of agricultural research and, in accepting his resignation, President Shantz said:

> The state and the people of the Southwest owe you a great deal for the years in which you have carried on this administrative work so successfully and helped Arizona develop from a cattle range to one of the leading agricultural states of the Union.

Just as President von KleinSmid had brought the slogan, "A Greater Arizona," so President Shantz brought one of his own which he used when he first met the students in the fall of 1928. He said in part:

> It is the hope of everyone of us that 1928–29 will be the best year the University of Arizona has ever had. The fulfillment of this hope lies within the reach of the student body, the faculty and the administration. But we must PULL TOGETHER. We cannot and should not always look at things from the same point of view, but our differences should be healthy differences and we can all be reasonable about them, and give or take a little as the case may be . . .
>
> A selfish interest on the part of one member of our football team would weaken the whole team. It is just the same in the University and applies to organizations as well as individuals. WE MUST PULL TOGETHER.

The student body greeted the new President with a ten per cent increase in registration in the fall semester of 1928, and the football squad, which was spoken of lightly as the "starless team," pulled together so successfully that it opened the season by playing UCLA to a wholly unexpected 7–7 tie in Los Angeles.

President Shantz fitted into the university picture without ruffling a feather, and the Board of Regents made approval of him a matter of record in 1929 in the resolution:

> Whereas Homer LeRoy Shantz came to the University of Arizona the first day of July, 1928, and in assuming the duties of his office he found many onerous, disagreeable and burdensome questions to solve, and by untiring zeal, patience, good humor and exceptional ability he has brought the University a prestige which has reestablished confidence within the organization and throughout the State, now therefore be it resolved that the Board of Regents of the University commend Homer LeRoy Shantz for his diligence and faithful service in behalf of the University of Arizona and pledge him their fullest and united support for the future.

The year 1929 saw the School of Music made a college under Professor C. F. Rogers, the College of Law building was remodeled at a cost of $40,000 and *The Wildcat* bragged that $300,000 was being spent on campus structures. Dr. Shantz reported to the Regents that he was planning a complete study of the state's resources and at the same time opened a campaign to acquire two sections of saguaro forest lands for the University. He explained he felt it essential that a large area of saguaro forest lands be preserved in their natural state for future study and that it might be wise to move the Steward Observatory there in the future. Toward the end of the year the Regents established a chemical laboratory in Phoenix, in cooperation with the water-users' association, where tests of the soil and water of the Salt River Valley as well as studies of citrus blight could be carried on.

But the big event of 1929 was the dedication of the new stadium which had progressed from a dream to a reality through the fighting zeal of the alumni. Homecoming Day in October saw the dedication crowned by a crushing football victory of 35 to 0 over California Institute of Technology before 8,000 fans. The guest of honor was former President Rufus B. von KleinSmid.

Almost two years had passed since the Regents accepted the plans for the stadium but left the task of paying for it to the alumni with the stipulation that $100,000 would be needed in gifts before contracts could be let.

What transpired after that action will always be a tribute to the dedicated leadership of a committee comprised of Dr. E. P. Mathewson of the College of Mines, Coach James F. McKale, A. Louis Slonaker, secretary of the Alumni Association, William Bray, superintendent of buildings and grounds, and the president of the University.

The committee was interested in a complete athletic plant and asked for bids on a stadium with dressing rooms, a baseball grandstand and field, and a men's swimming pool. The lowest bid was $133,600 which did not include a turf field, track, water, or lights.

The question had been where to get the money, and although alumni, faculty, and students had contributed about $25,000, the goal was still a long way off. There had been a hope that the mining companies might make sizable contributions but someone was needed who knew how to approach the copper kings and fortunately the University had the man in Dr. E. P. Mathewson, chairman of the stadium drive. Before coming to Arizona to round out many years of practical experience by teaching in the College of Mines, Dr. Mathewson had been with the Anaconda Copper Company for thirteen years and was famous for his operation of its smelters. He had a wide and close acquaintance with the top men in the great mining properties of the southwest, and now he personally appealed to them. A list of the big contributors shows how well he succeeded and additional evidence is found in the dedication program in which A. Louis Slonaker wrote:

> Too much credit cannot be given to Dr. Mathewson who served as chairman of the drive committee. He was personally responsible for raising a goodly portion of the $75,000 and his optimism was a tonic for other committeemen when it seemed that all possibilities had been exhausted.

It was impossible to publish the names of all contributors to the athletic fund, but the dedication program printed the names of those who gave $250 or more, and the vital part they played can well be acknowledged here. The list follows:

United Verde Copper Company, $20,000; Phelps-Dodge Company, $7,500; Inspiration Copper Company, $7,500; Colonel and Mrs. Boice Thompson, $5,000; New Cornelia Copper Company, $4,370; Miami Copper Company, $4,000; Calumet and Arizona Copper Company, $3,790; Nevada Consolidated Copper Company, $3,000; Magna Copper Company, $2,500; Roy Place, $2,500; American Smelting and Refining Company, $1,000; J. E. Thompson, $1,000; Apache Powder Company, $500; J. Ivancovich Wholesale Grocery Company, $500; Tucson Gas, Electric Light & Power Company, $500; Byron Cummings, $250; H. L. Shantz, $250; Mountain States Telephone & Telegraph Company, $250; Monte Mansfield, $250.

An unexpected contribution came from the Board of Regents which decided to spend $40,000 and enclose the back of the stadium. This created a two-story building the length of the football field which when divided into rooms gave the University, at an extremely low cost, much needed space.

The concrete stand of 1929 ran from end zone to end zone on the west side of the field and accommodated 7,000 spectators. If it failed to seat the crowd there were wooden bleachers east of the gridiron.

It was not much of a stadium by present standards, but it was a wonderful addition to the University in its time, and there was room for more seats to be added as they were needed. There was good green turf that a man could get his cleats into. Growing that green sod had been no small accomplishment. The land had first been leveled and six inches of good soil and fertilizer spread over the field. Then came hundreds of pounds of Bermuda seed and finally an irrigation system. The athletic department was $20,000 in debt when the field was completed.

Mention should be made that except for the farsightedness of the Regents, who bought two blocks of land on Cherry Street during Dr. von KleinSmid's administration, there would have been no land for the stadium that is so greatly admired by visitors today.

It was 1937 before most of the wooden bleachers were replaced by 150 feet of concrete stands which the Associated Students built at a cost of $80,000. Nine years later these were extended to 360 feet and again the cost, which was $95,000, was financed by football receipts. Finally, the east and west stands were connected on the south in 1949 by a section that raised the seating capacity of the stadium to 22,731. The University then built dormitories under the east and south stands at a large savings in comparison to the price of conventional buildings.

The dedication of the original unit of today's stadium was not only a time of jubilation, but it marked a time in which the administration had high hopes of making rapid progress during the coming year. The nation was enjoying prosperity which was expected to last indefinitely. Stock market profits were fabulous. Everyone hoped to become a millionaire and a great many made it, temporarily. Even housewives pinched a little money from their food budgets here and there and turned it into fur coats on tips they picked up at the bridge table. But two weeks after the dedication of the stadium, the New York stock market collapsed as 19,000,000 shares changed hands on the Stock Exchange and Curb. Five days later stocks plunged again in what is remembered as the blackest day in market history, and by November 13, 30 billion dollars in capital values had been swept away.

President Shantz had been at work on a ten-year building program that called for the expenditure of $2,000,000; but the market situation did not discourage him completely, for he said:

> We believe that if the state will adopt a conservative and definite building development, the University will be able to look forward to safe and economical development to meet present and future needs.

Dr. Shantz wanted buildings for chemistry and physics, language and literature, the social sciences, College of Music, Arizona State Museum, infirmary, an auditorium, and new dormitories for men and women. The last he said, were imperative if the University were to house the growing freshmen classes on the campus.

Nor was all this, for the President pointed out that there were buildings that had not been painted or repaired for eight and even ten years and something had to be done about these immediately.

But the depression grew more acute month by month. The price of cotton dropped and copper hit its lowest point since 1895, while an unprecedented drought swept the Midwest and the South in the summer of 1930 and the national income fell from a high of 81 billion to less than $68 billion. Thirteen hundred banks failed and on December 11, the Bank of the United States in New York City, with sixty branches and 400,000 depositors, closed its doors.

There was not a chance now for the President's program. The Legislature ruled out new buildings but did provide an appropriation of $1,002,500 for 1931–32 and $927,500 for 1932–33. This was expected to cover operation and maintenance and included $90,000 for improvement of old buildings and an extension of the underground conduits.

These were actually liberal appropriations, considering not only the national picture but also the situation in the state where tax collections were falling off at an alarming rate. The Board of Regents must have thought the skies would clear, for they authorized the president to spend $6,800 in cash and give notes for $16,000 to acquire title to 3,520 acres of land in the cactus forest. They also adopted a group life insurance plan for the faculty and other employees under which the insured paid $43.20 a year for a $6,000 policy. The University was to pay the balance of the premium.

Then came the year 1932 and the nation plummeted to the depths of what was known as the secondary post-war depression, carrying Arizona with it. Stocks dropped to 10 per cent of their 1929 value. Farm products fell to 40 per cent, unemployment rose to 15 million and the national income, which had been $81 billion, sank to $42 billion.

So far as the University was concerned, the only bright spot in 1932 was the admission of the College of Law to membership in the American Association of Law Schools. It was a great honor for the University and a credit to Dr. Shantz who had worked for four years to strengthen the law faculty.

A night course in law had been taught as early as 1911, but President Wilde didn't think much of it and said it should be made a regular one-year course with a second and third year to be added as soon as possible. One of the old catalogues listed an introductory study that emphasized commercial law in 1912–13. It was taught at night by William James Galbraith, a Tucson lawyer, and was given principally for the benefit of Tucson citizens. Coach J. F. McKale, who audited the course says it was taught in the basement of the old library and that Galbraith doubled in brass by teaching boxing as well as law.

President Wilde discontinued the class in 1913 and the subject was not taught again until 1915–16 when Samuel M. Fegtly joined the faculty and law was re-established in the College of Letters, Arts, and Sciences. From that point on progress was rapid. A department was established in 1918 with

Old North Hall, 1897. On site of present geology building.

Old Main, 1890. Note incomplete roof.

Former home of University presidents.

Gardener's cottage, 1919. First home of domestic science.

University of Arizona student body, 1896.

St. Patrick's Day Strike, 1904. Old Armory Park bandstand.

THEODORE B. COMSTOCK
1893–1895

University Library, 1891. Located in Old Main.

Section of campus, 1915. White building under "A" Mountain marks the corner of Third and Park.

HOWARD BILLMAN
1895–1897

MILLARD MAYHEW PARKER
1897–1901

FRANK YALE ADAMS
1901–1903

KENDRIC C. BABCOCK
1903–1910

ANDREW ELLICOTT DOUGLASS
1910–1911

ARTHUR HERBERT WILDE
1911–1914

RUFUS BERNHARD VON KLEINSMID
1914–1921

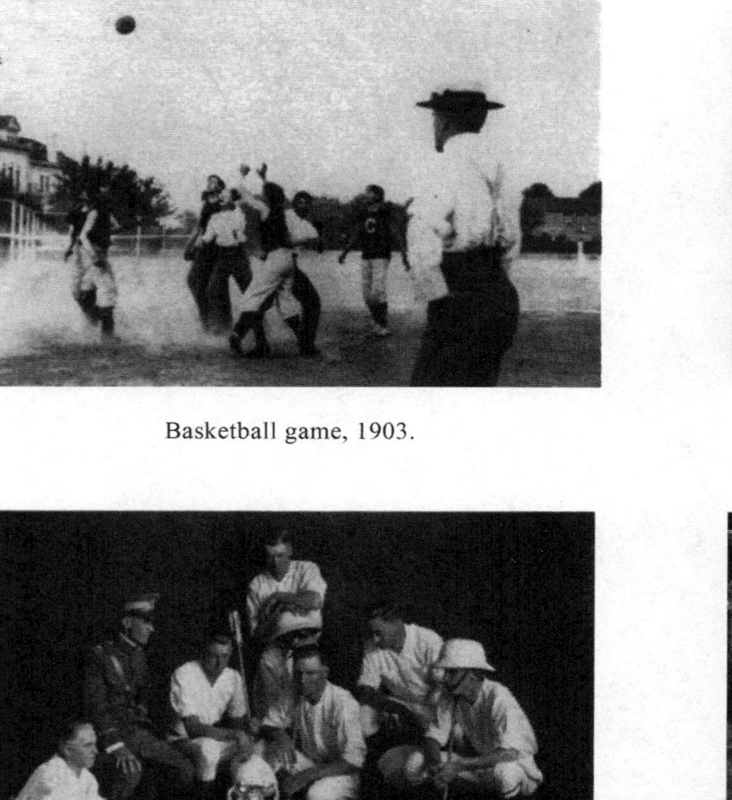

Basketball game, 1903.

Girls' gymnasium class, 1905.

Dance pageant, 1925. Lawn of Maricopa Hall.

Student battalion of National Guard, 1899.

Boots and Saddles, 1936.

"USS Bear Down," 1942, ready for Navy.

Last Navy battalion presents colors, 1944.

Third Street Entrance, 1905.

Third Street Entrance, 1959.

1366 students graduate in stadium, 1959.

Football field, 1926.

Stadium completed, 1950.

University Library, 1959.

College of Agriculture, completed in 1915.

FRANCIS CUMMINS LOCKWOOD
1922

CLOYD HECK MARVIN
1922–1927

BYRON CUMMINGS
1927–1928

HOMER LeROY SHANTZ
1928–1936

PAUL STEERE BURGESS
1936–1937

ALFRED ATKINSON
1937–1947

Bette Falk, '42, on famous army jumper, "Old Snowball."

Intercollegiate Rodeo Week. Annual Spring event.

Flag-raising, 1942. Navy student officers.

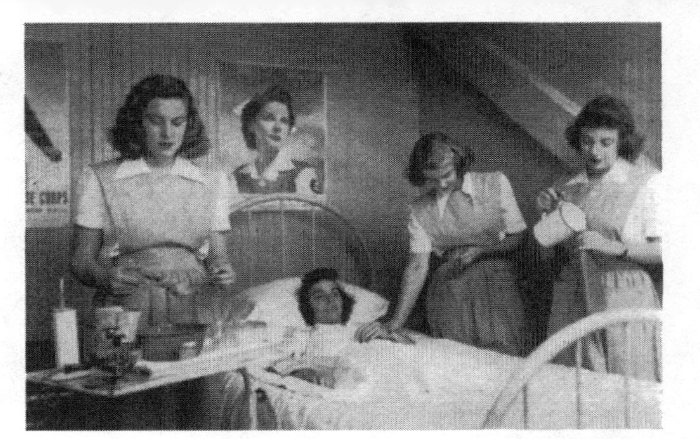
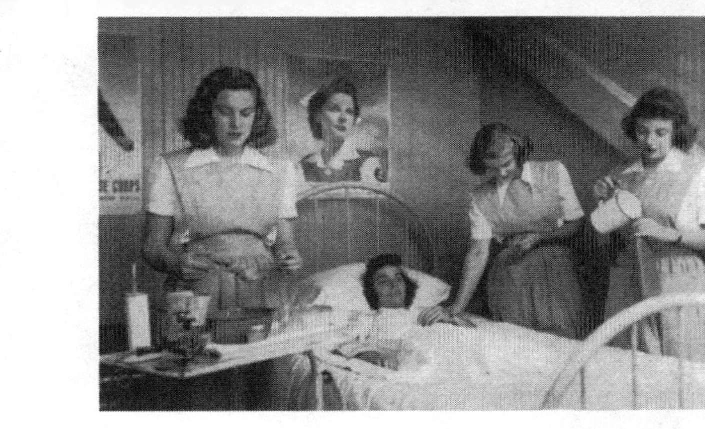

Student Nurses' Aide Training, 1942.

Wildcat Mailing to service men, World War II.

Bill Bishop Day, 1942.

JAMES BYRON McCORMICK
1947–1951

Old Main, 1959.

College of Law, built as library, 1905.

College of Education, formerly Liberal Arts.

University Administration Building.

Humanities Class in main auditorium, 1959.

Radio-Television Bureau in Herring Hall.

Graham, Greenlee, men's new dormitories.

RICHARD ANDERSON HARVILL
1951—

The Student Union, a World War Memorial.

Business and Public Administration.

The new geology building.

Fine Arts Center with theater and gallery.

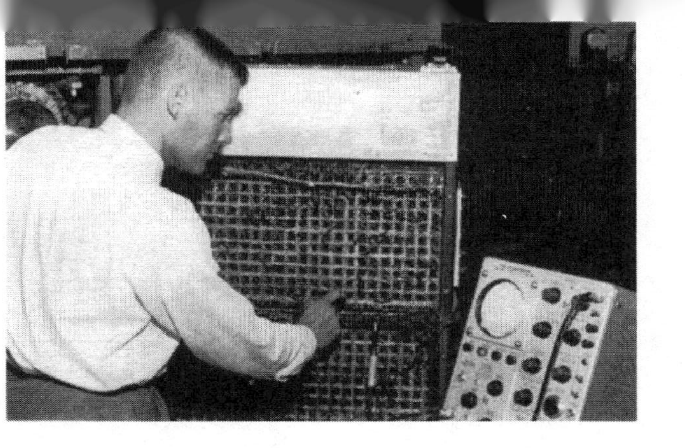

RAMAC computer.

Solar House Institute of Atmospheric Physics.

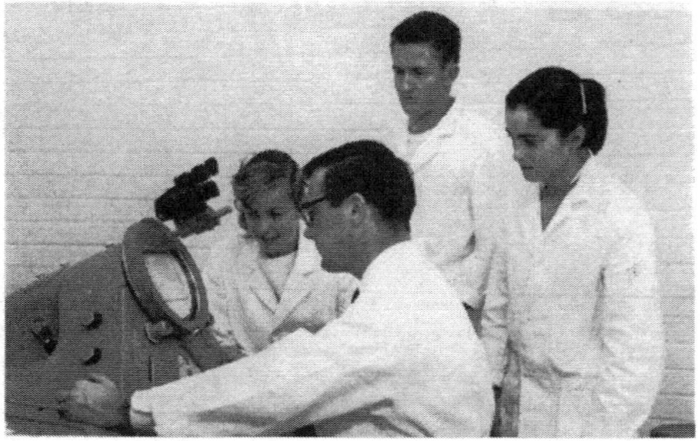

One of the two electron microscopes.

Archaeologists at Point of Pines.

Steward Observatory, landmark since 1921.

The Steward 36 inch telescope.

Liberal Arts.

TRIGA, the University's nuclear reactor.

New Home Economics building.

New Mathematics-Physics Building.

New Law Building.

Addition to the Steward Observatory.

Professor Fegtly as head and in 1929 it was made a college over which he presided as Dean.

Early in 1932 it became obvious that the state could not afford the $937,500 appropriation the Legislature had allowed for 1932–33, and the Regents not only cut the budget to $800,000 but made additional economies as well. Of this big saving, $92,573 came from the faculty which volunteered to take a 10 per cent cut in salaries above $1,200.

Heads of the University and the two state colleges now met to consider ways to eliminate duplication of work, but the principal suggestion was that Arizona State Teachers' College be made a trade school and that the teachers' college be transferred to Flagstaff. The College at Tempe naturally rejected this and countered with a proposal that all intercollegiate athletics be abolished. The University with its new stadium couldn't see that, so nothing of any moment was accomplished. Later the three presidents met again and this time they agreed that in 1936 the colleges at Tempe and Flagstaff would prepare teachers for grade schools, while the University would concentrate on instructors for high schools.

Dr. Shantz had not forgotten the cactus forest, and in spite of the depression the Regents were sympathetic to his plea that since this was the only forest of its kind in the world it must be preserved in its natural state for generations of future botanists and as a possible site for the Steward Observatory. The University already owned 480 acres and had state titles to 3,040 more; but these acres were in parcels, and this was not an ideal situation in the view of Dr. Shantz, who wanted a vast tract preserved. Before he finally persuaded the Department of the Interior to make the cactus lands a national monument, the Regents had invested $55,000 in buying acreage and clearing titles.

Eventually the Department of the Interior wanted the lands the University held, but years passed before a deal was made and it was 1958 before the cactus lands were actually traded to the government for 3,340 acres on the Ajo Road. The investment paid off, for the Ajo Road tract was worth a million dollars.

Austere as 1932 had been for both the administration and faculty of the University, the year 1933 was to be worse. Dr. Benjamin B. Moeur, who was elected Governor in 1932 after defeating Governor Hunt in the primaries, met the Eleventh Legislature on January 9, 1933, and announced in his message that the state budget must be cut by $4 million dollars. Half a million dollars of this saving, he said, should come from the appropriation for the University and the two teachers' colleges. In this connection, he noted that the state debt was $63,140,000 and interest charges were $6,781,560.

Among the suggestions made for boosting the state economy were a moratorium on delinquent taxes, the levying of a general sales tax and income tax, a reduction of 40 per cent in the cost of operating and maintaining all departments and programs of instruction, the abolition of the highway commission, and a limitation of road building to the sum collected in gasoline taxes. One legislator wanted the state to close the colleges at Tempe and Flagstaff; another suggested 90 per cent of all Arizona teachers must be graduates of Arizona schools and must have been residents of the state for five years, while a third recommended that workers who were not U. S. citizens must pay a license fee of $300.

The legislative galleries were soon filled with disorderly crowds that cheered or jeered, depending on the arguments heard. The members of House and Senate also heard from mass meetings where jobless men and women demanded a state dole of $3.50 a day.

Governor Moeur made an attempt to alleviate the problems of the unemployed by announcing that all state employees would be expected to give one day's pay a month for the relief of the jobless. This hit the faculty again, for Dr. Shantz later said that they contributed approximately $75,000.

In May, 1958, in an interview he gave when he visited the campus, the former president said:

> I persuaded the Governor to allow me to spend this money in Tucson and we used it to pay city laborers $2 a day for work on the campus. Some of the money also went to needy students who were having a hard time in spite of the fact that the Regents had cancelled their dormitory room rent.
>
> The case of some of these students was pathetic. We found one boy staggering from hunger who had been trying to live on a crate of apples a month. Girls at Pima Hall were getting their own meals and they had their expenses down to $18 a month. The dean of women looked into the matter and reported that the girls were not getting enough food. So I had two of them put on government relief at $15 a month. They turned this money into the house fund which gave them an extra dollar a day. I used to buy groceries for the girls and I remember that I once stopped outside Phoenix and bought a quarter's worth of lettuce. I got 30 heads for that quarter.
>
> We made that $75,000 go a long way. For one thing we excavated the north basement under the agriculture building

> and finished the stone fence which had been built along Park Avenue. Men students earned all they got. They filled in low spots, dug trenches for drains and chipped holes for trees.

Although the Regents had voluntarily cut the university budget from $937,500, to $800,000 for the year 1932–33, and knew this was as low as they could go with any safety, they offered to cut off another $50,000; however, they found this would not satisfy either the Governor or the Legislature. As Dr. Shantz remembers it:

> They sent down a special committee which was determined to make another deep slash. When I learned what they wanted to do, I went to a blackboard and proved that if we abolished music, art, agriculture, engineering, and liberal arts we couldn't save what they had in mind. So they said, "All right, we'll start by cutting faculty salaries again and go on from there."

While this was going on, President Franklin D. Roosevelt called for the closing of all banks on March 4, 1933. This holiday lasted until March 14 and was a disagreeable experience for the faculty and all other state employees. They had been having a hard time since September, 1932, when the state began paying them in warrants. In many parts of the state, banks cashed these warrants at a discount, although in Tucson the Southern Arizona Bank had accepted the warrants at face value until February 1, 1933.

The state then paid off in $25.00 warrants which were more flexible than one large warrant and could be spread among a number of merchants.

President Shantz issued a statement at that time in which he said:

> The Southern Arizona Bank has made it possible for the University to receive its money from state warrants when other State institutions throughout Arizona have been cashing their warrants at a discount. The Southern Arizona has practically carried the University since August and we deeply appreciate this.

Once the Southern Arizona Bank and Trust Company was forced to change its policy, the faculty members had to take what they could get; when the banks were closed they were forced to deal directly with the merchants, most of whom were caught with very little cash. Some stores did give a teacher half the face value of his warrant in cash and half in trade. Others accepted the paper only on a trade basis. But the worst was yet to come.

Urged by the Governor in February, 1933, the State Legislature began planning extremely heavy cuts in appropriations and by March the friends of the University were waging a bitter fight to save the University from a crippling blow. The House agreed to accept the Regent's request for $750,000 but the Senate said this must be cut to $650,000.

Heavy taxpayers were said to be in control of the senate and even Tucson merchants sent wires to Phoenix approving of the senate attitude. *The Arizona Daily Star*, however, was not at all pleased with the work of the upper House and said editorially: "The appropriation bill as passed by the Senate is a disgrace to the State of Arizona."

Although they fought the powerful forces arrayed against them to the last, the University's friends could push through only an additional $27,500 so that the institution finally got $627,000. The administration then adopted the following items of policy.

1. All non-essentials in academic courses to be eliminated.
2. The cost of absolutely essential features to be reduced to the lowest margin consistent with safety.
3. Every college and subdivision to be reviewed to provide for elimination and consolidation.
4. Extension and experimental work carried on for the good of the state to be cut to meet conditions.
5. The wages of the entire personnel to be reviewed and eliminations and adjustments made on the basis of working loads, ability, service, and contributions to the state.

Once this was decided, the cutting began with the salaries of the faculty and staff. As these employees had voluntarily surrendered 10 per cent of their wages in 1932, the blow was cruel.

There had been no replacements in faculty or staff for a year, and now both were reduced by dismissals until the total number of personnel on the payroll dropped from 343 to 256. Those who survived suffered cuts in pay as high as $500 plus 5 per cent for the best-paid people and down to $100 plus 5 per cent for instructors and others drawing lower salaries. This brought the average of the over-all pay cuts to 17 per cent.

President Shantz took the biggest cut of all. His salary was cut from $10,500 to $8,500.

Those who believed that their pay would be restored to the original figure when the depression passed were in for years of disappointment. Some waited as long as fifteen years before they were back on the old schedule. As a matter of fact, no promises were made of dates on which salaries would go back to normal. Instead, the Regents warned that if anticipated federal funds were reduced, there would be another slash, and that if the University encountered a deficit the faculty might have to serve without pay.

Drastic reductions were made in the cost of University operations. Administration lost $36,840, Agricultural Extension $38,597, and the Agricultural Experiment Station $41,218. The College of Letters, Arts, and Sciences, which was the largest college on the campus, suffered a slashing cut of $82,840.

The best picture of the condition of the University in this period is that in the report President Shantz presented in the October, 1934, issue of the *Arizona Alumnus*. In this he said:

> During the last 10 years we have added very little to the class room, laboratory and office facilities and have been forced to utilize every room in the library and all other buildings. At the present time there is no unused space on the campus. Office rooms have been rented off the campus and our classrooms and laboratories are overcrowded.
>
> The teaching staff of the University has increased in numbers in that time from 135 in 1924–25 to 175 in 1934–35. Several organizations have become affiliated with the University, notably the southwestern forest and range experiment station of the United States Forest Service, the bureau of biological survey and the southwestern plant introduction and plant propagation station of the United States Department of Agriculture. The University, especially the agricultural extension service, has been called upon to perform many functions incidental to the New Deal in agriculture and the staff had to expand to meet the increasing demand.
>
> The personnel of the University proper increased from 243 in 1924–25 to 314 in 1934–35. Student enrollment has risen during this period from 1,617 to 2,400 regular students or, if we include summer school, correspondence and extension students, the increase would be from 2,329 to 3,750.

> Therefore student enrollment has increased 48 per cent and the University staff 29 per cent.
>
> This rapid increase has been accompanied by a decrease in money appropriated by the State from $837,498 in 1924–25 to $627,680 in 1934–35, or 25 per cent reduction. . . . It is evident to anyone who knows our condition that we cannot long go on without a very material increase in classroom space and other facilities if we are to avoid sending students away who wish to register here.

Tucson was now feeling the full effects of the depression. *The Arizona Daily Star* printed its own scrip and Steinfeld's store missed a payroll. Organized charities were trying vainly to raise a fund of $25,000 and, as usually happens, well-meaning people came up with impractical relief suggestions. Tops for Tucson seems to have been a plan to give a jobless man a card that permitted him to beg for work at sixteen homes. Householders were asked to give the applicant two hours' work a week for which they would pay him at the rate of 12.5 cents an hour. This meant that if all the householders were generous, the jobless one could earn $4.00 a week. The plan was carefully explained in the press but apparently died quickly and quietly, for it was not mentioned again.

Serious as was the situation at the University, President Shantz and the Regents were not willing to give up all hope of a university building program, and on September 3, 1934, Dr. Shantz explained to the Board a plan that he believed might make it possible to meet the needs. He said the University could get $800,000 from the Public Works Administration. Thirty per cent of this would be an outright gift, the remainder to be repaid over thirty years. There would be no payments during the first three years. To meet these payments, which started at $12,000 and went up $1,000 a year, the Board pledged itself to pay as much as necessary out of gross income, fees and other income. Dr. Shantz reported,

> We had a great time getting that WPA appropriation. In the first place the Governor was opposed to it. He wouldn't consider it and he wouldn't call the Legislature. Even some members of the Board were opposed.
>
> General Frank H. Hitchcock was here then, publishing the *Citizen.* He favored the idea so we went up to Phoenix to interview Ellinwood. He said we would not only need a special session of the Legislature but would have to take

> the matter to the Supreme Court to see if it was legal. The Governor upset the applecart several times when we were trying to get the Legislature together so that it could pass an enabling act. I might mention that he was pretty proud of it when it went through.
>
> We had a man named T. D. Tway, chairman of the House appropriations committee, and we talked the matter over with him. The Senate was bound to be the stumbling block but Tway said, "I believe the majority of the senators would favor this bill if I could get around to see them. I think I could handle it."
>
> "Well," I said, "if I spend one dollar of state money sending anybody around I'll end up in Florence, and it will be the end of the University so far as the state is concerned."
>
> But Monte Mansfield heard about it and said, "I'll furnish you a car and the gasoline." So away Tway went. He found that the senators were favorable and that we could say to the Governor, "We've got the votes." So he called the Legislature, they passed it and the Supreme Court said it was legal. But if it hadn't been for Monte we might never have got the money. As a matter of fact, the loan and grant was $1,020,000 before we got through with it, while the State of Arizona got a total of $5,000,000 which was spent for the University, the teachers' colleges, roads, some irrigation projects, and municipal work.

President Shantz now dusted off his 1928 building program. He asked for and got a science building and greenhouse. The women's gymnasium and recreation building, an auditorium, a classroom building, the State Museum, the infirmary, cavalry stables, an addition to the power plant and heating system, plus additions to and remodeling of farm facilities. Rising prices ran the cost of all this construction up to $1,002,000. It was the greatest building bargain the State of Arizona had ever seen.

Turning his attention to reorganization, Dr. Shantz formed a School of Business and Public Administration under Dr. E. J. Brown with courses in economics, business administration, sociology, advanced courses in secretarial work, and a degree of bachelor of science in public administration. The College of Education was reorganized as a professional school, and a College of Fine Arts was established in which drama, rhythmics, music, and speech were grouped together under the direction of Dean Charles F. Rogers. The College of Music became a part of the new College of Fine Arts, and the old College of Letters, Arts, and Sciences became the College of Liberal Arts. The Graduate College was reorganized with R. J. Leonard as dean, and the Department of Home Economics was reestablished as a school in the College of Agriculture. The School of Home Economics continued to grow through the years, and in 1959 it moved into its own new building.

The most important change in personnel during these years was a change in the nature of Dr. A. E. Douglass' affiliation with the University. Under a co-operative agreement with the Carnegie Institute, he was to engage in full-time research in tree-rings. The Regents insisted that some connection must be maintained with the University and after Dr. Douglass' resignation continued to keep him on the faculty, and to provide him with quarters. The name of the institution he had served so well appeared on his publications, and in 1938 he resumed full-time duties with the University and renewed his work here.

Great arguments soon arose over the location of the new buildings, particularly over the site of the auditorium. Some wanted both the auditorium and the museum erected at the east end of the campus. This was Dr. Shantz' idea and he was deeply disappointed when overruled, for he regarded these as buildings to be used irregularly and he thought the space at the west end near the library should be devoted to structures that would be used daily by students.

One opinion was that the auditorium was so big that it would never be filled to capacity and therefore should not be built at all. The minutes of the Regents revealed this, but they do not reveal that there were others who agreed and who spoke of the building as "Shantz' folly." How wrong they were has been often demonstrated.

Records of December, 1934, show that the old science building east of the library was being remodeled for the College of Liberal Arts, Herring Hall was being changed from the women's gymnasium to a theater for the Fine Arts College, and the building of the Law College was also undergoing alterations.

All this growth represented a tremendous accomplishment. The hard years of the early thirties had failed to stop the soft-spoken President and his Board of Regents. Despite the depression and the resulting shortage of funds, they had expanded the University's plant and raised its academic standing.

But it takes money to operate new buildings as well as additional colleges and departments. Having succeeded in cutting the University appropriations to a drastic degree, the Legislature evidenced no intention of changing that policy. As Dr. Shantz recalled:

> I remember one meeting of the Regents, held in January, 1935. We had decided to ask for $800,000, but President Robert E. Tally said he had been before the Legislature and had agreed, in view of the necessity for economy, to cut this to $700,000. Governor Moeur said he would not approve more than $664,235 and [one regent] said he would support the Governor. The motion to ask for $800,000 was defeated and so was the motion.
>
> *The Arizona Daily Star* then carried an editorial under the heading, A DISGRACEFUL REQUEST, in which it said:
>
> The decision of the Regents of the University of Arizona to make a request for an appropriation of $800,000 a year for the next two years is a mistake. The State of Arizona in its present condition cannot bear such an appropriation for every dollar represents taxation. Moreover if the University of Arizona should be granted such an increase then every other institution and department of the state government would have the precedent to justify additional increases. Then all the economies made by Governor Moeur and the previous Legislature would be lost. . . .
>
> Arizona cannot possibly stand a further expenditure for government. Instead of setting the example of intelligence which should come from the Board of Regents of the University of Arizona, the Board has set a glaring example of stupidity and greed which is a reflection on the character and ability of each member of the Board. The extravagant request the Board has made should be refused to conform to the recommendation of the Governor's budget.
>
> It is not a question what the University and other institutions need, it is a question of what the state can afford.

This was scarcely in line with Governor Moeur's address to the Legislature in which he said that warrants could now be cashed at full value and that "Arizona is definitely on the road to recovery."

The House finally gave the University a biennial appropriation of $1,400,000. The Senate tried to cut this but failed.

Succeeding meetings of the Board were unpleasant for the President. The Board cut the salaries of leading professors, voted not to pay any part of the faculty group-insurance fees, and dismissed teachers. As Dr. Shantz remembers:

> Those were terrible weeks in the history of the institution. The Board which had been appointed by Governor Hunt was gone and there was no one left who had served when I was appointed. After the meeting at which the Board tried to tear the University to pieces I felt there was no use of staying. That finished me. I felt they were whipping the University over my shoulder and perhaps could not do that to a man of their own choice.
>
> One of the Tucson radio stations offered me $600 in time if I would go on the air and explain what was going on, but I refused to do it. I wrote a long resignation explaining my act. Then I tore it up and wrote a short one which merely said:
>
> I hereby resign my position as President of the University of Arizona to become effective June 30, 1936 in order to take charge of the Division of Wild Life Management of the National Forest Service.

The move came as a complete surprise to the state, and the Regents immediately countered by writing a eulogizing resolution which said in part:

> Under most trying economic conditions he has established a school of business and public administration, a graduate school, a school of home economics, assisted in raising the ranking of the Law College to among the highest in the United States, established the College of Education as a professional school, broadened the staffs and curricula of all departments, developed a Fine Arts College and raised every standard with the University. In addition he has stayed within his budget.

The Regents added that the building program providing for approximately $1,000,000 was in the main due to the vision and untiring efforts of Dr. Shantz. In addition to which he had been responsible for setting aside the Saguaro Forest as a national monument and had been personally instrumental in persuading Washington to approve the Gila-Yuma reclamation project. They closed the resolution with this: "He will live long in the heart of the people of Arizona."

The Gila-Yuma project called for the expenditure of $4,500,000 in federal funds on a major irrigation plan that would carry Colorado River water to thousands of acres of dry lands. It had been set up once and then cancelled by the Secretary of Agriculture when he received unfavorable reports from engineers who wanted the money spent in other ways.

Dr. Shantz had presented his resignation to the Regents but was still serving as president when he heard the bad news. Since his duties called him to Washington he went personally to Secretary Henry A. Wallace to try to resell him on the great value of the plan. So eloquently did he plead the cause of Arizona and so firm was his grasp of the true facts that the Secretary recommended the reactivation of the project to President Roosevelt and the Gila-Yuma project was saved. Governor Moeur was liberal with his praise of this service, and the residents of the Yuma Valley showered the retiring President with telegrams of congratulation.

President Shantz spoke his last word of farewell in the pages of the *Arizona Alumnus*. There, under the simple caption, "Adios," he said:

> During our eight years of residence on the campus of the University of Arizona, Mrs. Shantz and I have enriched our lives by friendships established with students, alumni, and many other Arizona residents.
>
> The president of a state university must forget himself and live only for the welfare of the institution and in the satisfaction of seeing the students, faculty, and physical plant develop. Probably no period in the history of our institution has been as trying as that through which we have just passed. Support from the state dropped below the level of 1930–31 although our student body had increased two hundred and fifty per cent. Both students and faculty have sacrificed to carry on their work. Both have striven constantly in the interests of the University. The alumni have done more to help than can ever be known. In every crisis they could always be counted upon.
>
> My classes have tied me to the University of Arizona. One cannot easily lay aside a work that has consumed every waking and many of the sleeping hours as well. I may change my work but a coat that has been worn so long cannot easily

> be laid aside. It must be torn off and left behind. With it will remain a part of me, perhaps the best eight years of my life.

The building program and greatly expanded curriculum for which Dr. Shantz had been largely responsible were not the only legacies he left, for his successor was greeted by a 14 per cent increase in enrollment which brought the registration up to 2,485. Nor was this all, since PWA in the fall of 1936 provided an additional $481,818 which was enough to build Pima Hall and a dining hall known as the Commons. The University had been regularly turning away between 150 and 200 women students for two years, and the new dormitory, with Gila Hall which soon followed, solved a vital problem. New buildings completed and in use at this time were the humanities building, the infirmary, the State Museum, the women's building, and the ROTC stables. The auditorium was opened on April 22, 1937, with a cantata, "Land of Light."

The Board of Regents named Dean Paul S. Burgess of the College of Agriculture as acting president following the resignation of Dr. Shantz and tendered him the appointment of president in October, 1936, but he was not eager for the honor, although it carried a salary increase of $2,000. He had accepted the post of Acting President with reluctance, and he still hoped to serve again as Dean of Agriculture, so he named Dr. Ralph S. Hawkins Acting Dean until he could return. Board members were meanwhile deadlocked in the choice of a president between faculty members from the University of Michigan and the University of California. That indecision would last another year.

While serving as President, Dr. Burgess had the support and admiration of the student body, though it could not understand his decision in opening the campus streets to public traffic. Students were upset principally because when they broke the fifteen-mile-an-hour regulations, they lost their cars for two weeks and had to pay storage on them, while townspeople and visitors merely went before a Tucson justice and paid a fine. *The Wildcat* reported that 60 per cent of the violators were from Tucson and asked in an editorial, "If the University is expected to consider the townspeople's wishes in keeping the campus open, won't the folks of Tucson co-operate by obeying our traffic regulations?"

With Dr. Burgess established as President, the Regents asked the Legislature to grant them a $200,000 increase in the appropriation for the University so that the 10 per cent cut in salaries the faculty had volunteered to take in 1932 might be returned in 1937 and 5 per cent of the additional cut be restored in 1938.

In this they had the support of *The Arizona Daily Star* which ran a strong editorial that said in part:

> There are no employees of the state more deserving of recognition by the Legislature. They, along with other employees of the state, are entitled to restoration of their pay cuts. To deny them that and grant it to others would be grossly unjust discrimination.

The Legislature refused to grant the request in full and cut it to a point that permitted only a 5 per cent increase, so it was a matter of no surprise when the faculty asked the American Association of University Professors to send in an investigating committee. The AAUP sent a committee with instructions to "look into friction and apparent insecurity of tenure." The visitors investigated the reasons for two specific dismissals and reported that in view of the financial situation they could not wholly condemn the actions of the Board but added that there could well have been a money settlement. As for the faculty as a whole, the committee found "distinct fear and distrust" that could be corrected only if the Board of Regents issued a reassuring statement of what its future policy would be on academic tenure.

This was refused in letters from Regents Ellinwood and McCluskey, who said the Supreme Court of Arizona had ruled the Board had no authority to "fix times of notice for the discharge of employees." That closed the door, and the AAUP could only notify college teachers of the United States that nothing had changed in Arizona and that tenure remained doubtful.

There was money for some purposes, if very little for salaries, and the Legislature agreed to give the University $70,000 for repairs on buildings and for an experimental farm in the Gila Valley. Legislators said President Burgess had made such an excellent argument when he appeared before them that they could not refuse him.

The President, who was an ardent sports fan, got a pleasant surprise that month when the football team closed a "suicide schedule" by playing the Red Raiders of Texas Tech to a 7–7 tie. This gave the University of Arizona five wins, three ties, and two defeats for the season.

January, 1937, ushered in the first of a series of lectures by peace propagandists who were making the circuit of colleges in a drive to arouse students against compulsory ROTC training and military service. The student peace council sponsored Art Casaday, a youthful peace worker from Los Angeles, who was coast secretary of the Emergency Peace Campaign, and students were invited to a luncheon given for him by Blue Key. Dr. Warren Graft, a Los Angeles clergyman, Miss Maude Royden, who was billed as the world's greatest woman speaker, and Leonard Miall, a Cambridge student, were other attractions. Senior students of ROTC met the challenge by presenting "a program designed to interest the entire student body," while the Peace Council and Scabbard and Blade, the ROTC honorary organization, finally held a test poll of students and faculty at the flag pole. The result was inconclusive, since only 608 votes were cast and the peace advocates, who did most of the campaigning, won by only twenty-four votes. If *The Wildcat* reflected the situation clearly, the students appeared to have conducted themselves with considerable restraint and there is no evidence that the administration interfered with editors.

The Wildcat staff, however, went on what the columns of the paper spoke of as a "sit-down strike" when the offices of the publication were moved to quarters under the stadium. According to the news stories, the staff refused to work for three weeks; but the files show no issues missing.

Two weeks before commencement in 1937, President Burgess sent his resignation to the Regents. He stressed that he had originally accepted the presidency on a temporary basis and now felt he should resign. In retiring he recommended Dr. Alfred Atkinson as his successor, and the Board accepted both the resignation and the recommendation.

Dr. Shantz died at the age of 82 while on a field trip over the Great Plains of the middle west. A final measure of his greatness in his chosen field may be found in the fact that when he was seventy-seven years old his reputation was still so outstanding that the Botanical Society of America formally designated him as one of the greatest botanists of his age.

CHAPTER 9

1937–1942

DR. ALFRED ATKINSON, who had served Montana State College as President for eighteen years, became the twelfth president of the University of Arizona upon the resignation of Dr. Paul S. Burgess in the Summer of 1937. The son of Canadian pioneers, he attended the public schools of Canada and then studied for three years in the Agricultural College of Guelph. He left Canada in his senior year to enroll in Iowa State Agricultural College, where he was made head of research in the Department of Agronomy before he graduated in 1904. The ink was scarcely dry on his Bachelor of Science degree when he headed west to become a member of the faculty of Montana State College. On leave, he did graduate work at Cornell, where he not only received his master's degree but also became an American citizen. Iowa State College conferred the D.Sc. degree upon him, and after returning to Montana he again served as agronomist before being named president.

Eight of Dr. Atkinson's years in Montana were devoted to the study of the effects of environment on changes in plant character. These studies he carried on in co-operation with the American Society of Agronomy. It was in this period that he wrote thirty bulletins for Montana's agricultural experiment station. He was one of the first educators to become a leader in the Farmers' Institute and Farm Congress movements, and was elected president of the Association of Land Grant Colleges in 1937. Societies and fraternities that honored him were the American Genetic Association, American Society of Agronomy, Phi Gamma Delta, Phi Kappa Phi, Sigma Xi, Gamma Sigma Delta, and Alpha Zeta. He was named food administrator for Montana during World War I and in 1924–25 was district Governor of Rotary International.

Resident enrollment was 2,827 when the President entered on his duties in Arizona. This enrollment represented a gain of 666 students since the primary post-war depression had reached the state in 1930. These figures did not include summer school, night classes, extension, or correspondence.

The new President came at the beginning of a difficult period in university history. It was a time for reconstruction and growth, yet the institution was pinned down by limited financial support from the state. Salaries were low, and the expense of maintaining the physical plant had increased.

Looking back on these years Dr. Atkinson once said, "You had to buy coal and light and sweep the building out, and by the time you paid for absolute necessities your money was gone. I think I can say truthfully that the institution was beset with grave financial and other problems during the depression and war years of my administration."

President Atkinson was formally inaugurated on April 12, 1938. The opening event of the day was a symposium entitled, "The University and the State." Dr. Francis C. Lockwood spoke on "Arizona's People"; Dr. Melvin F. Coolbaugh, President of Colorado School of Mines, took as his topic, "The Mining Industry in Relation to the State and the Nation," while Dr. Robert H. Forbes, Dean Emeritus of the College of Agriculture, sketched the early history of the University. Representatives of 190 colleges and universities and special guests marched in the academic procession.

C. Zaner Lesher, registrar, introduced the delegates to the President, who was welcomed to Arizona by Governor Rawleigh C. Stanford. Dr. G. M. Butler extended greetings from the faculty, after which Lee Lowery spoke for the student body and Aaron Levy for the alumni. E. E. Ellinwood, president of the Board of Regents, then inducted Dr. Atkinson into office.

In his speech of acceptance, Dr. Atkinson said:

> The responsibility of the University of Arizona is primarily to the people of Arizona. It is the people of the state who provide most of the support of the institution, and it is the sons and daughters of Arizona who make up a large part of its student body. . . .
>
> An acknowledgment of responsibility to its immediate constituency does not mean a limitation of the horizon and interest of the University. It has brought to its libraries the knowledge of the ages, and its faculty members and research workers are not concerned with geographic boundaries in their teachings and investigations. Knowledge is universal and young men and young women who go through the classes and who work in the libraries and laboratories of the University must be impressed with the universality of knowledge.
>
> The University has made large contributions to the betterment of agriculture, mining and other pursuits and it hopes to enlarge this work and to conduct investigations that will be of increasing importance. . . .

> Mr. Chancellor, with a high sense of appreciation of the honor conferred, and with some recognition of the responsibilities involved, I accept appointment as President of the University of Arizona and pledge to you and the other members of the Board of Regents, as well as to the University and the state, the best of whatever I possess in the way of attainment and ability. I may say that people are not efficient if their prerogatives and responsibilities are not clearly defined and fairly protected, and I shall make every effort possible to maintain a standard of fairness and tranquility that will insure effectiveness.

The last act of the academic drama was the conferring of the honorary degree of Doctor of Science on Andrew Ellicott Douglass, "scientist, author, administrator, world-traveler, investigator in pioneer fields, and leader in his chosen field of work."

An informal reception was held on the lawn of the library, and the Department of Drama closed the day by presenting *The Merry Wives of Windsor* in the evening to an audience that filled the auditorium.

Immediately after his inauguration, the President appointed a committee to make plans for a student union building and the Regents agreed to use a $45,000 surplus left from President Shantz' building program to build a block of concrete stands on the east side of the football field. It would increase the seating capacity of the stadium to 11,000.

Enthusiasm created by this move was dampened before graduation by an announcement that Old Main, the original home of the University, had been condemned by the building inspectors and that the Board of Regents would abandon the structure before classes resumed in September.

This put added pressure on the space in other buildings and resulted in moving the School of Business and Public Administration and transferring the thirty women students in Pima Hall to a large house on North Euclid. The offices of the U. S. Forest Service and the Agricultural Adjustment Administration were moved off the campus, and their quarters in the Agricultural College were assigned to some of the departments of the College of Liberal Arts, the College of Education, and the Department of Speech. In 1941 a new women's residence hall was completed and named Pima Hall, making the second use of this name in the University's history.

Twelve years before the abandonment of Old Main, the Legislature had refused to appropriate $80,000 to repair the landmark that had cost only

$35,000 to build, and there was no hope that the Legislature would change its mind. Not even the protests of 5,000 alumni who loved it could prevail. It was "Old" Main now, in fact as well as name, and it seemed doomed forever.

September of 1938 brought hopes for another university building program when the Legislature passed, and Governor Stanford signed, a bill giving the Regents authority to accept another Public Works Administration grant and a 55 per cent loan amounting in all to $1,167,530. The money was to be spent on self-liquidating and non-liquidating projects. The self-liquidating projects were a student union, a dormitory for men, and a dining hall. Rated as non-liquidating were a classroom building, a $40,000 home for the President, a physical plant shop, a new university well, and removal of the poultry farm to North Campbell Avenue. A separate item was the sum of $106,000 for maintenance, upkeep, and repairs.

PWA's Arizona office signed the necessary papers and the Regents hurried an attorney off to Washington to speed up final arrangements. Four months dragged by and then the bright dream exploded. The PWA decided that Arizona's allotment was exhausted, which meant that hopes for the grant and the building program were gone. There were other problems that same year, as the President's report showed. Dr. Andrew E. Douglass, Dr. Byron Cummings, and Dean Samuel M. Fegtly had retired and had to be replaced. The College of Mines and Engineering was in great need of a new building, and the Bureau of Mines had seen its financial support mutilated to a point where it was unable to meet the needs of the State for surveys and laboratory work. Director E. F. Carpenter of the Steward Observatory reported that the glow reflected from Tucson street lights was interfering with the studies of faint stars, for which the big telescope was built, to such a degree that the work was about as practical as looking for a firefly in the glare of an aviation beacon, and Dr. Atkinson noted that a men's dormitory and a classroom building were imperative needs.

All of this hurt the University, but the real blow came when Robert T. Jones, the new governor, notified the Regents that their proposed operative budget was not acceptable and must be drastically reduced. The Board had voted unanimously to ask $1,004,831 for 1939–1940 and $1,033,904 for 1940–1941, but these sums were slashed to $835,179 for 1939–1940 and $835,178 for 1940–1941.

Years afterward, President Atkinson made the wry comment that there was a vast difference between the way some of the Regents voted in their meetings and the advice they passed on privately to members of the Legislature.

The spirit of the University soared on May 27, 1940, when a new mining and metallurgical building was dedicated. The handsome structure, which had been built and completely equipped by the Phelps Dodge Corporation at a cost of $194,000, was known as the James Douglas Memorial Building.

With a true understanding of the stature of the man whose name was honored and the significance to the mining industry of the gift, the program was marked by noteworthy addresses of historical value and these were fully documented.

Walter Douglas, chairman of the board of the Southern Pacific Railroad Company of Mexico, and son of Dr. Douglas, spoke with "respect, admiration and love" of his father and sketched the life and accomplishments of the man who had left his bold mark on the hills and in the mines of Arizona.

Louis S. Cates, president of the Phelps Dodge Corporation, said:

> It is particularly appropriate that this building is being dedicated to the memory of Dr. James Douglas. It was through his broad vision and leadership in the field of mining and metallurgy that the mining industry of Arizona made the rapid growth and great progress that is its history.

Lewis Douglas, grandson of Dr. Douglas, was unable to leave his duties in Washington as Director of the Budget because of the international situation. He did, however, forward a message in which he said:

> A life—indeed a civilization—displays symbols of its moral nature. Dr. Douglas personified the best of the period in which he lived. He sought of public authority no bounty, no tariff, no subvention; for he understood only too well their stultifying effects on human character and their ultimate consequences on individual freedom. If he was a disbeliever in a government of unlimited powers, he was equally resistant to abuse of personal privilege and the administration of prices by corporate enterprise. He believed that the ownership of property was a private trust to be enjoyed only by those who could perform a useful service.
>
> Just as he was a disciple of the free exchange of goods and services in the market place, so was he a believer in the unfettered and voluntary exchange of scientific and technical knowledge. It was his crusade that stripped from metallurgical operations the veil of secrecy in which they had been clothed. If he thereby gained knowledge, he gave far more in return.

A notable symposium of high historical value provided addresses on "Early Mines and Mining," by Dr. Francis C. Lockwood; "Sixty Years of Copper Mining in the Southwest," by A. B. Parsons, Secretary of the American Institute of Mining and Metallurgical Engineers; and "The Development of Metallurgy in the Southwest Since 1880," by T. G. Chapman, Professor of Metallurgy at the University.

In responding for the University, Dr. Atkinson said that it accepted the gift with a sense of high responsibility; he declared: "The world's greatest mining school should be located in the most important mining state in the Union and that mining school must be at the University of Arizona."

The completion of this building made possible the division of the College of Mining and Engineering into a College of Mines, of which T. G. Chapman was made dean, and a College of Engineering under Dean G. M. Butler.

Reports covering September, 1940, show that twenty-one new courses were added to the University curriculum in speech, anthropology, history, agriculture, botany, accounting, political science, music, as well as a major in journalism. In addition, the graduate program added master's degrees in music, agriculture, education, and home economics. Requirements for the degree of Juris Doctor were stiffened in the College of Law, and the College of Engineering raised the standards for a professional degree.

Over the years, the good name of the University of Arizona had spread to all parts of the country and many parts of the world. Students from other states and countries came in ever-increasing numbers. During the years 1937–1940 this increasing popularity led to the unfair suggestion that social life and other recreational activities were overemphasized. One writer went so far as to characterize the University as "the collegiate country club of the Southwest."

The unexcelled climate of Southern Arizona was probably at the bottom of such erroneous ideas. For at least seven months of the academic year it is unexcelled for outdoor recreation.

It is impossible to answer charges that the weather is wonderful in Arizona except by admitting that it is, and everyone is glad of it. But the implication was silly that standards and cultural interests simply had to be low because the weather was so fine.

Another factor which helped to glamorize the University was the national prominence of its polo program. The team made the sport pages of the eastern press while society pages played up reports of social leaders who attended the polo matches and horse shows. Physical education for women and military training for men featured equitation.

Just prior to World War II, the University of Arizona had the largest all-cavalry ROTC unit in the country; the Army supplied the horses, and a military review in those days was something that stirred the blood when at the shouted order, “Line, draw sabers, trot, gallop, CHARGE,” the troop thundered down the field with trumpet screaming and sabers extended in a long line of glittering steel.

Tradition-minded upperclassmen paddled freshmen who neglected to wear beanies. The football team was playing and beating big time opponents, and women students fussed with the Dean of Women over the right to wear bobby sox.

The Blue Moon was a favorite rendezvous for dancing couples on Wednesday night. Oracle held square dances with music by old-time fiddlers, while Nogales was an irresistible attraction that kept the girls writing home for parental permission to cross the border.

And, of course, there were always the picnics at Sabino Canyon and desert ranches, and the long rides home under night skies filled with stars.

It was charged, and it was true, that there was drinking at football games and that liquor appeared now and then in fraternity houses. In this, the University was no different from similar institutions, but President Atkinson took cognizance of the situation during his first year. He made it a point to call a special assembly at which he warned students that the use or possession of liquor on the campus or in fraternity houses was illegal, and promised that those who broke the law would be disciplined.

The young College of Law announced that sixty-five of the graduates were serving in public life as judges, state attorneys general, county attorneys, city attorneys, and legislators. It added with pride that 100 per cent of the 1940 graduates had passed the State Bar examination. In the same year the College of Education reported that every graduate had been placed in a teaching position.

This was 1940 and the country was on the edge of war. The officials of the University knew that the government expected to draw on the military departments in land grant colleges for officer material and that many students would be drafted into the armed forces. At the same time one finds a strong student peace council organizing public meetings for speakers such as Marquis Childs, Kirby Page, and Robert Morse Lovett.

It seems, however, that student life seems to have moved along traditional channels and to have shown little concern over the spreading clouds of war. One doubts that the student body knew the significance of an extensive survey the university scientists had made of the critical and strategic materials the state could provide, or was even informed that the War Department had been supplied with a list of all men who had graduated during the previous five years.

This was also the period when the Board of Regents established the first international scholarships for students who, because of racial, religious, or political persecution, were unable to study in their own countries.

The University Artist Series presented Helen Traubel, Ezio Pinza, Gladys Swarthout, Jan Peerce, Fritz Kreisler, Yehudi Menuhin, and Ted Shawn's dancers.

The drama department gave such plays as *Romeo and Juliet*, *Taming of the Shrew*, *Pride and Prejudice*, *Winterset*, and *Ah, Wilderness*, while the School of Music sang *Faust* and *Iolanthe*, and Charles Wakefield Cadman conducted a presentation of his opera, *Shanewis*.

In one academic year the faculty gave 624 lectures in sixty-two communities to 63,478 people. This does not include the 44,000 people who attended lectures given by county agents or the 37,000 who attended the meetings held by home demonstration agents. Neither does it include the professors who appeared on 313 radio programs.

As for the standards of instruction, they may be judged in part by results in the College of Mines where the records show that 80 per cent of all graduates were employed in their profession, and members of every graduating class were in high demand.

Minor attention had been paid by *The Wildcat* to a ground school training program for aviation that was given under the authority of the Civil Aeronautical Administration, but on the whole it got less attention than the polo team.

It was not until classes resumed after the 1940 year-end holidays that student editors showed any real concern over the prospect of war touching the campus. At that time the paper welcomed the students back to classes with black headlines announcing the opening of a sixteen-week course for students who wished to train for employment in national defense industries and with the news that a survey had been made of the services faculty members could contribute to a national defense program.

In the same issue, *The Wildcat* editorialized on the re-opening of school and said frankly that while it might seem the same as it had in previous years "there was something different down underneath" and admitted that this "something" was the fear of war.

One month later Dr. Atkinson returned from a conference of 500 presidents of colleges and universities who had been called to Washington to confer with War Department officials on the drafting of students and on the services the institutions could give the nation. He brought the news that college students would be deferred from military service only until July 1, 1941. This ruling, however, was subsequently changed several times.

Graduation in May, 1941, saw 446 students receive earned degrees; eighty-one won College honors. This was sixteen fewer than the total of the previous year, but twenty-six students had dropped their books to enter military service. One of them was William Bishop of Cleveland, Ohio, who received his degree in absentia. He had enlisted in the Royal Flying Corps in Canada and became the first Arizona student to lose his life in World War II when his troopship was torpedoed enroute to England.

Forty-seven seniors were sworn into the ROTC as second lieutenants at commencement in 1941, and *The Wildcat* had an editorial message for the new officers:

> We cannot predict what will happen as a result of your efforts to stop those who would rob you of your personal ideals. But you who hold the ideals of fair play, decency and 'pursuit of happiness' will know that you are not going to want to see those things taken from you.

The ferocity of the war grew and the tempo of American preparations quickened during the following summer. The government organized the Office of Civilian Defense. A U. S. merchant ship was sunk without warning by a submarine, and President Roosevelt called the attack "an act of intimidation to which we do not propose to yield." On July 4, the President broadcast a message to the nation in which he said, "The United States will never survive as a happy and fertile oasis of liberty surrounded by a cruel desert of dictatorship." A little later he was to meet with Prime Minister Winston Churchill on a battleship where they drew up and signed the Atlantic Charter, "an eight-point declaration of principles for a post-war world."

College opened in September that year to learn that the basic military classes would be taught modern infantry drill in place of the cavalry training they had received in the past. Seniors, however, would continue to respond to the call of "boots and saddles."

Then came Sunday morning, December 7, 1941, "a day which will live in infamy." It was a quiet morning on the campus, for students were depressed by the 12–6 defeat the Wildcats had suffered at the hands of the University of Utah Redskins on Saturday night. But the radio soon changed all that as it began to carry excited flashes on the news of Japan's attack on Pearl Harbor. There was no argument now over whether we would enter the war. War had been brought to us, and there was no escape.

There was no talk of peace or unwillingness to submit to military training. Campus headquarters of the ROTC were filled with students who wanted to take military courses. A delegation called on Dr. Atkinson to offer its services in any work that needed to be done, and there was much talk of enlisting. *The Wildcat* took almost two columns of space for an undergraduate editorial that reflected students' reactions, fears, and hopes. It was written by Jim Bohannan who would become the University's first post-war Rhodes scholar. Now he wrote:

> Classes have been rather wretched yesterday and today. The intricacies of biochemistry, the anthropology of Africa and higher calculus have lost their charm. Because we're at war. The student body divided into little cliques around portable radios and listened to the final condemnation of decency in the world.
>
> We heard Roosevelt make his terse declaration. We are glad that's over. We know now where we stand. We heard about tears—quiet, serious tears—in some of the sorority houses and halls; we saw straight faces, serious eyes and occasionally heard an outburst of "I'm going to enlist."
>
> It's hard to believe that this is the same weather we've always had, that the campus is the same 40 acres, that the dark, ominous, mad feeling is within us . . .
>
> Those of us who think now—and we all have to think and trust, or we'll go mad—those of us who think know that we must look forward to a day when this war is over. Because wars do end.
>
> And we know that ours is the task of FIGHTING this war. We know that in a political sense we have to WIN this war; but we also know that in a humanitarian sense we have to MAKE THIS WAR STICK.
>
> No, we're not wanting to make this a war to end wars. We know that's a lot of poppycock of a generation ago. But when we do declare a peace may it be a righteous and humane peace. Let's make our war as terrible and unholy as Dante's Hell, but let's make our peace honorable.

> "But when peace comes, the University of Arizona will still be here; many of us will come back. And that's what counts. We've been sheltered and we have to go out and get kicked around a little—so that it can't happen again in the same way—so that at least we'll have moral progress in our wars. But when we get our kicking around we're coming back to our old sense of values and to the world that we've been fighting for.
>
> "Oh, yes, we'll be back, because you can't stop progress just by a piddling little war. It may ruin our lives, our culture, our whole generation, but you can't stop progress.
>
> We're coming back, we're coming back and we're going to make this a generation who learned by EXPERIENCE. We can do it. Just watch us.

The administration moved swiftly to alleviate the natural uncertainty on the campus. An immediate meeting of the advisory committee was held for the purpose of arranging a program under which students who enlisted would receive credit for incomplete work. When a state of war was declared with Germany and Italy, Dr. Atkinson called for a special assembly and asked for calmness. He said:

> Students should be deliberate. The prospects are that this will be a rather long war. Wherever we can bring our talents to bear most effectively to aid in this war, we will serve best. Some feel it is a stigma if one does not enlist at once. Yet no one can satisfactorily advise as to whether a young man should enlist now or wait. The decision is one he must make after consulting with his parents. The government is calling for enlistments. Men are needed, but the opening period of war is an emotional one and I charge you to be deliberate. If you are studying mathematics, physics, chemistry, engineering and kindred subjects, high preparation will make you better able to serve the nation in the war and in the period to follow. After all, the United States Army will tell us when it needs men.

It was probably difficult for the students to be deliberate in those first, strange days when *The Wildcat* was featuring such headlines as *War Upsets*

Arizona University Life, First Aid Classes to be Open for Men and Women, Eat for Health, Not Fun, Women Wanted to Knit and Sew for Red Cross, and *Details of Blackout Completed.*

Authorities thought there was little chance that Tucson and the University would be bombed, but Tucson citizens began to take precautions against air raids and established blackout rules. President Atkinson said the University was willing to co-operate, and students were soon startled to find air raid instructions in their college paper calling on them to form patrols. Shovels and buckets of sand appeared in the halls of campus buildings, and 900 blankets and stocks of surgical dressings were supplied to the emergency hospital that was established in the women's building. Red Cross first aid workers were assigned to posts, and air raid drills were held.

It was decided that women students were to be sheltered in the tunnels that carry service lines through the campus, and the entrances to these were marked with signs. All power lines running through the tunnels were to be cut at the main switches so that while the women might shiver with fear in the darkness they would not be in danger of death by electrocution.

Between the attack on Pearl Harbor and commencement night on May 12, 1942, the University lost 172 students to the armed forces. Among the 381 students about to receive degrees were fifty-two young men who would be commissioned as second lieutenants in the U. S. Officers Reserve Corps. Miss Mary Lauver, who was assistant secretary to President Atkinson at the time, remembers well that he signed their diplomas with tears in his eyes and that he said, "How sad, how sad, that these fine young men must sacrifice their hopes of a peaceful life and go out tomorrow on the paths of war."

His heart was heavy with that thought on commencement night when he arose to address the graduating class. It was a moment replete with drama in which the class and the audience shared. For although they were surrounded by the peaceful desert lying quietly beneath heavens filled with brilliant stars, they knew that far beyond the mountains the guns were thundering and men were dying. Only six days before General Wainwright had surrendered the torn, starved remnants of his forces at Corregidor. They too were American boys and whether the uniformed men in the graduating class would share such a fate no one knew.

It seemed right, therefore, that the dignified man on the platform should put aside the precise dictum of a college president; that he should speak from his heart in tones charged with emotion as he turned first to those who were soon to go from the campus to the battle lines and said:

At this commencement of 1942 I desire to pay special tribute to the young men before me who are wearing the uniform of the United States Army, to the others in the student group who will soon wear this uniform, and to the more than one thousand former students and graduates who are now in the armed services of the nation.

In the poem, "Flanders' Field," which Jack McCrea wrote just before he made the supreme sacrifice in the first World War, we find a challenge in the lines—

If ye break faith with us who die
We shall not sleep,
Though poppies grow
In Flanders' Field.

To the memory of those who established this nation in its early years, and to all others who have preserved its freedom in the different crises of its history, I want to say that this generation has not broken faith. It has seized the torch of freedom, flung to it by the men of the first World War and earlier wars; and is carrying it worthily.

The graduates of 1942 are completing their college careers under conditions which are quite different from those in which they expected to establish themselves. Young men and women have devoted themselves to preparation for important service in the pursuits of peace, in a world where peace prevailed. On this graduation night, these young people find that peace has ceased to prevail in most of the world, and that they must turn their efforts to the preservation of the way of life established in this nation and toward which mankind has striven through the centuries. When the emergency has passed and normal ways of life have been reestablished, under the security that our success in the present crisis will insure, you will return to the pursuits and interests which you had in mind when you entered the University.

Young ladies and gentlemen, your university experience has equipped you to meet the present emergency situation with courage and effectiveness. We have confidence that you will make your contribution in the crisis, and in the period which will follow. . . .

May God bless you.

Much would be expected of the new lieutenants if they lived up to the traditions of the University of Arizona men already on active duty, for university records show that 1,267 alumni had enlisted. Of this number 350 had received ROTC training and were serving as commissioned officers. The commandant at the University had said of them:

> Informal reports received indicate that they are rendering valuable services in all parts of the world and are reflecting great credit on their Alma Mater. This has more than substantiated every claim ever made concerning the value of ROTC in our scheme of national defense.

An inspection of the University's military unit in 1942 brought a rating of "excellent" and a statement from the War Department inspector who said:

> The seriousness with which all students perform their duty, due to a state of war, is reflected in improvement in the unit in every respect.

New courses of study were added for those who were entering or would enter the armed forces, and the Fall of 1942 found such additions to the curricula as military law, navigation, spherical trigonometry, training in army and navy typewriting problems, military astronomy, economics of war, and geography of world areas. Physical education courses for men stressed bodily contact and included boxing and wrestling. Health education for women gave first-aid training to all women entering the University.

New courses in small arms and military service were added by the Department of Military Science and Tactics, and the Civil Aeronautics Administration ground course could report that 331 students had enrolled in its classes since September, 1939.

The CAA work was actually the first national defense activity to be carried on by the University. Under the contract with the CAA, Dean G. M. Butler of the College of Engineering and nine members of his faculty taught and administered the ground school course. Private flying companies taught thirty-five hours of flight training and awarded private pilot licenses to those who successfully completed ground and flight courses. Only regularly enrolled University students or former students who had completed two years of academic studies were accepted for the CAA training.

This training was closed by the War Department in September, 1942, since the Army, Navy and Air Corps had started their own training facilities and because all students at the University were either enlisting or giving all their spare time to the ROTC. The work, however, had been worthwhile, for eighty per cent of the graduates saw service.

The University lost two popular features in 1942. One was the polo team and the other was the women's riding classes. Colonel A. W. Holderness, in disbanding the team and discontinuing the classes, said in stiff military language, "These activities are discontinued due to an increase in ROTC riding activities incident to additional military instruction." What he did not add was that the order closed a ten-year period in which the polo team had ruled without a break as western collegiate champions. It was the end of a type of activity loved by students and remembered fondly by the alumni, for while riding classes for women were renewed briefly in 1943–44, the Army sold the horses at the end of that college year.

President Atkinson petitioned the War Department to reinstate the cavalry unit, but jeeps, trucks, and tanks had supplanted the horse cavalry, and cadets never again galloped down the field while a trumpet blared.

By March, 1942, four months after Pearl Harbor, the student body had recaptured some of its enthusiasm for traditions. The annual rodeo drew an audience of 3,000 spectators. Tommy Dorsey's swing band played a concert in the auditorium, and the engineers held their cherished celebration of St. Patrick's Day. Nevertheless the campus was not quite the same; not with recruiting officers very much in evidence, a naval flying squadron organizing, and young women who hoped they might sometime serve as ambulance drivers taking courses in first aid and in the care and operation of gasoline motors.

The College of Agriculture actually began its war work as early as September, 1940, in co-operation with the state and county war boards established by the U. S. Secretary of Agriculture. Director Charles U. Pickrell of the agricultural extension service reported on this in June, 1941, when he said:

> In September [preceding Pearl Harbor] the State war board was given quotas for increased production goals in various farm commodities in the State, consisting of dairy products, poultry, eggs, hogs, hay, beef, pasture crops, as well as small grains to meet the demands of the lease lend features of our defense program. These goals were increased in December to take care of the added demands of our military forces. The extension staff, in cooperation with the

> experiment station staff was given the job of breaking down the state goals for these various commodities into county goals. Work in land use planning previously done in the various counties was a great assistance here.

The annual report for June, 1942, shows how rapidly and extensively the College of Agriculture was adapting to the demands of total war. One of the requests of the U. S. Department of Agriculture was for a survey of farm labor and farm machinery. This was vital if the government found it necessary to establish a federal rationing program, and both the extension and experimental services of the University performed valiantly.

Rubber was in short supply and the experiment station carried on work with forty desert plants but found that only guayule gave any promise of producing in commercial quantities. The search for rubber was accompanied by a similar survey of plants that might yield me-dicinals, insecticides, resins, and oils.

War had shut off imports of vegetable seeds, and this, too, became a project for the scientists who were able to show that Arizona could produce many of the needed varieties. Even the tamarisk trees that flourish so abundantly in the State were studied as a possible source of fence posts and lumber for furniture.

The research often called for scores, sometimes hundreds, of experiments. Under normal circumstances these would have been all that the scientists in the experimental and extension services could carry. But this was war and somehow they also found time for such projects as the fattening of beef cattle, control of cotton pests, constant tests of new strains of vegetables, and always the study of ground water problems.

No one could deny that here was a practical demonstration of the fact that the State's tax dollars and the federal grants that had made the University possible had not vanished as they were spent, but had become investments that yielded a high return in a time of need.

The faculty was shrinking in number as teachers withdrew to enter war services. Twenty-five members had left to enter military service or government bureaus by June, 1942, yet C. Zaner Lesher, the registrar, could report that the work in classrooms, laboratories, libraries, and in the field went on without delay and that the morale of the faculty was commendable.

It was obvious that neither faculty nor students were shirking the obligations that war had brought. They set up informal joint committees that engaged in defense and relief activities and established a key center of war information in the library. Very early in the struggle the Associated Students and the

Alumni Association began to keep in contact with the men and women in the services. Copies of *The Wildcat* and *Arizona Alumnus* were mailed free to former students in all parts of the world. A. L. Slonaker, who had been graduate manager for twenty years and secretary-treasurer of the Alumni Association for seventeen years, had turned over his alumni duties to J. Melvin Goodson in 1940, but Goodson went off to war in 1942 and Slonaker shouldered both jobs again. This time he took on the duty of answering every letter and postcard from service men and women. It was a heavy task, for in 1943–1944 he handled 51,376 pieces of service mail in addition to carrying the work of his dual positions.

If change in the life and work of the University was marked in the first five months of war, it was actually only a prelude to what was coming in 1942–1943. Students learned this when President Atkinson addressed them as they returned to school in September on the subject, "The University and Total War." He said:

> In the everyday routines the University has not been especially conscious of the war demands. Except for those who have to do with the special defense work most of us have gone our ways without much adjustment. That period has now come to an end on the campus of this University and in a few weeks we will become more definitely conscious of the demands which grow out of the needs of total war.
>
> It is expected that the work of the University will go forward much as usual during the year, but everyone connected with the institution will find it necessary to make certain adjustments and adaptations.

It was well known at this time that the Navy was about to set up an indoctrination training center on the campus for young commissioned officers. The first 500 of these men would arrive on October 15, and the second class was scheduled for November 15. Each class would remain sixty days, so that within a few weeks there would be 1,000 men training. The student officers were to be quartered in the gymnasium while Arizona Hall was to become a medical and dental infirmary. Navy instructors would live off campus.

A mess hall that would seat 600 men was being built on the parking lot between the Commons and the Women's Building where University cooks would prepare meals under Navy supervision. The young officers—their average age was 27—would use the university classrooms, auditoriums, and the stadium, but the hours would not conflict with the schedules of regular college work.

The naval officers faced a tough course. Revielle sounded at 5:30, breakfast came at 6:00, sick call at 7:40, color formation and inspection at 7:50, and colors at 8:00. The first classes opened at 8:05, and regimental drill was held daily at 11:00 before the noon mess. A busy afternoon with study periods preceded evening mess at 5:30, which was followed by an hour of recreation. Evening lectures were closed at the sound of a bugle at 10 P.M.

Of special significance, as far as the campus itself was concerned, was the fact that the Navy had let a contract for the rebuilding of Old Main. This was no mere facial job to be accomplished with a coat of paint. Main roof trusses were replaced, new floors were laid in the basement and on the second floor porch, old plaster and lath came down, and all interior walls were refinished. A new metal roof topped the job, and by the time the workmen moved out the Navy had spent $89,000 on the building.

It was plain that the Navy meant business. Coach Miles Casteel discovered this for himself one morning when he entered his office in the gymnasium and found a fast-moving night crew of government carpenters had shifted a wall four feet, reducing his space and robbing him of one window.

Not all the construction work done on the campus, however, was for the use of the Navy. Yavapai Hall, a men's dormitory that had been delayed by the shortage of building material, was completed in the summer of 1942. It cost $250,000, accommodated 220 students, and was financed by self-liquidating bonds. For the first time in years the University could house its male students. The new dormitory, however, could not compensate the college men for their difficulty in competing with naval officers for co-ed attention. *The Wildcat* touched on the point in a feature article which read:

> Intrepid student officers—one month after arrival—have raided the various girls' dormitories and the mutual loss of hearts has been severe. Also on the casualty list are the male students who are seeing their heart's desire captured by the swashbuckling future Nelsons.
>
> Lack of acquaintance with girls bothers these hardy lads of Mars not at all. After a reconnoitering mission on the intended female object they clear the deck for action with the standard navy introduction, 'Baby, this is war and red tape is out of date. I'm Ensign . . . and I'll be by for you at four bells.'

Associated Students now proposed that President Atkinson and Student President Jack Ogg appoint a faculty-student committee to "coordinate activities which should properly be part of the work of students and faculty of the University during the present conflict." The suggestion was accepted and the two presidents named Ogg, William Lindawood, Tom Ellinwood, Loree Collins, and Lois Garber Epley from the student group. Faculty members were Director J. F. McKale, Colonel A. W. Holderness, Dean A. H. Otis, Miss Florence M. Bond, and Miss Ina T. Gittings. *The Wildcat* welcomed the committee with an editorial captioned "At Last We Begin to Move," which said:

> At last the University has taken 'it out of neutral' and in another week or two a fully combined and co-operative campus will move into high gear to aid in the war effort.
>
> The first big step was taken last week when a joint faculty-student war aid coordinating council was set up. The choice of Mr. McKale as chairman was a wise one. With his training, experience, and personality, there will be no waiting policy.
>
> An all-out campus war drive requires the combined efforts of Greeks and independents, halls and dorms, faculty and staff members, honoraries and social groups. No one group can carry the entire burden, nor can one group exclude itself from the work.

There was an immediate speed-up in war work after the committee took over. A scrap drive promoted by the Greeks turned in twelve tons of metal, and a cotton-picking contest was a real success. Two hundred men and women students climbed into levis, donned straw hats, and took off for cotton fields which were short of pickers. The men averaged seventy-five pounds, but the women had trouble doing better than twenty pounds. They all came back to the campus with aching backs but happy in the assurance that they had picked enough cotton for eighty-five parachutes.

The committee's greatest achievement was a war bond and stamp sale sponsored by *The Wildcat* and staged around the flagpole in honor of William (Bill) Bishop, the first student to die in World War II, and twenty-two others who had given their lives since he went down with his torpedoed ship in the North Atlantic.

The goal had been placed at $10,000, but when Abe Chanin, editor of *The Wildcat*, finished the count, the final figures tallied better than $15,000. Few who witnessed the rally would soon forget it. Administrative officers, faculty, students, and staff gathered before Old Main on Thursday, November 12, 1942, to watch with bared heads while a bugler sounded "taps" and the flag sank to half-mast. The University led off with $6,000, Associated Students followed with $1,000, and Phi Delta Kappa led all the honoraries with $500. *The Wildcat* reported, "The faculty did more than its share to make the drive a success."

December, 1942, brought two rumors that caused such a wild furor on campus that they had to be dealt with officially. One tale was that Christmas holidays would be cancelled and the other was that the University would not re-open in January. President Atkinson issued a formal denial of the first and the Board of Regents took care of the second with a statement that the institution would be maintained and operated even if registration were greatly reduced.

Some of the fraternities had been so thoroughly sold on the idea that the University would not re-open for classes in 1943 that the members hoarded rationed gasoline to make sure of getting home. It did them no good, for Tucson firemen learned about the hidden gas and seized it in a series of raids.

The first year of war closed on the campus with a Christmas tree assembly and then students went home to family celebrations. But there were no holidays for the naval officers. A class of 555 left for active duty and 500 more men took their places.

CHAPTER 10

1942–1947

ALTHOUGH the military program developed at the University during World War II is remembered chiefly because of the large U. S. Naval Indoctrination School set up on the campus, this is far from being a complete picture. A summary is needed and, following this, there should be a more detailed recital of activities.

Briefly, therefore, it may be said that more than 11,000 men were trained here for warfare on land, at sea, and in the air. Included in this total were 10,000 young officers assigned to the naval school, 591 men in the naval aviation school, 283 in the Army Specialized Training Program, and 331 in the Civil Aeronautics Administration's civilian pilot and war training classes. The figure does not include those enrolled in the ROTC, the Enlisted Reserve Corps, 704 men and women who enrolled in special vocational courses, or the University's college-grade short courses in engineering, science, and war management.

The tragedy at Pearl Harbor and the swift series of Japanese smashes in the Pacific had left the Navy in no condition to fight a war on two oceans. It needed everything—ships, guns, ammunition, and aircraft—but first of all it had to have trained men, and it wanted them in a hurry. This meant a speeding up of industry, a new program of vast and coordinated effort on the part of the scientists, and tremendous demands on institutions of higher learning.

The Naval Academy at Annapolis could not hope to train men fast enough to set the program rolling, even though it cut its course from four to three years. Accordingly a crash program of indoctrinating naval reserve officers had to be established, and early in 1942 the government set up special schools at Harvard, Dartmouth, Columbia, and Princeton. It was then decided that a western base was needed, and the University of Arizona was chosen because its location, climate, buildings, and teaching facilities met the Navy's requirements. September 4 found a representative of the Secretary of the Navy and a staff of naval officers surveying the campus. President Atkinson took the visitors on a tour of the buildings, drill fields, and laboratories. He said afterwards,

"I was wondering all the time how we could meet the housing program, including the question of where we would get 500 double bunks to accommodate 1,000 men. But when I put the question to one of the officers he said, 'Don't worry about that. The bunks have been shipped.'"

Considerable concern was expressed in the state over the possibility of the Navy's interfering with the regular academic program, and the Board of Regents felt that this should be answered. They issued a formal statement in which they said that the usual academic program would continue throughout the war even though 40 per cent of the space was absorbed by the Navy.

The men's gymnasium was taken over immediately and became the home of the young naval officers. It accommodated 1,000 men, the majority of whom wondered over the slogan, "Bear Down" painted on the roof. That slogan, a campus tradition for sixteen years, was Greek to men from other states. Once its significance was explained, however, they immediately adopted the phrase as their own, and the gymnasium became known as the *USS Bear Down.* Navy brass eventually thought enough of the story to include an explanation in the official history of the school and explain why it had been an inspiration to men who were preparing for battle. The history included these paragraphs:

> Back in 1926, the story runs, John Byrd Salmon was quarterback on the University of Arizona football team, catcher on the Wildcat baseball nine and an outstanding student. Early in the gridiron season, October 2, 1926, "Button" Salmon overturned his car returning from Phoenix, rupturing his spinal cord, an injury which attending doctors knew would result in death before many days had passed.
>
> Near the end—"Button" died October 8—Athletic Director J. F. McKale went to pay a last visit to the courageous Salmon who knew that he had not long to live. Salmon faced death as he did everything else—with a stout heart.
>
> "Have you any message for the team?" McKale inquired of "Button." He looked intently at the dying youth.
>
> "Any message?" asked "Button" gazing up at McKale. "Tell the team to bear down!"
>
> Learning of this story the student officers unconsciously bore down a little harder, inspired by the courage and tenacity of purpose which another humble American youth had displayed.

The student officers in the indoctrination school came from every state in the nation and from practically every profession. There were college professors among them, including Lieutenants Laurence A. Muir, Russell C. Ewing, and A. Boyd Mewborn of the University of Arizona. But whatever their training had been in civilian life, they all took the tough Navy ninety-day course, which included 446 hours of study and instruction as well as hours of tests, interviews, drills, and guard duty.

Discipline was strict, and it was relaxed only during liberty weekends. Then the citizens of Tucson and members of the faculty opened their homes, clubs, dances, and teas to the young officers. This liberty was limited to definite hours, and a co-ed who danced with a young officer on Saturday night was greeted with a blank stare when he marched past her to class on Monday morning.

The Twenty-fifth and last battalion trained was graduated December 20, 1944, in the auditorium, and presented its colors to the University in a ceremony held on the library lawn. The flags occupy a place of honor in the lobby of the library today. Decommissioning came January 10, 1945.

The school was closed when the Navy stopped commissioning officers from civilian life, and as suddenly as the first battalion had arrived, the final unit disappeared from campus and classroom. Yet in their departure they left behind a treasured memory and a warm farewell from Captain W. E. Cheadle, their commanding officer, who wrote:

> From the point of view of the Navy, the University of Arizona furnished an ideal location and adequate facilities for an indoctrination school.
>
> Naturally the introduction of a Navy School with its own staff, curriculum and routine as an integral part of a state university presented certain problems, ordinarily not easy to solve. Due, however, to the cooperation and competence of the President, faculty and staff of the University of Arizona the expected difficulties failed to materialize.
>
> During the commissioning of the school the most cordial relations were established and continued throughout the Navy's tenure on the campus. We of the Navy feel highly honored to have been accepted as a part of the University.
>
> In leaving we will carry with us fond memories of our many friends and their unfailing kindness to us during this tour of duty.

To this letter of thanks and farewell, President Atkinson penned a reply reflecting sentiments that prevail to this day. He said, in part:

> The University has greatly enjoyed its contacts with the 10,000 young men and the training officers who have been stationed on its campus. Their fine exemplification of citizenship and preparation for defense, along with the cooperation of Captain W. E. Cheadle and his staff of officers, has been a matter of very great satisfaction. We are pleased that the Naval Training School was established at the University of Arizona, and are gratified if its officers found conditions here favorable for their work.
>
> The training staff and student officers of the school have exemplified the meaning of "an officer and a gentleman" in such impressive fashion that their stay on campus will continue to be one of the rich memories of the University.

As has been noted, the University's participation in civilian pilot training under the Civil Aeronautics Administration of the Department of Commerce was the first national defense activity organized on the campus. It opened in the Fall of 1939 with ground school instruction on campus and flight instruction at private flying fields and continued until September, 1942. Dean G. M. Butler was coordinator, and nine faculty members served as ground school instructors of 331 students. No military commitments were required until war was declared. After that the students were required to take military training and finally to enlist in the national reserves. Before the courses were closed, men in military duty were reassigned to them for pilot training. In addition to its own work, the University aided a commercial flying company to establish and operate a non-University, elementary flight course at Globe and another in Tucson. The government finally cancelled the program because of a shortage of instructors and prohibitive priorities on planes.

Although not the most important of the University's defense activities, the pilot training program performed a valuable service. Because it was inaugurated before the war, men began training before being called into service and before the government had facilities for instruction. In addition, a high percentage of the students went on to take actual military training and passed their tests as pilots. Finally, the experience gained in training civilian flyers became the foundation for a naval aviation school on the campus that would enroll 591 students.

There was a shortage of instructors qualified to teach military flying, and the CAA had done so well that the Navy set up six schools at various universities to prepare men for this service. The actual flight training in Tucson was carried on at the Gilpin Air Lines field, and the University was responsible for rooms, meals, physical education, and ground-school studies. Dean Butler, the coordinator, had a staff of eight civilian instructors in addition to the faculty members who assisted.

This work was supplemented in May of 1943 by a highly specialized, long course for instructors. The class was small and the course was difficult and ran for twenty-four weeks. The curriculum included mathematics, physics, civil air regulations, aerial navigation, general servicing and operation of planes and motors, communications, aircraft recognition, meteorology, theory of flight, plotting cross-country flying, and teaching methods. Students received 576 hours of ground school work and from 140 to 170 hours of flight instruction.

This course was followed in a month by a different type of training for naval aviation cadets. It gave three months' training for V-5 Navy pilots and a total of 501 men enrolled in the classes. Three hundred and twenty-five men received elementary pilot training and 176 took intermediate work. The courses closed in August, 1944, when the Navy was no longer in desperate straits for instructors and pilots.

Military reserve programs at the University produced more headaches than the Navy's big school and its 10,000 graduates had ever created. University administrators, headed by C. Zaner Lesher, military co-ordinator, cooperated whenever possible, but it was sometimes difficult to keep pace with the changes occasioned by the varied and shifting needs of the armed services. Some requests could not be met because a land-grant college was not authorized to participate in the problems. There were also times when the University did not have the facilities to absorb more men.

The Navy once sent a group of officers to the campus to find out whether it could increase its trainees. The group spent three days investigating before it was discovered that the Army, which had priority in a land-grant college, had already been turned down in May, 1943, on its request that the University accept 400 additional men immediately. Since the Spring semester was in its final weeks and the dormitories were filled, nothing could be done. In June, however, the Army was back, this time with a request that the women's dormitories be turned over to 700 men in September. The University compromised and offered to quarter 200 men in Cochise Hall.

These men were the best officer material in motorized, engineering, and air corps units and were to be relieved from active duty while they took engineering courses of college grade. The Army would direct their military training but the university faculty would have to teach the college courses. All preparations were made to accept additional responsibilities in the Fall, but late July brought a telegram informing President Atkinson that the time of arrival had been advanced and the 200 men would arrive on August 9. This would normally have been an impossible situation, but it was war and the University met the challenge. Telegrams were dispatched to the faculty of the College of Engineering, ordering them to cut their vacations or drop all other work and hurry back. New instructors were found, class schedules were rearranged, and supplies were purchased. Double-deck cots were installed for the students and sleeping porches glassed-in for the officers of the new unit, converting Cochise Hall into living quarters for the contingent. Arrangements were made for the university dining hall to begin serving breakfast and dinners to the engineers on August 9. Lunch they would get at the Navy mess.

The course was known as the Army Specialized Training Program, or ASTP, and the curriculum was the equivalent of college work, except that the Army insisted on the quarter system. The faculty consisted of all the teachers in the College of Engineering, eleven professors and instructors from the departments of mathematics and physics, and the Dean of the College of Mines. That made a faculty of thirty teachers, and even this did not include those from physical education, the School of Military Science and Tactics, and the four army officers and staff of sixteen men in charge of the group.

Although the civilian enrollment in engineering had dropped to 113 students, the civilians were the particular responsibility of the University and had to be accommodated. One result was that they took classes with the army men on the quarter system. This was made imperative when an ROTC unit of fifty-nine former University of Arizona students was relieved of active duty and included in the ASTP program. They were quartered in the stadium rooms, for Cochise Hall was already bulging with men.

The university officials had just about time to draw a long breath after establishing the quarter system when another telegram arrived. It notified the President that the ASTP would be cancelled on March 11, 1944, because of an urgent need for men in active service. This meant that with graduation six weeks away, all but the ROTC men and the regular students would drop their studies.

Important as was its work with the armed services, the University made another contribution of such significance it cannot be forgotten. This was the training, between the years 1940 and 1945, of 1,900 men and women for work in war industries and on the farm. In this effort it participated in a national program.

Oddly enough, the United States had discovered suddenly that despite its mastery of mass production, the war plants could not operate their machines without many more trained men at the controls. There was a similar labor shortage on the farms where the draft had reached in and taken the youngest and strongest workers, and the University was given the task of meeting these problems in Arizona.

Lights soon burned all night in the university shops where groups of citizens were taught the skills demanded by aircraft factories, shipyards, and munition plants. Others took courses fitting them to work as rodmen and chainmen for civil engineers. Only those who displayed aptitude were accepted, but even severe screening did not discourage applicants, and there were always more of them than the shops and courses could handle. The College of Engineering trained 702 civilians in college-grade short courses and 704 in non-college vocational skills. Somehow the time and teachers were also found to carry on extension work in Phoenix and Yuma.

While this went on, agriculture and home economics cooperated with the Arizona Department of Vocational Education and the U. S. Office of Education in a food production and conservation program. There were courses in auto mechanics, tractor repairing, and metal work which were designed particularly for farmers and ranchers. A total of 394 people were trained in these classes. Home economics developed a teaching program that trained seventy-eight teachers qualified to conduct community and high school courses in food preparation. They in turn gave 300 courses throughout Arizona.

Service demands for trained nurses grew so rapidly that the homes and hospitals of the nation were soon suffering severely and here again the University was able to be of service on the home front. The school of home economics gave a course in home nursing and the administration instituted the first college course in the United States in nurses' aide training to be established on any campus. Out of this effort came 236 young women who were trained in the non-technical phases of nursing to relieve registered nurses for their special duties. The program was offered first in the Fall of 1943 and continued until January 1946. During this period the University also gave training to fifty cadet nurses from St. Mary's Hospital. College credit was allowed them for satisfactory standing.

Only one plan that the University worked out for the government seems to have been a failure. This was a correspondence course for men and women in service under which the Army paid half the cost of tuition and textbooks. It was opened to the Navy, Marine Corps, Coast Guard, and women's divisions and was known as the Army Institute Plan. Of 388 men and women enrolled, a mere twenty-four finished the work and received credit.

In opening his report for 1942–43, President Atkinson quoted President Roosevelt's admonition:

> War is not a matter of armies and navies alone. War is something in which everyone participates; every institution contributes to it; a University above most other institutions gives of its resources in staff and facilities to train men for the responsibilities which highly trained personnel must carry on in winning a war.

Like other colleges and universities, the University of Arizona met that challenge and did its share in writing a proud record of achievement.

Dr. Atkinson pointed out, in this connection, that while forty-seven members of the faculty had been taken by the government, 42 per cent of the floor space in the buildings was occupied by defense services and twenty-nine contracts had been signed, "all problems were met and the regular work went forward."

The President was too modest to mention that in spite of the crushing weight of his administrative duties, the U. S. Department of Agriculture had sent him to Mexico City to represent this country at the Second Inter-American Conference on Agriculture. As one of the leading agronomists of the United States, he had delivered a major address there on "The Integrated Scientific Approach to Agricultural Policy."

Nor did he speak of the fact that his advice was sought by national and state cattle and other agricultural groups and that he spoke and wrote for radio and newspapers. This, too, was part of the war effort of the University, and he took it in stride.

One problem that could not be met, however, was the drop in registration. It had been 2,513 the second semester of 1940–41, had fallen to 1,870 the second semester of 1942–43 and had hit bottom in September, 1944, with 1,540. This was the smallest registration in seventeen years and might have gone even lower except for a sharp increase in the enrollment of women students.

A summary of the reports of the colleges in 1943–44 illustrates the situation. Dean T. G. Chapman of the College of Mines showed a loss of 32.2 per cent in undergraduates and 76.8 in graduate majors. Dean Gurdon M. Butler of the College of Engineering reported that while 317 students had enrolled, enlistments and the draft had cut this almost in half. Dean P. S. Burgess said the College of Agriculture had only eighty-five students. The College of Education, according to Dean J. W. Clarson, Jr., was in difficulty because the number of majors at the graduate level had dropped from thirty-nine to twenty-one.

Dean J. Byron McCormick of the College of Law reported that he had lost twenty students and now had a total of thirty-three. This, he said, was normal for accredited law schools. It is interesting to note that the College of Law kept a military record that showed twenty-two per cent of all graduates and forty-one law students had entered the services since Pearl Harbor. Of these, eighty-three were commissioned officers.

The College of Fine Arts, according to Dean A. O. Anderson, lost 189 students. The band, which played for the baccalaureate and commencement ceremonies, had only twenty-four members.

There were occasions when classes were extremely small. But the Board of Regents kept its promise that no Arizona student would be denied an education, and even though only one or two students faced a professor in a class, that class was continued. Registration could have been increased if the Board had been willing to lower requirements for out-of-state students. This it refused to do. The registration might fall, but not the standards, and all courses and grades required for degrees were continued.

In one specific case the Board of Regents failed to cooperate with a government agency. The War Relocation Administration made several appeals for the University to provide extension courses, lectures, and books for the Japanese who were confined in relocation centers. Dr. Atkinson reported the following:

> Those representatives [of the War Relocation Administration] wanted free correspondence courses for the Japanese, a service which we cannot give to our own Arizona citizens or our men in uniform. They also wanted us to set up . . . a system under which camp instructors would conduct the courses for which this University would give academic credit. That was impossible. The University would not do that for the citizens of Phoenix or any other city of Arizona. We cannot do this even for soldiers in military camps in the state.

The Army and Navy used accelerated teaching methods, but the University made little use of them. There were, of course, scores of academic adjustments in subjects and schedules. No college, department, or course escaped changes necessitated by the loss of teachers, lack of essential materials, addition of subjects foreign to peacetime curricula, and the steady drop in civilian registration.

Freshman English dropped from twenty-nine sections with 864 students in 1942–43 to twenty-one sections with 624 students the following year.

The Department of History and Political Science revised its lectures as governments and armies wrote new history. Zoology changed its courses to step up the work of pre-medical students. The College of Law offered summer classes to students who wanted to get their degrees before entering military service, while the Department of Astronomy added marine and aerial navigation as well as descriptive astronomy. The College of Education, hard-pressed as it was for graduating majors, might have coasted, but it made nineteen curricular changes in one year to prepare the teachers it sent out for the new demands that would be made on them in secondary schools. Urged by the American Institute of Physics to keep its standard high, the Department of Physics held to its regular pace but in chemistry the call for graduates was so insistent that seventy-one students were crowded through three semesters of intensified work in two semesters.

It would be useless to attempt to tell in detail the story of the contributions and sacrifices in time, energy, and health the members of the faculty made on and off the campus. They served on government boards and met with military authorities. They picked cotton and provided entertainment for the men in military camps.

Once, in October, 1942, the War Labor Board permitted the Regents to pay the faculty a bonus that would help the teachers meet the increased cost of living, but it was not money that held these men at their tasks. Many of them could have entered industrial concerns that would have paid them far better salaries than they were getting. They chose to stay and serve where their particular talents counted most.

Despite the handicaps under which the overloaded faculty labored, a number of research problems were carried on in several fields. The faculty of the Department of Physics had lost good men in the months following Pearl Harbor, yet despite the plea that it maintain high academic standards, the department still met government requests including a program of research on the effects of rapid increase and decrease of pressure on fliers.

Chemistry, botany, zoology, agricultural chemistry, and plant pathology carried on a sustained effort to find rubber-bearing plants. Another long search was for a substitute for carob-bean mucilage which had many uses and was in short supply. One hundred and sixty-five species of legumes were analyzed and 125 with mucilage seeds were found. The best was guar and the University experts persuaded Arizona farmers to raise this plant in quantities with the result that it was on the market by 1944. General Mills laboratories praised the University highly for this work.

The Department of Chemistry was working under high pressure, yet with help from agriculture and mechanical engineering, it analyzed gasoline from defective bombers in a search for evidence of sabotage. Thirteen carloads of fuel were checked at Davis-Monthan, and the University scientists were able to prove that the wrong gasoline was being shipped to the field through error. Then came a hurry call asking the College of Engineering to find out why hydraulic landing gears on the B-24's shipped to the Soviet Union were freezing. The need for the facts was urgent since the government had stopped all shipments until it had the answer. The engineers came through with proof that the fluid being used in the mechanism was not suited to the job. Other problems were corrosion of de-icing equipment and water lines, failure of sealing compounds in oxygen supply lines, and inadequacy of anti-freeze fluids. All had to be answered, and there was no rest for the engineers. Even when summer closed the classrooms, the government put the engineers to work on tests of aluminum rivets and welds, or on making improvements in floating and fixed bridges for the Army.

Most of this work was never publicized. No generals on leave from the front came to pin decorations on the engineers, chemists, and agronomists, or hoist a "well-done" pennant on the University flagpole. But this did not concern University scientists.

Student body life had changed as completely as had that of the faculty and staff. Sororities adopted austerity programs, pledged the purchase of war bonds, and enrolled 100 per cent in Red Cross classes and work. Simplicity was the rule at the few social events. There were no decorations or name bands, and dances were held on the campus instead of at downtown hotels.

The Wildcat took note of the situation in the Spring of 1943 and said:

> Social activities during a war cannot necessarily be as splendid as those in the past. . . . The Desert dance is a big step towards solving what to do when the gas runs low in the tank. The dance will be held in recreation hall. You won't need gas or tires to get there—just four bits and a date. Similar dances will be held each week if you want them.

No football was played in 1943 because no lettermen came back to the University, nor did the game return until 1945 when a team took the field and played five games. A little basketball was played in Tucson High School gymnasium against teams of factory workers.

The freshman class created some commotion in 1943 when the few remaining upperclassmen ordered it to repaint the letter on A Mountain. Two sophomores who went along to assist the traditions committee were whitewashed from head to foot, one boy suffering a serious head wound, and the other temporarily blinded when a freshman shampooed him with lime. A tradition that was shattered the same Fall was the defeat of male candidates for student officers. Miss Edith White defeated her opponent for the office of president of the Associated Students by sixty votes, and women also captured seven editorships on *The Wildcat*. The men took these defeats with good humor, but the elimination of their cavalry drills was saddening. The last mounted drill was held March 24, 1944, before a crowd of 1,000.

In saying goodbye to 240 graduating seniors in May, *The Wildcat* reviewed the year:

> Petticoats, the sorority and hall variety, have been at the helm of the social campus this year with the masculine half of the campus putting in a strengthening oar as the second semester advanced.
>
> Cut to the minimum, social activities have nevertheless continued to adapt themselves to a war campus.
>
> It has been a problem year to the socially minded—no men, no gasoline, no cars. . . . The man problem is the touchiest. Campus fellows are running a noisy second to service men in co-ed dating.
>
> Rushing was simplified yet more co-eds wore pledge ribbons this year than ever before. Informal rush was cut during the second semester. Fraternity rushing was spasmodic.

Three new deans were appointed in the Summer of 1944. Dr. Robert L. Nugent, who had been Dean of the Graduate College, was made Dean of the College of Liberal Arts, and Dr. John F. Walker was appointed to fill the vacancy. Mrs. Hazel MacCready was appointed Dean of Women. Eighteen new members joined the faculty, and two professors returned from leaves of absence.

President Atkinson called attention repeatedly to the G.I. Bill which would provide fees and living allowances for veterans, and the Board of Regents began making budgets and plans for a postwar building program. A special committee of the Board recommended an aeronautical building, two dormitories for women, one for men, a fine arts building, and a dairy building. The total cost was estimated at $1,000,000.

Three women enrolled to every man in the Fall of 1944, when the registration reached 1,850. Commenting on this at the first assembly, Dr. Atkinson said that there would soon be a heavy increase in the number of men on campus and that the administration was looking to its building program. The records show that the Regents not only wanted authority to raise $1,000,000 by issuing self-liquidating bonds but also expected to ask for a direct appropriation of $1,182,096 for instructional buildings if the government would make a grant of 30 per cent. One month later the President sent his resignation to the Regents, but on their insistence that he remain until the war closed and current plans materialized, he agreed to stay until June, 1947.

Although *The Wildcat* promoted a straw vote during the Roosevelt-Dewey campaign—faculty and students voted for Dewey—the old enterprise and sparkle of the past had drained away with the passage of the war years. A shortage of paper had cut the publication to one four-page issue a week, and the editor apologized for *The Wildcat*'s general dullness but said nothing about the reason, which was obviously the low state of campus morale. One short feature story, however, did present a brief picture of a student body with an overload of gripes. A bitter complaint concerned the time students lost standing in line for food at the Commons and there were objections to what were spoken of as the "monstrous" 7:40 classes. Only one hope of a happier future bloomed that year when a committee was organized to try to perfect plans for a student union. An attempt made in 1938 had failed when the government refused to grant a request for a loan, and President Atkinson said now that there should be no further delay. Alumnus B. G. Thompson was made chairman of the new committee, with Graduate Manager Louis Slonaker as secretary. Other members were Dean J. Byron McCormick, Dean Hazel MacCready, Director J. F. McKale, and students Miss Rayma Babbitt and Harry Bagnall. The Board of Regents gave the project its blessing and said that if the committee could raise $500,000 the Regents would arrange for the balance. The thought was that the building should be erected on the triangle west of Old Main.

A milestone in the progress of the University and state colleges was reached in 1945 when the affairs of the three schools were placed in the hands of one Board of Regents. Fourteen states had adopted this plan of simplifying and unifying control of their institutions of higher learning with the expectation that it would eliminate duplication and encourage economy. For guidance in outlining working plans, the Regents then employed Dr. George A. Works, who was a national authority on educational surveys, to study the Arizona problem. He employed two qualified educators as associates, and after a careful study the three men turned in a seventy-three-page report, which was based on the theory that "competition among institutions undermines public confidence and jeopardizes continued development of higher education."

The experts summed up their theory of the administration of state universities and colleges in a single paragraph, which read:

> Funds made available for higher education should be expended in such a manner as to bring the maximum return to the State and programs of publicly supported education should be developed from the viewpoint of the State's needs rather than those of the immediate community in which an institution is located or the basis of the ambitions of administrative officers in charge of higher education.

The Board of Regents studied this report carefully, but in the last analysis did not make any major changes.

In student affairs, the effects of more than three years of war conditions were beginning to be evident. There were very few editorials and little news on the war or war efforts on campus in the Spring of 1945. Even a statement from the Regents that they were planning to ask the Legislature for an increase in appropriations got little attention in *The Wildcat*. Student spirit was still dropping, and the first student to recognize it was Hal Slutzky, a returned veteran, who wrote a letter to the college paper in which he said:

> Let us wake up before we become absolutely incurable. I'm sure when the boys who left school to enter the service return they'll never recognize this as the same U of A they once attended. I know I didn't. Are we going to continue the 'who cares' attitude or shall we take the first step in ridding ourselves of this harmful mood of indifference? Let's go Wildcats.

The Wildcat had the courage to admit that the veteran was right. It said:

> War should not have created a campus where the most notable point is a lack of spirit.
>
> We have been on the downgrade so far. We can start the upgrade now if we do something about it. . . . The elements are here. It is up to us, the student body, to furnish the spark.

It may be that the letter of a single veteran touched off a revival of the old time Arizona spirit, or perhaps the time was right for a change. In either case, *The Wildcat* began to reflect a different attitude.

In quick succession the rodeo committee was roundly criticized for inefficiency and lack of enterprise, another Bill Bishop bond drive was held and shot past its $15,000 goal by $4,100, a Red Cross drive raised $1,600, Bobcats and Blue Key were revived, and more than sixty per cent of the students voted in the annual election.

Grumbling over delays in service and the quality of the food served on the campus finally blossomed into a boycott. The President suggested that students meet and draw up a list of complaints and they complied with a rousing rally around the flagpole where they found fault with prices and quality of the food as well as the compulsory purchase of meal tickets. A committee then called on Dr. Atkinson, who ruled that the purchase of tickets should be a matter of individual choice. The "cuisine rebellion," as the students called their boycott, was said to have resulted in only a slight improvement in the quality of the food.

Then came the morning of May 8, 1945, when sustained blasts from the powerhouse siren announced the anticipated surrender of Germany. Radios were tuned to catch the speeches of President Harry S. Truman and Prime Minister Winston Churchill, and all University people attended a solemn assembly in a spirit of thanksgiving. Dr. Chester Smith of the College of Law was the principal speaker, there were prayers for lasting peace and Professor Rollin Pease led the audience in singing "The Battle Hymn of the Republic."

The war in the Pacific remained to be fought out and won, but President Atkinson and the Board of Regents were making plans with all possible speed for the readjustments that would be essential when the veterans came streaming back to college.

Old Main was revamped and converted into a temporary student center that would have to serve until a student union could be built. Student officers, campus publications, and the bookstore all moved into quarters on the ground floor. A games room, fountain, and lunch counter were installed and suites were set up for the graduate manager and alumni secretary. The second floor of the building was converted into nine classrooms that would help pick up some of the growth in enrollment.

Enrollment increased that Fall, the total registration being 2,220. Fraternities began to show modest signs of recovery and there was evidence that athletics were reviving. Coach Casteel produced a team that defeated Arizona State College at Flagstaff, San Diego State College, Williams Field, and California Polytechnic Institute, while the basketball squad won the Border Conference title.

The Student Union committee appeared to have attracted little attention during the year, but it had been meeting regularly and had accomplished a great deal, particularly in arousing statewide alumni groups. The result was that it launched a formal campaign on December 14, 1945, at a dinner attended by 300 enthusiastic graduates and friends of the University. Books showing the plans for the Student Union Memorial, as it was to be called, were distributed for the first time. The plans would undergo many changes and the building would not rise on the proposed site, but the 20,000 copies of the book carried the encouraging news that the money raising campaign had opened under the direction of W. R. Wayland of Phoenix, and that gifts of $100,000 were already assured.

It was obvious by June of 1946 that the G.I. students would begin arriving by September, and there was a frenzy of planning. Dr. Atkinson announced that the University would conduct laboratory classes until 10 o'clock at night and would repeat morning lectures in the afternoon. To accomplish this, he said, forty-seven members would be added to the faculty. The Legislature, which had been warned by educational authorities and by a congressional survey that thousands of veterans were heading for college, called a special session in which it made a direct appropriation of $380,000 and authorized $350,000 in bonds for new housing.

Plans had been drawn, the President said, for four dormitories, including one to be built under the east stadium, but it was a little late to be making plans. What the University had to have was housing, and the Federal Public Housing Administration came to its relief with a promise to erect enough Quonset huts on the practice polo field to house 248 married men and to erect more, if needed, on the polo field proper. The University spent $55,000 providing utilities for the Quonset huts, but the government did not finish them for weeks after the opening of the 1946–47 year. Eventually, 100 trailers that had been occupied by war workers were made available and 300 cots were set up in the gymnasium.

President Atkinson asked deans and heads of departments to express their views on the teaching buildings needed in the order of their importance. The answers favored a chemistry-physics addition, new quarters for home economics, and large buildings for liberal arts and business administration. But none of these were more than dreams when Japan sued for peace on August 10, 1946.

Tucson held a parade of civic and military groups that day, and Dr. Atkinson was the principal speaker at an evening program given in Tucson High School stadium. The celebration on campus was marked by pride in the fact that 4,613 men and women had served; the occasion was saddened by the memory of the 270 students, alumni, and faculty who had given their lives for their country.

Three weeks later a total of 4,484 students enrolled at the University. Of these 2,262 came in under the G.I. Bill and were responsible for the 100 per cent increase over September, 1945. Only fifteen of the promised Quonset units were completed and there were no roofs on the two one-story dormitories for men, so temporary expedients had to be adopted to care for the enrollment. President Atkinson made a successful personal appeal to the people of Tucson for 400 private rooms. Cochise Hall was re-established as a dormitory for men, and fraternities made room for some unaffiliated students who had no place to live.

The shortage of classroom space was as serious as the lack of housing. To help solve the problem, the administration obtained wartime wooden barracks, which were trucked to the campus and set up west of the gymnasium. Huge classes forced Psychology 1a and Humanities lectures into the University auditorium. Psychology 1b classes were so crowded that students sat on window sills, while Freshman English had 1,840 students in fifty-five sections.

Cold figures are sometimes interesting, and they can be used here effectively to explain why there were not enough dormitories or classrooms ready for the veterans when they arrived.

During the first war year, 1941–42, the Legislature allowed the University only $793,420 for operating expenses, and it stuck to those figures during the three succeeding years. It is difficult to understand this attitude, because it was evident to all that the University had its back to the wall and that conditions were going to get worse. It had given up 42 per cent of its space to the military services, collection of student fees was low, and much of the equipment needed repairs or replacement. Finally, the long-suffering faculty was definitely entitled to a raise in salary.

Dr. Atkinson often commented on these days after he left the University; and a few weeks before his death, he said laughingly, "They gave us just about enough money to heat and light the buildings and to cut the grass."

Even for 1945–46, when registration increased to 2,222, and in 1946–47, when it hit 4,484, the Legislature had increased the appropriation by a mere $70,000. This made a total of $863,475, which was $57,416 less than it had given the University in 1929–30 when it had 1,899 students.

Since the policy of the state was to accept all qualified Arizona high-school students at the University, and the registration figures would clearly pass the 5,000 mark, it finally became evident that permanent increases had to be made in appropriations.

Not all the enrollment was due to the influx of veterans, for Arizona experienced a heavy growth in population and prosperity when the government's defense efforts went into high gear after Pearl Harbor. Davis-Monthan field was crowded with bombing planes and men in training. Fort Huachuca was active, and there were aviation fields and training camps in many parts of the state. It is estimated that these war facilities turned out 200,000 trained men. Of much less importance in a military way were the camps for war prisoners and the relocation centers for Japanese-Americans.

Because of the climate and its relatively protected position, Arizona was a good location for war plants. Manufacturing had grossed merely $17 million the year before Pearl Harbor, but in 1942 it touched $50 million and by 1945 it reached $105 million. As the production of manufactured goods rose, so did the population and the number of young people who wanted a college education. There was a temporary drop of $19 million in the value of manufactured products in 1946, and it was estimated that 15,000 of the new residents had left the state. But a year later population and production had soared again, and it was evident that an industrial era had been established on a sound basis. In population and industrial growth, Arizona became the pace-setter for the nation and fifteen years later its busy plants produced annually $400 million worth of manufactured goods.

During Summer of 1946, plans were made with the Veterans' Administration to set up guiding and testing centers for G.I. students and arrangements were completed to accept the VA proposal for vocational rehabilitation training. Faculty salaries also came in for some attention, and President Atkinson reported that there might be a five per cent increase. This was far from satisfying to the faculty. One finds an editorial in *The Alumnus* of December, 1946, which said that the teachers had launched a campaign through the Arizona Chapter of the American Association of

University Professors "to inform the people of Arizona of the need for increased salaries at the State University." The editorial read:

> *The Arizona Alumnus* supports these efforts to increase faculty salaries on the one hand and to inaugurate a uniform salary policy at the University on the other. It believes these changes to be absolutely necessary to prevent the decline of the University to a second-rate school, turning out second-rate graduates.
>
> The policy adopted by many universities of setting a minimum salary for various classifications of faculty members should be instituted.
>
> The University is on the threshold of an expanded future. Enrollment increase, added facilities and equipment all combine to form a tremendous postwar growth already under way. But expansion as a first rate institution is dependent on maintenance of standards. These standards are seriously threatened.
>
> The campaign is not a move against the administration of the University. It is an attempt to educate the Arizona public to the needs of the faculty at their State University. It is an attempt to show them how they would be affected should the University enter the decline now threatened. It is an attempt to arouse the State and the Legislature to grant an appropriation high enough to be consistent with the rising costs of living. Only the people of Arizona can bring that about.

There was great enthusiasm in the Fall of 1946 over the return of sports and record-breaking enrollment, but there was a day of sadness when thousands took time to grieve over the passing of William J. Bray, superintendent of buildings and grounds. Through good years and bad, he had kept the campus a thing of beauty. He had not been widely praised and he would not have wished it, but now there came words of gratitude from the Regents, President Atkinson, former President Shantz, the newspapers, the college publications, and the students.

Said *The Arizona Star*:

> A flag flew at half-mast at the University on September 5, in respect to William Joseph Bray, UA's oldest employe. In

> the University auditorium funeral services were held for one of the best-known and best-loved men in the city.
>
> Bill Bray, on the staff of the University for 39 years and superintendent of buildings and grounds since 1914, leaves as a fitting memorial the beautiful grounds of the University which were a result of his management.

Perhaps the tribute Mr. Bray would have liked the most came from *The Wildcat*:

> During the year 1944–1945 a series of posters appeared on the campus which read, 'Hurrah for Bill Bray.' A letter written to *The Wildcat* by Dan Ricker explained that the posters had been put up by students who appreciated the services of the man who was responsible for the comfort and beauty that surrounds our campus.
>
> So we say, 'Goodbye to you, Bill Bray. Thanks for everything and Hurrah.'

President Atkinson announced on Jan. 3, 1947, that he would end his service the last of June, and the Board of Regents named Dean J. Byron McCormick to succeed him. At the same time they created the new post of vice-president, choosing Dean Robert L. Nugent to fill it. Dean Richard A. Harvill, of the Graduate College, moved up to the dean-ship of liberal arts, Dr. David L. Patrick took Dr. Harvill's place, and a fifth deanship went to A. L. Slonaker who became Dean of Men. "Slony," as every student has called him for generations, stepped into the office vacated by the death of Dean A. H. Otis.

A member of the class of 1921, Mr. Slonaker had served for twenty-five years as graduate manager of student body affairs and seventeen years as alumni secretary. He had spark-plugged most of the accomplishments of both groups, including the current drive to build the student union, and behind those years of service was an unforgettable period when he had been the university's outstanding athlete with fourteen letters and the Freeman Medal to his credit.

The new President went into office under more agreeable conditions than had existed for several years, for the Regents announced in April, 1947, that they would establish an improved schedule of minimum salaries. This, however, was not the only mark of a change in the Legislature's attitude toward higher education because it granted the Regents' request for an increase in the operational budget and gave them $1,389,956.

Dr. Atkinson's resignation as President did not actually mark the end of his connection with the University. The Regents appointed him executive adviser in budgetary and financial matters, and he held the post until July 1, 1955, when he terminated fifty-one years of service in the educational field. The Board then made him President Emeritus and closed the record with this tribute which was spread on their minutes:

> You have served the State of Arizona efficiently and well. Under your ten-year guidance the University of Arizona has considerably expanded the physical plant and has almost doubled in student attendance. Because of your insistence upon intellectual accomplishment, educational programs and research procedures at the University have been stimulated to higher levels and in the field of cultural leadership the institution is exercising an increasing role in the life of the State.
>
> Through the war years you have set a high standard of administrative achievement under most onerous conditions and at the Board's insistence you subordinated your own desire to resign at an earlier date until the difficulties of that period were past. We will regret your departure from the campus but we offer our thanks for a job well done and we wish you Godspeed as to any plans in the future.

The tribute is not complete because there should be a mention of the important gifts that came to the University in the last years of Dr. Atkinson's administration.

One of these was the T. E. Hanley collection of books which was first presented to the College of Fine Arts and then transferred to the main library in 1938. The original collection consisted of 2,500 books, and large annual gifts from the donor brought the total to 34,700 books in 1959.

Another contribution was the Pfeiffer collection of contemporary American art. Consisting of more than 100 paintings, it was the first of the University's famous art collections. The donor was Charles Leonard Pfeiffer, a New York business man and an alumnus, who felt that his alma mater should be the center of artistic development and the home of outstanding art in the Southwest. The collection was exhibited in the Metropolitan Museum of Art in New York City and the M. H. de Young Memorial Museum in San Francisco before it was shown on the campus.

There were also munificent gifts that provided a fund to be used in attracting outstanding high-school graduates of the State to the University of Arizona. James Baird, a distinguished building contractor, who had made his home in Tucson, was deeply interested in broadening educational opportunities and was persuaded by Dean A. Louis Slonaker to consider establishing a scholarship fund for Arizona students. With President Atkinson's aid, Dean Slonaker drew up a plan of operation that satisfied Mr. Baird, the Regents, and the scholarship committee. This grant has exceeded all expectations, for the original $207,000 was increased to $250,000 and then to $300,000 before Baird's death. The market value of the stocks and bonds in the fund had increased to $750,000 in 1959, and its income finances forty-five annual scholarships of $500 each.

CHAPTER 11

1947–1951

THE UNIVERSITY OF ARIZONA was fifty-four years old when Dr. J. Byron McCormick, Dean of the College of Law, became its thirteenth president on July 1, 1947.

A native of Illinois, he attended Western Military Academy and was graduated from Illinois Wesleyan University with an LL.B. in 1915. He practiced law in Peoria and Emden, Illinois, for ten years and served for two years as director and vice-president of the Farmers' State Bank of Emden. In 1926 he came to the University as assistant professor of law. Continuing his studies, he later received his master's degree from the University of Southern California and then his degree of Doctor of Judicial Science from Duke in 1933. The year 1930 saw Dr. McCormick advance to an associate professorship in Arizona, and in 1933 he was raised to a full professorship. Five years later he became Dean of the College of Law and thereafter served as acting President during the absences of President Atkinson.

The basic problem that faced the new president and his Board of Regents when they sat for the first time on July 26, 1947 was how to meet the demands that the growth of the state were making on the University. Walter R. Bimson, President of the Valley National Bank and a member of the Board of Regents, was to sum the situation up in hard statistics when he participated in a symposium during Dr. McCormick's inauguration a few months later. He said in part at that time:

> When admitted to statehood, Arizona had a population of about 200,000. Our population now totals better than 700,000 . . . A generation ago our total income from agriculture was less than $20,000,000. Last year it was nearly 10 times as great. A generation ago the deposits in all the banks in Arizona amounted to less than $30,000,000. Today their combined bank deposits are more than $400,000,000, or 15 times as much.

This spectacular growth not only increased the state's need for services and for academic expansion but also created a primary problem of how to expand the physical plant of the University fast enough to provide classrooms and housing for students who were knocking at the doors.

Only a generation before the University had had 463 students. In 1942–43 there were 2,500. Now the total was 5,000, and the Board knew it would continue to increase. It was clear that the Legislature faced the responsibility of providing for the needs of the young people of the state.

The first message of Governor John M. Goodwin in 1864 had called for common schools, high schools, and a University. Education, he said, must be "as free to the people as the air they breathe." The result was that the Legislature established a University by law, a constitution for it, and outlined a curriculum. The legislation lapsed, but twenty-one years later, in 1885, the Thirteenth Legislature adopted a new university bill which provided in its second section:

> The object of the University and all other state educational institutions shall be to provide the inhabitants of this Territory with the means of acquiring a thorough knowledge of the various branches of literature, science and the arts.

Again, when the Territory became a state, the constitutional convention called for a university that would be open to students of both sexes with the assurance that education would be as free as possible.

The question in 1948 was whether the young people were to be barred from their heritage because the University had no classrooms in which to teach them. If not, then a building program was an absolute necessity; and President McCormick told the alumni, "The immediate future must be a 'brick and mortar' period." He said also that he did not favor the present plan of limiting enrollment of out-of-state students and felt this policy should be dropped as soon as necessary buildings were completed.

The cost of instruction per student in 1946–47 was $276.08, of which $76.20 was provided from state sources. In contrast, Dr. McCormick pointed out, "Our non-resident tuition is sufficiently high that these students pay their way entirely."

Before the new administration was fairly under way, the Associated Students launched a vigorous new administration of their own under the leadership of Morris Udall, a returned veteran who had been elected student president on a "new deal" program. Udall outlined the proposed policy in a forthright statement in which he said:

> With the growth of the school the student council feels it is of importance that it actively and constructively represent student opinion on living conditions, campus regulations, and all other University activities which affect the individual student.
>
> The student council is also interested in furthering better school-student relations. It is felt that when student 'gripes' are ignored they magnify and create bitterness. The surest cure for student dissatisfaction, it is believed, is to take notice of it, presenting any justified and constructive suggestions to the University administration.
>
> Particular concern is felt about the high cost of campus living . . . These conditions are being studied and constructive suggestions will be made.

The students charged that the Commons, as the dining hall was called, was charging unreasonably high prices for food, and here they met a sympathetic response from the President, who instructed the Commons to issue a monthly meal ticket for $37.50 which provided seventeen meals a week. Then came a question as to whether the Associated Students could legally lend $2,500 to G.I. students who were planning to open a grocery store at Polo Village. The University officials and their attorney said this would be an illegal use of funds.

The students then amended their constitution, giving them the right to invest their funds in the store, and the loan was made.

There were no complaints now over lack of student spirit. The influence of the veterans was felt everywhere. They were not actually challenging the administration, but they were asking, "Why?" and would continue to do so; yet on the whole the relationship was mature. Udall testified to this on leaving office, when he said that while there had been serious differences of opinion, President McCormick had been reasonable and fair.

Years later, after he had resigned and returned to the College of Law, Dr. McCormick was to say:

> Student relations were never a real problem. I think it is probably true that a President doesn't have time to give

> as much attention to either student or faculty problems as they deserve. A President's time is so taken up with financial matters and long range policy that he can't take care of all these matters, although if it wasn't for the students and the faculty the institution wouldn't be here.

The faculty took no part in the controversies raised by Associated Students. They had problems of their own, including retirement and an argument over the library's condition. This situation had made the headlines because of a critical report written by Librarian Fredrick Cromwell. Cromwell charged that the previous administration had been reluctant to purchase books and had held the library expenditures to between 2.4 and 2.7 per cent of the university budget. This figure was below the 4.0 per cent average of land-grant colleges and far below the 5.0 per cent standard the U. S. Bureau of Education had said was necessary to build an adequate library. The report revealed also that the Arizona Chapter of the Association of University Professors had protested without success to President Atkinson in January, 1947. The administration came back with a different set of figures and the subject was argued back and forth without decisive results. Eventually, however, the library budget was increased.

President McCormick's first year opened in September, 1947, with an enrollment of 5,147 students of whom 2,444 were veterans under the G.I. Bill. The number would have been higher, but the lack of campus facilities had made it necessary for the University to limit new enrollments to Arizona students and to hold the number of out-of-state co-eds to one-third the total registration. Hopes of starting the work of building new dormitories failed to materialize in September because building costs had risen and all bids were rejected. New bids, however, were asked for classroom buildings.

Hard usage during the war had damaged dormitories and halls to such an extent that the Regents found it necessary to raise rentals fifteen dollars a year to pay for repairs. This caused considerable complaint, but the Board told the Inter-hall Council that the buildings must be self-supporting and refused to reconsider the ruling.

A top football team might have given the students something to take their minds off their grievances that year, but the best the Wildcats could do was to win five, lose four, and tie one. Practically nobody was happy about it because Hardin-Simmons whipped the Wildcats 35 to 7. Texas Mines was beaten by a single point, 14 to 13.

Another problem facing President McCormick when he took office was the campaign to raise funds for a Student Union. A committee first appointed in December, 1944, had worked ceaselessly, but the drive was a long way from its objective. Dr. McCormick felt that the Union was an absolute necessity and was firm in the belief that the half-million dollar fund still necessary could be raised. It was a problem that was not to leave him for almost two years; but nobody gave up, and a new drive was opened in the midst of a hot argument over the site of the proposed building. In recalling this later, the President said:

> I can't remember whether it was the committee or the Regents who first thought the Student Union should be built in front of Old Main. But we brought in a noted architect who had designed similar buildings and he said it ought to replace Old Main. The majority of alumni approved but the oldest graduates said, "No!" and they were in a vociferous mood. So the architect told us that if it was impossible to raze Old Main the new building should replace the Commons and face the cactus garden, which is now the mall.

Unable to get an agreement between the students and the alumni, the Regents turned the problem over to the faculty. The faculty favored the Commons site, providing the area occupied by the cactus garden was filled and turned into a lawn that would give a feeling of spaciousness. The students, however, continued to insist on removing Old Main, and eventually the Regents settled the whole matter by deciding to build on the area occupied by the Commons and the power plant.

President McCormick had entertained a private idea that Old Main could be saved and given a facial treatment that would make it a positive ornament to the campus. He referred to this once in a review of the years he spent as President and said:

> One thing which has disturbed me was that I had the consent of the Board to authorize architects to draw plans for the job and they came up with plans I thought were good. These called for replacing the wooden railings and posts with ornamental iron, giving the walls a stucco job and replacing the tin roof with tile. Both the east and west stairways, which are rather steep, would have been broken with a landing while the interior of the structure would have been beautified with tile. My idea was that if we had to keep the building it should be a thing of beauty that preserved the

> outlines of the original architecture. The cost, as I remember it, would have been around $125,000 and while the Board approved the idea it never got around to asking the Legislature for the necessary appropriation. I think if I had stayed in office I might have pushed that idea through.

A University retirement plan for faculty and staff went into effect the day President McCormick took office. It was actually similar to the system that had been initiated ten years before but which had lacked any arrangements for the University to pay a share of the costs. The same semester saw the Board of Regents approve a new faculty constitution that marked a long step forward. This constitution established a faculty chairman, a faculty senate with legislative powers, and a planning committee known as the Committee of Eleven. The chairman, a majority of the members of the senate, and all members of the Committee of Eleven were to be selected by faculty vote.

President McCormick said in his first annual report that both plans had been well received. He noted also the marked increase of interest in the operation of the University among students and attributed this to the mature group of veterans and the leadership of student officers. He did not mention it at this time, but the faculty was highly pleased over the scholastic records being made by the veterans.

A significant improvement in housing marked the President's first year. Hopi and Papago Lodges were completed as was the extension of the east stadium with its dormitory below the stands. These buildings accommodated 362 men students and, when added to the 248 Quonset hut apartments for married students, they eased the housing problem. Work began that year also on the additions to the College of Law and the chemistry-physics building as well as on a cooling system for the main library.

But while housing for men students had improved, there remained a very definite need for more classrooms for the colleges. Reports of the deans showed that the physical plant was practically bursting at its seams. The College of Business and Public Administration, with an enrollment second only to that of the College of Liberal Arts, had crowded its staff into a remodeled dormitory and was holding day and night classes in Old Main, as well as any other place where it could find the space. Greatly needed was a bureau of business research, but there was no place to put it. The College of Education was crying for its own building, and the dean said its facilities were inadequate. In the College of Liberal Arts, which hoped to have a new building soon, fourteen of the departments lacked adequate office space and secretarial assistance. Engineering reported that unless more speed could be made in completing plans for the promised aeronautical building, there would be little chance of providing for junior and senior enrollments. Agriculture, crowded beyond endurance, wanted the space in its building now filled by other colleges and added that it must have a building for home economics. The library suggested that, since there were as yet no funds for the additions needed to house its stacks, the basement ought to be remodeled for storage purposes and pointed out that the increase in enrollment called for a larger staff. Physical Education needed additional lockers and more tennis and handball courts, while the Steward Observatory appealed again for relief from the lights and smoke of Tucson through the removal of the big telescope to a "safe and tolerable site."

While these needs could not be forgotten, they were moved to the background on May 9, 1948. It was one of those bright spring days with a warming sun and a light breeze rustling the palms when the long academic procession moved over the winding road to the auditorium and the inauguration of President McCormick. Regents, faculty, and students had attended a morning symposium at which Dr. Alfred Atkinson, executive advisor to the Regents; Walter R. Bimson, President of the Valley National Bank and member of the Board of Regents; and William H. Westover, one of the first graduates of the University School of Law, spoke on "Arizona Today and Tomorrow."

Universities, colleges, and learned societies were represented by 250 delegates who came to bring greetings. They heard the new President receive congratulations from Governor Sidney P. Osborn; William F. Kimball, president of the Alumni Association; Dr. Melvin T. Solve, chairman of the general faculty; and Merrill Windsor, president of the Associated Students. Fifteen radio stations broadcast the induction of Dr. McCormick by Mr. Samuel H. Morris, president of the Board of Regents, and the addresses of President McCormick and Judge Justin Miller, the guest speaker. Judge Miller, a close friend of the President, was a former dean of law at the University of Southern California and Duke University. He had also served as associate justice of the First United States Court of Appeals in Washington, D. C., and at the time of the inauguration he was president of the National Association of Broadcasters.

Dr. Miller chose as his subject, "The Role of a University in the Atomic Age." In presenting his theme, he prophesied that the atomic age would present two alternatives. One was relentless war which might wipe out American cities, wreck the industrial system, and reduce the free and individualistic way of life in the United States to a regimented level of mere subsistence. The other was a struggle to preserve existing forms of freedom and self government; a cold war supported by the "confiscatory expenditure of national wealth," to meet an endless threat. He continued:

> Under either alternative the funds for universities will soon begin to dry up. Under the first the universities will be forced to develop skeleton organizations. . . . If the worst comes it may be well to concentrate on perpetuating the most essential knowledge on bronze and other imperishables and hiding it away in caves hoping for its discovery and use by a new and better race of men.
>
> If it is our fortune to experience the second suggested alternative—of a continuing 'cold war'—then we shall see a bitter, gruelling continuance of that race of which we have been warned so often between the discoveries of physical science, on the one hand, and on the other, of man's capacity for objective, farsighted, intelligent statesmanship. There can be no doubt that the discoveries of physical science are presently far ahead in the race and the universities are largely responsible for this fact. . . .
>
> Forty years ago William James, the great philosopher, gave the prescription for making a real university. He said:
>
> "It is the quality of its men that makes the quality of a university. You may have your buildings . . . you may spend money until no one can approach you, yet you will add nothing but one more trivial specimen to the common herd of American colleges unless you send into all this organization some breath of life, by inoculating it with a few men, at least, who are real geniuses. . . . Like a contagious disease, almost, spiritual life passes from man to man by contact."

It was Dr. Miller's firm belief that universities must find some way to train the cream of their students for service in government as well as in science. In supporting this he pointed to the fact that while every member of the Atomic Energy Commission and its advisory committee were men of high scholastic standing, this was far from the case elsewhere in government. Among the 550 men then in top level offices of the government, including the President, Cabinet, Supreme Court, Senate, and House of Representatives, he said, there were only twenty-nine members of Phi Beta Kappa, while in the executive branch not one man had won college honor for intellectual talent. His conclusion was:

> We must face squarely—and answer—two questions: first, is genius of too great value to be wasted on government; second, are universities willing and able to train geniuses for effective participation in government?

President McCormick acknowledged his induction with a brief address in which he outlined the responsibilities of the University, the State, and the graduates. On this subject he said:

> A university is an intricate institution, potentially capable of developing both the culture and economy of the area it serves. To be useful, education must and does give insight into how to solve practical problems. Education cannot get along without business and industry, but the reverse of this is likewise true . . .
>
> The need of a good job for every man is no greater than the need of a good man for every job. While there are times when the trades and professions are crowded, even then there is room at the top—the crowding is always at the bottom. There is justification, then, for this great demand for higher education, but the higher the education the higher the cost.
>
> The states will find it expensive to provide their colleges and universities with the necessary facilities to meet these demands, and there will certainly be those who will ask if we can afford it. We cannot afford to do otherwise. The college and university system of a democratic state should provide the widest possible variety of opportunities. Courses both in 'living' and 'earning a living' may, in academic respectability, be offered side by side and accorded equal dignity.
>
> At the same time the State has the right to expect that those for whom it has provided these advantages will develop a reciprocal attitude of individual responsibility and a well informed loyalty to the institutions of representative government which maintained a free society.

The President closed the ceremony by conferring the honorary degree of Doctor of Laws on Judge Miller. A public reception attended by hundreds of dignitaries, citizens, and students was then held in the library, and this was followed by the College of Fine Arts presentation of Sigmund Romberg's *The Vagabond King*.

A new and important faculty committee was at work on the campus when President McCormick was inaugurated. Before he left office, President Atkinson had established what was known as The Committee on Future Development of the University under the chairmanship of Dr. L. E. Roberts, giving the College of Liberal Arts four members and naming two from each of the others. In beginning its work, the committee had decided that it would follow two main approaches. The first was to be the study of areas into which the University might expand. This study was known as "the emerging needs of higher education" and would consider both the demand for such expansion and its value to the State. The next approach was to study the probable cost and the effect of such expansion on the already established curriculum. In plotting the second approach the committee agreed:

> The wisdom of undertaking new programs of work which might make considerable demands upon the limited resources of the University can scarcely be discussed without taking into account the needs and plans, the hopes and difficulties of departments already established. In fact, the term 'Future Development of the University' is interpreted to refer not only to expansion into new fields, but also, and even more importantly, to the growth and development of departments and colleges now in existence. The committee therefore considers that an important part of its work should be concerned with a story of past performances and present needs of existing departments.

This was a new approach to the study of academic problems, for it sought the opinions of classroom teachers who had often complained of being ignored by the administration when changes were made. Now that their opinions were asked, the committee members decided that the final report would "indulge in any criticism which seemed logical, wise, and necessary."

A preliminary study of the high birth-rate between 1940 and 1944, convinced the committee that despite the probable drop in G.I. registrations and the indicated growth of state colleges at Tempe and Flagstaff, Phoenix Junior College, and Gila Junior College, the University would soon be besieged by applicants. With that as a base, the committee reviewed all departments, making a file of comments and recommendations. Out of these came suggestions for new buildings, an unfavorable reaction to the appeal of an ambitious University school that wanted to be made a college, approval of an increasing program of research in some areas, criticism of unnecessary departments, and a strong recommendation that the University begin to reach out for young teachers who could take the places of many professors nearing the retirement age.

The Committee also had definite ideas about new buildings. It said that the University must have a large central classroom and office building for the College of Liberal Arts, which was crowding as many as five teachers into one office; it further reported that the College of Business and Public Administration was not only in great need of a building but also was "under-staffed, inadequately equipped, and overworked." As for the College of Education, the report stated that this division of the University was so badly housed as to influence unfavorably the morale of the faculty.

A building was requested for the College of Fine Arts and the School of Home Economics, but it was strongly recommended that no major building development be planned without inclusion of a new stack building for the library. The committee added that it was useless to buy new and greatly needed books if there was no place to put them.

The report also contained an interesting chapter on mistakes the faculty felt had been made by architects in the past, and it was urged that every effort to be made to avoid such mistakes in the future. Beauty and harmony, the report observed, warranted more attention in the future; and more care should also be given to planning interiors. While admittedly the Library was the most pleasing structure on campus to a casual observer, the truth was that trucks of books had to be hauled long distances between desks where staff and students were at work. The final complaints were that the Library had only one elevator, which opened into the staff workroom, the ventilation was poor, and so were the acoustics.

There were strong recommendations that haste be avoided in the future so that buildings at other universities could be studied and members of the University of Arizona faculty could be consulted on facilities they would be expected to use. All new buildings, the report said, should be air-conditioned and new dormitories should not be built on the campus because "no great hardship is imposed upon a student living in a dormitory off campus if he is required to walk a block or two to class."

Having disposed of present and future buildings, the committee turned to the curriculum and said:

> Certain guiding principles suggest themselves for determining the range and extent of appropriate curricular offerings at the University of Arizona. Supported by and responsible to the people of Arizona, the University's primary obligation is that of providing opportunities for higher education to the citizens of Arizona. This does not mean that the University is the tool of a popular majority. Nor should it respond to the whims of special groups. Rather it is the function of the University to provide educational leadership to the people of Arizona as a whole. . . . Work that cannot be done well when judged by reasonable standards is expensive and should be left undone.

Specifically included in this report was the decision that a medical college was "neither necessary nor economically feasible" at that time. Here the committee said:

> The amount of physical equipment and size of faculty required for creditable work are important when exploring new areas for development. For example, several state universities do not offer medical training because of the huge plant facilities and large faculties and staff personnel requirements in relation to the demands in the State for medical training. Duplication of medical training facilities accessible in schools already established requires resources that could much better be spent for other educational purposes.

The question of the need for medical education in Arizona is currently being studied under a grant made by the Commonwealth Fund.

It was high time to decide on the future needs of the University, for a few days after the inauguration of President McCormick it broke its record by graduating a class of 672 students, a gain of 149 over the previous year. Nor was this the only indication of great growth in the near future, for a second record was broken in September when 5,147 students enrolled for regular classes and an additional 529 entered night classes, extension work, and correspondence courses. Dr. Alfred Atkinson warned the Board at this time to prepare for rapid increases during the next ten years.

Two recurring problems faced the Regents at the next meeting of the Board. One concerned the press, which as usual asked that reporters be admitted to meetings. The other involved the Department of Athletics, which petitioned for permission to fly university teams to games with distant schools. The Board refused in both cases.

A more serious distraction was a series of conflicts between the Board and Mrs. Ana Frohmiller, the State Auditor. Mrs. Frohmiller consistently criticized and challenged university spending. Finally she refused to honor expense accounts of teachers assigned to attend academic meetings. Here the Supreme Court ruled against her, and when she then refused to approve payment of the costs of the inauguration of President McCormick, it ruled against her again.

December, 1948, brought the President before the Regents with a long list of requests for buildings he spoke of as "pressing needs." He asked for buildings for the College of Liberal Arts, the College of Fine Arts, the College of Pharmacy, for biological science, dairy husbandry, home management and nursery school, two dormitories for women, and a stock-judging pavilion for the College of Agriculture. He also suggested additions to the library and museum and more funds for the Student Union Memorial Building. The total cost of all this was estimated at $5,700,000 and the Board felt the sum was too large to win the approval of the Legislature. Nevertheless, it was willing to recommend a request for $5,000,000 covering the principal buildings.

A paramount problem in 1948 was the financing of the Student Union. The fund still lacked $500,000 and both the committee and the administration were investigating possibilities for raising the money. It was apparent that the Legislature would have to provide more help, and by March, 1949, it responded by passing a second appropriation for $150,000 and giving the Board permission to issue $400,000 in bonds.

This, with the $268,000 raised by students, alumni, and friends, plus the first legislative appropriation of $150,000, brought the total to $968,000. It would not be enough, but it was close and was far more than the originally estimated cost of $560,000 submitted by the executive committee in 1945. The University had grown and so had plans for the building.

No student who uses the Student Union Memorial Building today can have an adequate conception of the devoted service of the many men and women who made the Union possible. The administration, deans, professors, department heads, directors of student activities, friends of the University, and students were united as never before. The committee met three and four times a month to consider the facilities in the building and to hear suggestions from architects of national as well as local standing. Thousands of details had to be worked out, but this great task was accomplished in the atmosphere of faith that permeated the campus. Nothing seemed impossible after 1948.

One heard the satisfying sounds of hammers and saws and the rumble of power shovels and bulldozers. Wherever one looked there were piles of building materials and the rising walls and roofs of new buildings. The aeronautical engineering building was finished. So were additions to the law building and the east stadium. The Legislature passed appropriations for the College of Liberal Arts, the enclosure of the south end of the stadium with Navajo and Pinal halls, an addition to the library, and a new power plant and shops. Right behind these would come a new building for the College of Business and Public Administration.

As the buildings went up so did the scholastic standards. The rule had been that a student must have a grade of 3.0 or better in eighty per cent of his subjects; and if he had grades of 5.0 he was not considered for graduation. This was changed with faculty approval, and a grade average of 3.2, reached by averaging all grades including 5's, was made a graduation requirement. At the same time the College of Law average was raised to 3. President McCormick reported that 1948–49 had been the most important years in the history of the University from the viewpoint of scholarships, highlighted by the establishment by Mr. James Baird of the Baird Foundation with an annual income from $220,000 for scholarships and student loans; Mrs. Ann Rae Binney gave $25,000, while mining companies and others made annual grants amounting to $11,500. The College of Liberal Arts now had space to provide for a flourishing Department of Journalism, and the College of Business and Public Administration would get the long-needed Bureau of Business Research.

Dr. McCormick claimed no credit for the change in the attitudes of the Regents and the Legislature that had made all this possible. He talked about it freely in later years and said:

> I worked no magic. I think it was the spirit of the times plus the fact that we had a good Board and a good Legislature. All over the country legislatures were becoming more generous about that time. So I would attribute the heavy increase in appropriations for building and operation during the period I was in office to a reflection of the national trend. State universities were coming into their heyday while endowed schools were finding the going very tough

> because they had to get along on a lower rate of return from their investments.
>
> I'll say this: I may have been a little more extravagant in my requests to the Board than was usual, but the Board was inclined to raise its requests to the Legislature and the Legislature was more generous. The expanding economy of the State had a lot to do with the attitude of the Legislature. Revenues from manufacturing had gone ahead of both mining and agriculture. Agriculture first went ahead of mining and then manufacturing went ahead of both of them. We had practically no manufacturing at all previous to the war so I would believe that if you are making an accurate appraisal of this increase that came along in appropriations and buildings you'll find it was largely a result of the expanding economy. The State was growing rapidly and the population figure was rising. Denver had been the financial capital of the Rocky Mountain Empire. Phoenix took over that position with one bank alone carrying larger deposits than all the banks in Denver.

Dr. McCormick recalled with no pleasure that, before the building program had produced results, he had brought in a number of surplus army buildings to serve as classrooms. They were bleak affairs, inside and out, and as soon as possible he asked the Board for permission to remove them. He remembered:

> They were an eyesore and I was afraid we would wind up with them on our hands, as that is what usually happens. I got rid of all but two and I think those two are still there. There is always someone who needs more space.

One of the projects in which Dr. McCormick took special interest was air-conditioning university buildings, although on this he was unable to accomplish all he had hoped. The library was air-conditioned and a central air-conditioning system was installed, but all plans to cool the agricultural building failed. The building did not lend itself to this type of modernization, except at a price too high to be approved. The Liberal Arts College was air-conditioned, and so were the buildings that followed after Dr. McCormick's time. Even the old home of the College of Liberal Arts was made comfortable when it was redesigned for the College of Education.

President McCormick avoided bond issues whenever possible in his "brick and mortar" era. In discussing his reasons for this later, he said:

> My worry was that if we went very far with this matter of raising money by issuing bonds we were going to get to a place where, in order to meet our bond obligations, we might have to dip into our operating budget. The point is that it is very easy to get a Legislature to go along on a bond issue. What may happen is that if you do have to dip into the operating budget it will probably be at a time when things are not going along too well financially in the State and your appropriation for operating expenses is not going to be too heavy. Then you are caught both ways.
>
> With the exception of the Student Union, the buildings we put up in my time were built from outright appropriations.

Great as was the "brick and mortar" expansion on the campus, it was matched by the growth in enrollment. The academic year of 1949–50 saw 6,044 students register in all classes and for the first time in history 1,000 students marched to the raised platform in the stadium to receive diplomas.

There were people in the stands that night who had seen President Theodore B. Comstock present sheepskins to the first graduating class of three students 54 years before.

One of these pioneers was Mrs. Clara Fish Roberts, the first student to register at the University of Arizona. She said:

> It was wonderful to watch 1,000 young men and women follow the footsteps of the little group of students I had known by name so long ago. It meant my school had become a great institution and I was thrilled then as I always am today by any evidence of its progress.

The academic year of 1949–50 brought to a successful conclusion the long struggle for the Student Union Memorial Building when the Board of Regents accepted a bid of $898,827 and granted an additional $28,155 towards furnishings. The final campaign was over. Noted architects had said their last word. Now tired committees drew a long breath of relief as the builders who were to translate the dreams of years into brick and stone moved in to take up the burden.

Important events were now crowding the calendar. Mr. and Mrs. Harold S. Gladwin made the University a million-dollar gift of the Gila Pueblo Archaeological Foundation and all its collections, the Arizona Co-operative Cotton Growers Association praised the department of plant breeding for the successful research work done in improving strains of cotton suitable to Arizona, and the federal government finally contracted to exchange 3,340 acres of public lands along the Ajo road for the 480 acres the University had acquired in the Saguaro National Monument through the urging of Dr. Shantz.

Only football failed to keep the pace. The Wildcats were far below the winning standard to which the campus was conditioned by tradition. Coach J. F. (Pop) McKale, who coached from 1914 to 1930, had turned in seventy-eight wins against thirty-two losses. Coach Tex Oliver had a 35–11 record from 1933 to 1937, and despite Coach Mike Casteel's final three years in which his teams won only two more games than they lost, he scored forty-six victories to twenty-six defeats from 1939 to 1948. This was a total of 159 victories to sixty-nine defeats and fifteen tie scores.

So when Coach Bob Winslow took over in 1949, won two victories, lost seven games and tied one, the student body and other supporters were disappointed. The Wildcats improved in 1950 and 1951, winning ten games in those two years and losing eleven; but were practically run off the gridiron by Arizona State College at Tempe; which overwhelmed them by scores of 47 to 13 and 61 to 14. The only consolation was that fans continued to turn out and fill the seats in the enlarged stadium.

Basketball, however, reached a peak not equalled before or since, when in February 1951, the team, under Coach Fred Enke, was named by the Associated Press as eleventh in the entire nation.

Scholarship funds continued to increase and so did the enrollment, which passed the 6,500 mark. As had been predicted in every survey made, the institution was definitely on the march to heights that would have seemed fantastic to those men of vision who had called on the people of a pioneer territory in 1864 to prepare the way for a University.

President McCormick chose this time to step out of office, and on October 26, 1950 the Board accepted his resignation, at his request, and returned him to the College of Law as a professor. At this time he also replaced Dr. Atkinson as advisor to the Board of Regents. The search for a new president was short, and on December 16, Richard A. Harvill, Dean of the College of Liberal Arts, was appointed to fill the vacancy.

There was considerable speculation over the reason for President Mc-Cormick's resignation, but he always insisted there was no mystery and explained his action frankly. He said:

> I went into the office reluctantly and only on the promise that the Regents would appoint a vice-president. At my suggestion they named Dr. Nugent who, by the way, did a tremendous job.
>
> The burden on the President's office is just terrific. The office closes at six o'clock at night but after that there are what you might call extracurricular activities. A President has to make talks all over the state. It is natural that this is expected of him because he is a public servant. If somebody in Phoenix, Yuma, Benson, or Holbrook is holding a meeting you're often asked to speak. Of course they want you to speak of things in which they are interested so you can't talk, let's say, about law.
>
> It takes time to prepare a speech for these important dinners. Sometimes you aren't even told in advance that you are on the program and often it isn't made clear that you are the principal speaker, or even the only speaker, and that you will be expected to fill a half hour or 45 minute hole in the program. And you have to be in command. A President of the University can't afford to do a bad job.
>
> That's a part of the work which the average person thinks is so pleasant. He says, There is the President of the University at the head table here, there and everywhere,' but it is really a tremendous drain on your time and it becomes a great burden. So far as your daily work is concerned if you can't be in your office from eight in the morning to six in the afternoon you just can't keep work current. You can't be away too much and keep abreast. I know a lot of university presidents who are not on their campus more than 60 or 75 percent of the time but their work can't be current unless they have a lot of administrative assistants. If you are away a week the work piles up until you are busy day and night after you return. I know that I sometimes went weeks without getting home to dinner.
>
> There's the real reason behind my return to my chosen profession. The presidency was a great experience and I

> have only the finest memories of the people of the state, the Regents, the Legislature, the faculty and students and the help they gave in building a great institution.

During the years he was Dean of the College of Law, Dr. McCormick made it part of his work to visit groups of lawyers in every county in Arizona. This he had to give up when he became President, but he still believes the practice was worth the time it took. He takes this view:

> In the case of a professional or technical school, unless it is approved by the people of that profession in the state—whether it is a medical school, a law school, a mining or engineering college or a school of pharmacy—you have a hard battle. The success of our College of Pharmacy proves the point. We opened a school of pharmacy in 1947–48 under Dr. Rufus A. Lyman. That man sold the school of pharmacy to the pharmacists of Arizona. He did a terrific public relations job. He visited every drug store and within a year we had grants coming in that are not matched today in the College of Law. The result was that in 1949 we took the school of pharmacy out of the Liberal Arts College and made it a college with Dr. Lyman as the first dean.
>
> I've often said that a professional school or college is no better than the people think it is. If the people in that profession look down on it then for practical purposes it is a poor school even though it is actually one of the best in the country. You could have the Harvard law school here, but if the bar of the state looked down on it then it wouldn't be a good law school.
>
> That's true about the University. There are still people in parts of the state who don't know what a great University this is. One reason is that there are those who continue to think of the University as it was 25 years ago whereas it has changed in that time.
>
> In the last year over $2,000,000 in grants and gifts came to this institution. But those people remember when we didn't get a dollar in grants and gifts and they have no idea of the tremendous expansion which has taken place. The developments in the Institute of Atmospheric Physics

> and electrical engineering as well as many other similar developments have meant enormous progress.

President McCormick's year was to end on June 30, 1951, but he was called away by his duties as a member of the National Board of the American Red Cross, and on June 15 the Board of Regents gave Dr. Harvill full authority as acting President.

So closed an important period in the history of the University, but it would immediately be followed by one of even greater growth and service to the State.

CHAPTER 12

1951–1959

PRESIDENT RICHARD A. HARVILL was born in Centerville, Tennessee in 1905. He received the degree of Bachelor of Science from Mississippi State College in 1926 and the Master of Science degree from Duke University the following year. The degree of Doctor of Philosophy came from Northwestern University in 1932. Dr. Harvill concentrated his studies in the field of economics and taught that subject as an instructor at Mississippi State College and Duke University. At Northwestern he served as research assistant in the Institute for Land and Public Utility Economics and as teaching assistant in the Department of Economics.

Dr. Harvill appeared on the University of Arizona campus for the first time in 1934 as Assistant Professor of Economics. While on leave from this position he served as visiting Assistant Professor of Economics at the University of Buffalo in 1937–38, and a year later he returned to the University of Arizona as Associate Professor of Economics. This position he held until 1946 when he was advanced to a full professorship and named Dean of the Graduate College. Four of the World War II years (1942–46) were spent on war leave with the Arizona Office of Price Administration: one year as Assistant District Price Executive and three years as District Price Executive. In 1947, he succeeded Dr. Robert Logan Nugent as Dean of the Liberal Arts College, and in 1950 he was appointed President of the University, succeeding Dr. J. Byron McCormick. This appointment became effective July 1, 1951.

Important as the induction of a new president is in the life of a University, the inauguration of Dr. Harvill was lifted far above the traditional place reserved for such ceremonies in administrative and academic history because it marked three notable advances at the University. The first was the public showing of the newly acquired Gila Pueblo Archaeological Collection, the second was the unveiling of the priceless Kress collection of European masterpieces which the Samuel H. Kress Foundation had placed on indefinite loan with the University, and the third was the formal opening and dedication of the million dollar Student Union Memorial building.

The inauguration program occupied a period of three days. Thursday evening, Nov. 15, 1951, featured an open house at the State Museum, where the public was invited to view the Gila Pueblo showing. The monumental collection was the gift of Mr. and Mrs. Harold S. Gladwin. With its monetary value established at approximately $1,000,-000, it was one of the largest gifts in the University's history. From the standpoint of science, it was described as an incomparable assemblage of archaeological material that covered the Southwest from the era of 12,000 b.c. to the period of European conquest. It contained 50,000 specimens.

The donors had financed and formed the foundation at Globe, in 1928 and in 1950 decided to present the collection to the University. In that time, their scientists and staff had explored 8,000 sites, had wholly excavated thirty ruins, and had partially uncovered twenty others. Notable among the excavations were those at Snaketown, near Chandler, that had disclosed the cultures of the ancient people known as the Hohokam. These people had developed a sound agricultural economy founded on irrigation in the Salt River and Gila River valleys, and the collection bearing on their history is the most complete and important on that subject in the world.

Dr. Emil Haury, director of the State Museum, called the collection "the original manuscripts from the libraries of Southwestern archaeology" and added, "No archaeological collection representing the Southwest is more comprehensive than the combined Arizona State Museum and the Gila Pueblo artifacts."

Four former presidents of the University delivered addresses on Friday morning, November 16, in a symposium on "Arizona, Land of Promise and Fulfillment."

Dr. Homer LeRoy Shantz spoke on "The Geographical Background," and in the course of his remarks this famous botanist and world authority on arid lands warned that Arizona must conserve its water. He said:

> No problem facing the State of Arizona is as vital to its future welfare as the water problem. Every drop of water which falls in the state should, if possible, be conserved in the soil where it falls. Every watershed should be managed with this is mind; there should be no loss of flood waters and no unnecessary use of water for irrigation or for domestic or commercial purposes. Water is for Arizona the factor which will set the limits of growth and development.
>
> Nature has for eons of time built our state with its many natural resources, and civilized man in a mere moment of

> time has partially depleted our mineral resources, our watersheds, our vegetation cover, our underground waters, our soils and our wildlife.
>
> With the future undoubtedly making even greater demands than the past, wisdom and a desire to conserve are dictated as our method of approach to our natural resources.

Former President Rufus B. von KleinSmid's topic was "The Cultural Story." He called the Southwest "the happiest hunting ground of the American archaeological prehistorian" and praised the University for its museum and its excavation programs. These, he said, "place the state and the campus in the forefront of the commonwealths and campuses of America."

Retiring President James Byron McCormick gave "The Legal and Political Story," sketching the history of the state from Coronado to modern Arizona. He closed with a quotation from the message that Governor Thomas E. Campbell had sent to the Legislature thirty years before:

> From the mountain top of vision, the future of Arizona unfolds itself with panoramic vividness. Fertile fields . . . the wheels of factories and railroads . . . mines disgorging their wealth, and prosperous and virile people, is the picture. . . . The day is not very distant when the dream of this moment will be the actuality of tomorrow. The future, therefore, your future, my future and the future of the people of the State is committed to our care. We can measure up to the responsibility by united endeavor, and animated by a desire to be of constructive service, not only to this but future generations. In this worthwhile work of empire we can all play a part.

The final speaker was former President Dr. Alfred Atkinson, whose subject was "The Business and Industrial Story." After having presented a factual picture of the great growth in population, industry, agriculture, tourism, and the consequent increase of bank deposits, Dr. Atkinson turned to the rapidly developing emphasis on University research and said:

> In my opinion the prospect of attaining enduring peace rests in the hands of the research workers. Most of the people in the world are hungry. This shortage of food, along with growing populations, produces conditions unfavorable

> to stability and peace. The so-called backward areas of the earth have learned that hunger does not prevail in some other parts of the world, and this stimulates unrest and upheaval. To talk of world peace with the present population-food supply relations in many nations is idle babbling.
>
> At the present time approximately two billion dollars a year are being expended for research by institutions, government agencies, industry and privately supported foundations. This shows recognition of the need of investigation to understand the materials and forces of the earth and to make them serve the needs of mankind. Because of their highly trained and capable faculties, educational institutions are in a position to contribute to the body of important knowledge through research activities. The upbuilding of an attitude of research should be encouraged. Students should be impressed with the important fact that the results of the work of investigators are changing the world in which we live, and these changes have social and political repercussions.

A luncheon in the new Student Union Memorial building at which Governor Howard Pyle was the speaker followed the symposium. Governor Pyle said that if Arizona was indeed to be a land of promise and achievement the builders must be filled with the dedicated spirit of Father Kino, rather than the plundering aspirations of Coronado and asked that modern leaders approach their task with prayer.

Following the luncheon the academic procession formed east of the Administration building and followed the traditional path around Old Main to the University auditorium. Six former presidents were in the line with members of the faculty and 252 representatives of colleges, universities, and academic and professional societies. Dr. Robert L. Nugent, vice-president of the University, was in charge of the exercises which opened with greetings from Dr. Melvin T. Solve, faculty chairman; Douglas J. Ward, president of the Associated Students; Frederick R. Stofft, president of the Alumni Association; and Governor Pyle.

The speaker of the afternoon was Dr. James Roscoe Miller, president of Northwestern University where Dr. Harvill had received the doctorate.

President Miller dealt at length with the fact that through research and training in the universities, science had become almost paramount, but he brought a message of caution for the future in which he said:

I am not convinced that military might and technological and productive strength are enough to win the struggle for a free world. I incline to agree with the English military authority who recently wrote that the real victory would be won, not by fission of the atom but by fission of ideas.

This means that in the event of a prolonged cold war, the maintenance and development of our democratic institutions and democratic culture will be just as important as the maintenance of our physical might . . . From the long-term view, we Americans must plan our defense effort to include the maintenance and improvement of the quality of life in our nation. Civilization has been defined as a sense of values. The values of democratic civilization are our ideological bomb in the struggle with totalitarianism.

One of the members of Northwestern's faculty, Dr. Baker Brownell, recently pointed out the danger of our universities losing their cultural balance. He expressed the fear that they may become only seats of scientific development and thus pass from the scene as creative factors of the community. . . .

The modern university is concerned with training people for almost every conceivable vocation; with seeking after facts and figures, and with seeking after understanding and wisdom; with improving health, and with alleviating social ills; with pure science and with applied science; with the problems of business and the problems of labor; with the development of the spirit, the building of character, and the improvement of the intellect.

The strength of American education lies in this diversity—it is just as essential to our national life as diversity of creeds and opinions. All of these elements have a place in perfecting the design of civilization. But to give them their right place, we must have some idea of what we desire that design to be. Religion, literature, history and the arts—those studies generally grouped under the broad heading of the humanities—have an indispensable place in all education because they are our main source of knowledge about what is first-rate in human character and conduct.

Asserting it was his belief that more could be done to restore America's moral vitality by education than by congressional codes, Dr. Miller said:

> We shall do all we can toward strengthening education. That is our business. We shall try to keep it the right kind of education—well-balanced and morally forceful. We shall try to preserve the freedom of integrity of education. But the difficulty of doing these things is very great in a time of wide confusion, national mobilization and warring ideologies. Educators cannot carry these burdens without the help of citizens who realize the relationship between high education and American democracy.

President Harvill's address, which followed his induction by Cleon T. Knapp, President of the Board of Regents, dealt with the purpose and responsibility of a university to students and society. He said in part:

> In assessing the role of education in the maintenance of a free society, we must recognize that intellectual capacity of a high order is only one of the conditions that qualify individuals for their responsibility as citizens. Indeed, formal education and knowledge alone are not going to preserve our cherished and traditional values. Unless the purposes or ends of the entire social order are kept firmly in the foreground, the intellectual ability and effort of the people may be directed toward the attainment of a social system totally inconsistent with those of freedom and democracy. Indeed, the danger of collapse is recognized as never before in the history of Western man. To avoid catastrophe and to repair damage already done are our most compelling tasks. . . .
>
> A student's formal educational experience should contribute in substantial manner to the understanding of himself and the world in which he lives. It should equip him with the knowledge and skills necessary for professional and vocational services. But scientific knowledge and technical skills, though vitally necessary and increasingly important in our highly complex contemporary society, do not alone constitute the education required by free, responsible citizens. Personal

> excellence and social competence are demanded and these involve more than specialized technical education. . . .
>
> By reason of its location, the University of Arizona possesses special advantages and opportunities which influence its instructional and research programs. Mining and agriculture, long the two outstanding forms of economic endeavor in Arizona, have long engaged the attention of teachers, students and research scholars. Opportunities in these areas still abound. Business and industry, including a substantial volume of manufacturing, are becoming increasingly important. . . . Emphasis upon learning and understanding our own State does not mean that we are to limit our horizon or become provincial in outlook and interests. Geographic and political boundaries have no meaning for ideas and knowledge in the modern world. A university must concern itself with the entire range of knowledge, regardless of its extent of time and space. A compelling responsibility devolves upon all of us to understand as fully as is possible the powerful and complex forces at work in the world—some directed toward achieving turmoil and disunity, some directed toward achieving order and stability again. We must try to understand the ideas and methods of hostile nations that seek to undermine our spiritual and material strength. More importantly, we must understand the real nature of our own free society and the sources of its strength.

Following his address President Harvill conferred honorary degrees on Harold Sterling Gladwin, donor with Mrs. Gladwin of the Gila Pueblo collection; Rush Harrison Kress, who with his brother, Samuel Henry Kress, had entrusted the University with the Samuel H. Kress collection of twenty-five masterpieces of European art; Dr. Clifton Mathews, judge of the United States Court of Appeals in Arizona, and Dr. James Roscoe Miller, President of Northwestern University. Dr. David E. Finley, Director of the National Gallery of Art in Washington, delivered a formal address in which he said:

> Those in charge of the Kress Foundation feel that, in a country as large as this, works of art must not be concentrated in a few large cities but must be made accessible to people in all parts of this great and growing country of ours.

> And so they have brought to you, in this center of culture in the Southwest an important collection of paintings. . . . It is a unique conception, as grandiose as it is generous, and with unlimited possibilities for the happiness and moral and intellectual welfare of the people of this country. Furthermore, the carrying out of this program has come at a time in our history when it is greatly needed. For we have now reached a point in the development of our nation when our strength, both moral and physical, has placed the leadership of the free world in our hands.

The inaugural exercises were followed by ceremonies at the University library where the President and Regents held a public reception and the masterpieces of the Kress Foundation were viewed by the guests.

The long program closed in the evening with a production of *Brigadoon* by the College of Fine Arts. There was standing room only in the auditorium—which a Regent had once said would never be filled—and the event was a fitting climax to a day that would live long in University history.

The day following the Inauguration was Homecoming Day, November 14, 1951. One more noteworthy event remained. It was both the realization of a dream and the conclusion of years of effort on the part of the State, the Regents, the students and faculty, the alumni, and friends of the institution—the dedication of the Student Union Memorial. Honoring 285 former students and members of the faculty who had given their lives in World Wars I and II, the building was also a monument to the living spirit of an institution that had kept faith with the ideals for which its men had fought and died. A mere vision in 1944 during the presidency of Dr. Alfred Atkinson, there had been times when the campaign to raise the funds necessary to make it live had seemed almost hopeless. But the determination that this effort must not fail was greater than all obstacles.

President James Byron McCormick picked up the leadership when Dr. Atkinson stepped down as President and carried on with the help of forces completely united.

The final cost was about $1,200,000 for construction and furnishings. One third of this came from the State Legislature, which recognized the need to furnish dining facilities for the growing enrollment. One third was raised by alumni, faculty, students, corporations, and the general public, and the remainder came from the sale of bonds which were to be paid off with income from student fees and sale of services.

Two memorials were established to perpetuate the memory of the honored dead. One was a large bronze plaque listing their names. The other was the ship's bell from the Battleship U. S. S. Arizona, which had been sunk at Pearl Harbor. The bell was hung in the clock tower, the chief architectural feature of the building, where it tolls each December 7, as a reminder to today's students that the sacrifices of those it honors must never be forgotten. There are other occasions when chosen students are selected to ring the huge bell and send its reverberations over the campus in a message that another victory has been added to the long list of university honors.

Speakers at the dedication ceremonies were Dr. James Byron McCormick, Governor Howard Pyle, Dr. Alfred Atkinson, President Harvill, and Mr. Cleon T. Knapp, President of the Board of Regents.

Regent Knapp's dedication address was an eloquent tribute to the men whose names remain not alone in bronze, but in the heart of the University. He said in part:

> We now dedicate this beautiful building as a memorial to those who were once a part of the student body or faculty of this University of Arizona and who gave their lives for their country. The story of their sacrifice stretches from Flanders Fields—the beaches of Normandy—the islands of the Pacific—to the mountains of Korea. Upon those battlefields they gave the last full measure of devotion that this nation of freedom and liberty might live. We knew them in the days when they strolled about the campus—played their parts in our university life—won scholastic honors—and received cheers upon our athletic fields. This memorial will forever be their shrine. I should like to think that, even at this moment, their spirits hover over us in silent appreciation of the tribute we now pay them.
>
> But in a sense we also dedicate this memorial to the living. May it be an inspiration to those who become part of our university life. May it be the center and gathering place—the incentive to high endeavor, leadership and achievement of the better things in life. May it be the symbol of good citizenship. Citizenship that demands honor and honesty in high places in our national life. Citizenship that appreciates the freedom and liberty so nobly won for us by the founders of this nation. Citizenship determined to preserve

> our institutions and pass them on to posterity, strong and untarnished.
>
> A bell hangs in the memorial tower. A bell that was once on the battleship Arizona, which sank in the mud and slime of Pearl Harbor. The bell is clean now—it has been purified by the tragedy of a great war. It is the voice through which this memorial shall forever speak. In the hours of great national achievement in war or peace, it will speak in ringing tones of joy; it will ring with pride when honors come to this University. But when the bell speaks in its sadder moments, we shall know 'for whom the bell tolls.'

A moment of reverent silence followed the speaker's closing words. Then the memorial plaque was unveiled and the Arizona's bell began to toll a solemn pledge of the University's dedication to the American way of life for which students and faculty had given their lives.

So one administration closed and another opened.

Though the years between the closing of President Atkinson's administration and the inauguration of Dr. Harvill were few in number, Arizona had shown unmistakable promise of tremendous development. In Dr. Atkinson's last year, Arizona was second in the rate of increase in population and bank deposits. By the time Dr. Harvill took office, Arizona was the fastest growing state in the Union and led in the rate of growth of income, retailing, and bank capital. As the state grew so did the University, and Dr. Harvill's first annual report, issued in 1952, dealt seriously with the situation. He warned that while the G.I. enrollment was dropping, national studies indicated that increases at institutions of higher learning would soon double the peak figures of post-war years. He was the third successive president to warn the Legislature and the people of what lay ahead and to urge realistic preparations to meet the army of youth even then on the way to colleges and universities.

In addition to the Student Union, the academic year of 1951–52 had brought the completion of new stack space for the library and a new power plant. The new home of the College of Business and Public Administration was under way, and funds were available for a home management house and nursery school, an addition to the administration building, the construction of a home for the president, and extensive improvements and new buildings on the Mesa experimental farm. In addition to all this the Legislature had authorized the Regents to borrow $500,000 from the government for new dormitories.

It was quite obvious that the physical plant was growing, but if the president's report for 1952–53 was read with attention to the progress being made in the academic field, one might suspect that the brick and mortar program was scarcely keeping pace with the inner growth of the University.

Dean John Crowder, who had been brought to the campus from Montana State University, was rapidly reorganizing the College of Fine Arts. Departmental organization of the School of Music gave way to a single administrative unit. Two new programs were added to music education: a graduate program leading to a degree of Master of Music education and an undergraduate program that provided a degree of Bachelor of Music with a major in music education. These met the requirements of the National Association of Schools of Music and raised the standing of the college.

There were other important developments at this period in instruction and research. A Bureau of Ethnic Research was established to study all phases of the history and life of Arizona Indian tribes. The Bureau of Business Research began publication of a monthly *Business and Economic Review*. Journalism, which had been taught in the English department since the first class in 1926, had reached a position of importance which required departmental status and well-equipped newsrooms in the modern Liberal Arts building.

President Harvill's report revealed that the University was not only very busy at home but had entered into an agreement with the U. S. Department of State and the Department of Agriculture to lend help in developing Iraq's College of Agriculture at Abu Gheraib near Baghdad. The University sent four scientists out on this tour of duty in January, 1953. This work went on until political troubles in Iraq made it necessary for the University to abandon the project and to call its scientists home in February, 1959.

Of great importance to the faculty was the adoption by the Legislature in 1952 of a state retirement act which coupled federal social security with limited state aid that provided small prior service benefits. The faculty had fought strongly for state benefits commensurate with service rendered, but both the Legislature and the people failed to support it. In commenting on the plan as finally adopted, the President said:

> Surely, even with the very small prior benefits, it represents a distinct advance as compared with the uncertainty of the preceding three and one-half years, particularly from the view of the younger members of the faculty and staff for whom prior service benefits are of relatively small importance.

It is interesting today to note that the 1952 report was the first to dwell specifically on the university research activities. Heretofore the colleges and departments had made minor individual reports. Now the President treated them in one general report that showed that forty-five sponsored research programs were being carried on for government departments, the Army, Navy, and numerous private foundations and industries. The total amount of sponsored funds was $160,200 and the largest single grant was $29,350.

The new College of Pharmacy was exhibiting remarkable growth and was now accredited by the American Council of Pharmaceutical Education. The Agricultural Experiment Station noted that two-thirds of the 1,144,000 acres of Arizona agricultural land were planted to crop varieties that the University had produced or introduced. Dr. Edwin F. Carpenter, director of the Steward Observatory, revealed that the big telescope had been instrumental in the discovery of the smallest star ever observed by man.

Research divisions were busy carrying on special projects. Among these were the Agricultural Experiment Station, Engineering Experiment Station, the Laboratory of Tree-Ring Research, the Bureau of Mines, the State Museum, the Bureau of Business Research, and the Steward Observatory. Of great significance was the addition of two new divisions. They were the Carbon 14 laboratory, where a new technique of determining dates from material of organic origin was studied, and the Institute of Atmospheric Physics, which was to make the University a world leader in a field where man was reaching into the secrets of the skies for the first time.

The Carbon 14 laboratory was one of eight in the United States, but its location in Arizona was of particular interest to scientists because it supplemented the work already done by Dr. Douglass, who had established the science of dendrochronology, usually called the study of tree rings. Through Dr. Douglass' discoveries, man had learned to establish dates and to study rainfall cycles as far back in history as a.d. 100. While Carbon 14 overlapped this, the combined sciences made it possible to carry dating back 20,000 years. Great as was this particular advance of science at the University, it was of less importance to the future of man's way of life in semi-arid regions than the Institute of Atmospheric Physics.

Now and then in the history of the University of Arizona it sometimes seems as if a guiding hand pointed out one of the trails through the barriers to the unknown that the institution must take if it is to be worthy of being called a University. Certainly it happened now when good fortune brought it Lewis W. Douglas, world citizen and native son of a pioneer Arizona family that had often befriended the University in its early days.

Lewis W. Douglas had been the first man in the Southwest to invest imagination, energy, and capital in a serious effort to increase the rainfall in semi-arid lands. This naturally evoked comment, and there were those who thought it very odd that a former ambassador to Britain, director of the U. S. wartime budget, deputy war shipping administrator, vice-chancellor of McGill University, member of the board of directors of life insurance companies and great industries, banker, mining man, and Arizona rancher should be trying to make rain by hiring commercial flying companies to "seed" clouds high above the desert floor.

Actually it was not a sudden impulse that led Douglas to conduct these experiments, and they were definitely no game. There were motives behind them that were rooted in his past. One was a deep love for Arizona going back to the days of his boyhood. Another was the thought he had always given to the problems and possibilities of his homeland.

Let him tell the story in his own way:

> I studied geology in college and because Arizona was always close to my heart no matter where I went or what I did, I gave a great deal of thought to the water problem. It is scarcely necessary to point out that as the State grew and developed so would the need for more and more water and it was easy to see that if Arizona was to continue its development the problem of trying to supplement our vanishing water supply could not be ignored.
>
> It appeared possible at first that something might be accomplished by forcing clouds to drop their moisture. So, for two years, with other interested citizens, I carried on experiments in seeding clouds. These fell short of our early hopes.
>
> President Harvill had shown much interest in this type of research and with his assistance we sought the advice of noted scientists. As a result we were able in 1953 to bring about a conference of the leading scientists in the field of cloud physics. These were great men and we accepted their view that a program of basic, rather than applied, science must be established and carried on in a sound manner by an Institute of Atmospheric Physics. Such an institute, they said, should be established in a semi-arid land and this to me meant only the University of Arizona.

> I have always had a very strong conviction about the quality of education at the University of Arizona and have felt that the highest order of research was possible there. A college is a place where known facts are taught, but a true university is an institution which persistently inquires into the unknown.
>
> The scientists agreed that the University was the proper laboratory for the study of the problems which had to be solved; especially the problems of agriculture. It had carried on years of research in the problems of desert lands and in addition to this the State offered definite social and economic advantages.

This conference drew the attention of scientific journals and the world press for among those who participated were Dr. E. G. Bowen of the Commonwealth Scientific and Industrial Organization of Australia; Dr. H. G. Houghton of Massachusetts Institute of Technology; Dr. Joseph Kaplan, University of California; Dr. Verre Peterson, University of Chicago; Dr. R. M. Cunningham, Cambridge Research laboratories, Dr. Walter Hirschfield, McGill University; Dr. S. E. Reynolds of the New Mexico Institute of Mining and Technology; Dr. V. J. Schafer, General Electric Corporation; Dr. Horace Byers, University of Chicago, and Dr. Roscoe R. Braham, Jr., Dr. James McDonald and Dr. A. Richard Kassander of the University of Arizona. Douglas said:

> With the advice of our scientific friends the institute was established, a program outlined and a staff organized. Once again it was proved that while mediocrity merely perpetuates mediocrity, the best attracts men of the highest intelligence, for the University of Chicago joined the project. It not only contributed the data on studies which it made in the Chicago cloud physics project but shared its scientists with us. This set us firmly on our way.

Professor Horace R. Byers, chairman of the University of Chicago department of meteorology, and his associate, Dr. Roscoe E. Braham, Jr., were given joint appointments in the two universities and other men from Chicago received direct appointments. Douglas, who had been made a member of President Eisenhower's committee on weather control, served the University without salary as administrative consultant.

Financed by state and private funds, the new institute in 1954 began taking a cloud census in which it used radar and time-lapse motion pictures.

Some understanding of the wide appreciation with which the University program was received will be found in the material assistance provided by national foundations. All travel expenses of scientists attending the seminar were paid by the Rockefeller Foundation. The Alfred P. Sloan Foundation contributed $150,000 for research and the National Science Foundation added another $50,000. The Geophysics Research Division of the U. S. Army supplied costly radar and camera equipment, and the weather bureau, Davis-Monthan Air Force Base, the forest service, national parks, and the soil conservation service contributed aid that brought the rapid expansion of the research program.

Meanwhile, other research projects were multiplying at the University. Industry began bringing in problems and the signal corps at Fort Huachuca worked closely with campus research scientists. The $160,200 total of sponsored funds reported by the President in 1952 increased to $332,600 in 1953–54. This necessitated new policies and a complete system of reports and records. As a result, Dr. David L. Patrick, Dean of the Graduate College, was placed in charge as co-ordinator of research.

It was obvious that the University had crossed the threshold of a new day—the day of modern scientific research. But very few could have anticipated how surely and swiftly it would move forward.

The flood of students which economists and educators had warned taxpayers and lawmakers to expect was now rolling toward the colleges and universities of the nation, its speed and volume accelerated by public concern over the Soviet Union's technological and scientific achievements.

Fortunately for Arizona, the University administration had been alert, and the Legislature had not ignored the need for more technicians, more teachers, more courses, more classrooms and buildings. However, there were problems, outside the academic and brick-and-mortar fields that could not be immediately solved by money and good intentions, and the biggest extracurricular problem was undoubtedly football.

This most popular of all college sports had been at low ebb when Dr. Harvill took over the presidency in 1951. This caused a difficult public relations' problem that no one wanted to ignore. Coach Bob Winslow resigned, and his replacement was Warren Woodson. The situation improved slightly during the succeeding five seasons. There were three winning years, and the rivalry with Arizona State College at Tempe was settled to the satisfaction of the Wildcat supporters in 1953–54–55. In 1956 the team slumped again, winning only four games and losing six, including a 20 to 0 defeat by ASC.

Once more there was a change of coaches. Woodson resigned and the position was filled by Edward Doherty; but instead of improving, the Wildcats went into a tailspin. Doherty's teams won only one victory in 1957 and three in 1958, losing to Arizona State College at Tempe by heavy scores in both seasons.

The administration responded by revamping its physical education program. Professor Richard Clausen was brought from the University of New Mexico, where he had coached in 1956–58, to fill the office of director of physical education; and James LaRue, assistant coach at Southern Methodist University, was selected to replace Coach Doherty who had resigned.

The new director took on a task that had defeated his predecessors for a decade. Baseball would not be one of his problems, for Coach Frank Sancet had lifted his baseball teams to the ranks of national collegiate champions and had twice barely missed the crown itself. But there was work to be done on basketball as well as football if sport was to come even close to equalling the sudden lustre of the Graduate College and the academic divisions entering on new adventures in science.

Commenting in 1959 on the stature reached by the Graduate College, Dean Herbert D. Rhodes detailed its growth with interesting statistics. He said:

> Since 1954 the increase in graduate enrollment has been almost explosive in character, averaging almost 40 per cent a year. The overall enrollment for graduate studies between 1954–59 accounted for more than ten percent of the total enrollment at the University and the enrollment of the doctoral level increased by 700 percent. Sixteen doctors of philosophy and one doctor of education graduated in the class of 1959.

The capacity of the University to support advanced work is shown in the increased number of graduate offerings. In 1950 the master's degree was offered in forty fields and the doctorate in six. In 1959 the master's degree was offered in sixty-nine fields, the degree of Doctor of Philosophy was made available in twenty-nine, in addition to a doctorate in education and another in musical arts.

To meet this growing load, the administration revised its operations. The duties of the old committee on graduate study, composed of nine members under the dean, were changed and it became the graduate council, charged with administrative duties. A new and larger committee of forty members and the dean now assists the graduate council in an advisory capacity on such subjects as improvement in programs and the development of new ideas and fresh approaches to graduate work.

There was no lack of research projects to which the graduate students could apply themselves, for in 1956–57 sponsored research grants numbered 107, or more than double the total in 1954–55, and the funds made available multiplied more than six-fold, increasing from $318,263 to $1,954,362. Even this record did not stand long, for by June, 1959, the funds allotted to the University for teaching projects as well as scientific research reached $2,215,839. The institution had come a long way since the day when the Board of Regents had received an appropriation of $25,000 and was told to find free land for a campus or return the money to the State.

The new projects, supported entirely or in part by research grants, naturally brought problems, and one of these was the need for more teachers and research workers on the faculty. Speaking at the tenth anniversary of the Southwest Research Institute in 1957 on the growing competition for teaching and research talent, President Harvill said:

> Industry has bid the price up and offered other inducements beyond the present means of colleges and universities.
>
> In May, 1956 the National Science Foundation reported that nearly two-thirds of all the natural scientists were employed by private industry and about one-fifth by government agencies of all kinds leaving one-fifth for higher education. Private industry employed more than 90 per cent of all metallurgists, more than 80 per cent of chemists, more than 60 per cent of earth scientists, more than 50 per cent of physicists and more than 40 per cent of mathematicians.
>
> The plain and evident fact is that the United States today does not provide incentives for large numbers of the best creative minds to go into research and teaching in universities and colleges. . . . The attractions woefully needed are a greatly improved climate of attitudes and understanding that places the proper social value upon the work of teachers and research scholars. . . . It is a shocking fact that teachers in our society do not in 1957 enjoy the regard and esteem in which they were held 50 years ago, nor do they receive as high real income as half a century ago.

Important as were the projects on which University scientists and graduate students were working in 1959 there was one, known as "Interdisciplinary Research on Arid Lands Problems," that attracted world attention.

Science the world over believes that if man is to meet the problems of multiplying population and rising standards of living a way must be found to manage and bring into use the arid acres that now cover thirty per cent of total land area of the globe. Here in America, for example, it is no longer possible for the people of the United States to satisfy the need for more land by encouraging invasion of the fertile domains of its neighbors. The old doctrine of "manifest destiny" that built the West cannot be reinvoked. There is no longer a California, Texas, Nevada, Utah, New Mexico, or Arizona to be settled. There are no more Oregon lands to be seized from the British Crown with the threatening battle cry of "54–40 or Fight."

Whether he likes it or not, southwestern man must stop depleting and learn how to conserve and manage the resources of his arid lands where there is an abundance of sunshine but a shortage of water.

The United Nations recognized the vital need for studies of these lands in 1950 and appointed an advisory committee to plan an international attack on the problem. An international arid land meeting was held in New Mexico in 1955 under the auspices of the American Association for the Advancement of Science, following a meeting of the Association's advisory committee at the University of Arizona.

The University was well equipped for leadership in this field. It had sixty-five years of experience in the study of desert problems, and while it had gathered a vast library of information it was wise enough to know that isolated departments had worked only within the limits of their own fields, whereas the need was for a program in which the sciences would combine their research, using the State of Arizona as their laboratory. The Rockefeller Foundation was impressed by this approach and offered a grant of $208,000 to support a three-year pilot study of the "fundamental biological and physical mechanisms at work in arid regions."

An executive committee was then appointed consisting of directors and professors in the departments, institutes and laboratories of archaeology, biology, climatology, geochronology, the Agriculture Experiment Station, and the U. S. Geological Survey. Dr. A. Richard Kassander, director of the Institute of Atmospheric Physics, was named chairman and described the organization in his first annual report. In this he said in part:

> A monthly arid lands colloquium was organized. All of the personnel of the arid lands project were expected to participate for the general education of each other. The colloquia were to be open to all University people and to the general public.
>
> Personal contacts between researchers in different departments was guaranteed. Because of the formal disciplinary organization no researcher had to feel hesitant to ask a colleague to take time out to discuss a problem. Each scientist felt that he had a stake in the activities of each other group.

This first annual report, together with copies of University publications on arid land problems, and detailed studies of ground water in the state going back as far as 1897, were ready when a committee appointed by Governor Paul Fannin to consider desert problems met on the campus in July, 1959. The speakers were university scientists and their topics were vital and practical. Dr. Emil W. Haury spoke on "The Human Factor in Arid Land Research," and Dean Harold E. Myers of the College of Agriculture discussed "Agricultural Problems, Including Water, in Arid Lands." Other speakers were Dr. Kassander and Dr. John W. Harshbarger, district geologist of the U. S. Geological Survey. The gathering made no black headlines, but it was of great significance that scientists of the generation that had developed nuclear energy and put satellites into orbit were combining their technologies in a disciplined search for the answer to one of man's great needs.

CHAPTER 13

1959–1960

IT SHOULD NOT be considered that the growth of a university can be entirely measured by the new buildings that rise on a spreading campus or the growth of student enrollment. These sometimes reflect only a mass production of mediocrity. They are therefore meaningless in judging today's University unless they are coupled with three other measuring rods: the teaching and research standards, the libraries, and the equipment in modern laboratories.

The days are gone when college laboratories were marked only by test tubes, bunsen burners, scales, graduates, small microscopes, and bottles of acids. These will always be tools, but advanced undergraduate and graduate students who are preparing to enter the wide fields of science at the University now turn to modern mechanical miracle-makers. There is "TRIGA," the University's nuclear reactor that was made possible under a grant of $110,000 from the Atomic Energy Commission, and RAMAC, a computer whose mechanical brain is capable of storing and using 35,000,000 bits of information. Students also become well acquainted with SPACE—special purpose Arizona computer, experimental—which will teach them how computers work, and there are simpler digital and analog computers for use on many problems. Much of this equipment was made possible by $250,000 in grants and gifts from such representatives of private enterprise as the International Business Machines Corporation, General Electric Company, and Beckman Instruments, Incorporated.

Possession of such a computer as RAMAC was only a dream, and so was a laboratory for applied research in 1955 when the electrical engineering department of the College of Engineering received two contracts from the U. S. Army Electronic Proving Ground at Fort Huachuca. But by 1957 contracts for research projects were multiplying so rapidly that President Harvill authorized the new laboratory and provided the faculty and staff for its three components: the computer center, the data reduction center, and the research center.

The aims of the new Applied Research Laboratory were to bring outstanding scientists and engineers to the campus, to provide research problems for students and research services to the faculty, and to formulate a program that would not only assist the U. S. Army at Fort Huachuca but also bring increasing industrial growth to Arizona.

If the University had done nothing between 1954 and 1959 but establish the Institute of Atmospheric Physics, organize the Arid Lands Program, and set up the Applied Research Laboratory, it would have done enough to admit it to the select group of leading research schools. But these activities are far from the total of the University's achievements, and the stockholders of the University—the taxpayers of the state—can find reason for pride in the fact that the institution did not rest, but had the will and the wisdom to push ahead.

The University's next step in 1959 was to organize a supporting teaching facility for the College of Engineering by recognizing the growing science of computer technology within a department known as the Numerical Analysis Laboratory.

In the preface of an illuminating report on scientific and technological research at the University in 1959, President Harvill made it clear in the foreword that the basic policy of the University is and must remain two-fold. Dr. Harvill wrote:

> Never in the history of our nation have people demanded more interpretive knowledge of science and technology than they do at present.
>
> This demand is a product of times in which swiftly moving events bring all of us into frequent personal contact with the effects of scientific and technological advances. The gap between the laboratory and the layman has narrowed rapidly until today the discoveries of science and the applications of engineering have almost immediate impact on the social, economic, and political affairs of everyone.
>
> The exploration of space is an example of this trend. Events of the past two years have made many people aware that our nation has entered a new era, one in which we face an educational challenge particularly apparent in the fields of science and engineering.
>
> The challenge is not merely to educate more and better scientists and engineers but also to give laymen a greater opportunity to understand the concepts, methods, and objectives of science and engineering. Without this understanding, the non-scientist is handicapped in efforts to comprehend

> those fundamentals of science and technology which bear directly upon the future of mankind. In the field of nuclear energy, for example, these are fundamentals which may well determine whether mankind continues to have a future.
>
> A university must direct its efforts toward two major objectives. These are the discovery and organization of knowledge through research and scholarship, and the communication of knowledge through teaching. Clearly, research is an integral part of the educational process. In a broad sense, it is the basis of all knowledge. It follows that the measure of scientific and technological research in an institution of higher education is at the same time an evaluation of how well that institution is meeting the challenge of our times.

If further emphasis is necessary regarding the basic principles underlying teaching and research at the College of Engineering, it will be found in the words of Dean Thomas L. Martin, Jr., who has said:

> Active faculty and graduate student participation in research is the first requirement of a good instructional program . . . teaching and research are fundamentally inseparable.
>
> This philosophy guides all of the University's engineering research and accounts in large measure for an important dual advantage; the University's College of Engineering is Arizona's only accredited engineering school, one which is earning an outstanding record of research accomplishment.

To this the dean adds:

> This is a future world because today's freshman will not approach his maximum productivity as an engineer until about 1971. That will be a very different world from 1959. Engineering education must be based upon a recognition of this fact and the sure knowledge that the incredibly swift advance of science and technology will grow swifter yet.

While noted for the progress it has made in the last few years, the College of Engineering is by no means the only division of the University doing scientific and technological research. There are actually sixteen organized divisions, from agriculture to zoology, which carry on research. The Department of Bacteriology and Medical Technology is one of these, and, like engineering, it is working with the finest modern tools. Through several National Science Foundation grants, including one of $30,200, and state support, the department became the possessor in 1958 of two of the first electron microscopes in Arizona. One instrument is capable of magnification to the extent of 100,000 diameters, while the other magnifies up to 12,000 diameters. Photographic enlargements provide useful magnification up to 200,000 diameters in the more powerful machine and 50,000 in the smaller.

Dr. Kenneth F. Wertman, head of the Department of Bacteriology and Medical Technology, has said of these new instruments, "In our area of bacteriology these instruments are important tools which we will use in our study of human virus and rickettsial diseases. They will be of great value in the training of medical scientists."

The University emphasized the important part it expected to play in medical research through microbiology when it announced that Dr. Ralph W. G. Wycoff would join the faculty in September 1959. At the time he arrived on the campus to begin his work, Dr. Wycoff was a distinguished biochemist and one of the world's leading authorities on electron microscopy. His mission is to supervise the operation of the microscopes, assist other scientists in their use, and teach a graduate course. He also continues to do independent research.

Backed by $35,000 in research grants from the U. S. Public Health Service, Dr. Wertman's department carried on pilot investigations into various major medical research problems that influence human health and happiness. A second grant from the Public Health Service provided $60,000 which enabled Dr. Henry A. Freiser, head of the department of chemistry, to spend three years of research on anti-cancer agents. Dr. Mary E. Caldwell began research on a somewhat similar campaign in pharmacology. She is experimenting with the chemical ingredients of southwestern plants.

Latest of the research plans is the one which the University launched in September 1959 when it announced that the College of Engineering and the Department of Chemical Engineering of the College of Mines had joined forces in an effort to help Arizona business men bid for a share of the billion-dollar plastics industry. The first step was a conference at which representatives of Arizona business and industry met Dr. Donald H. White and Dr. James F. Carley, noted chemical engineers from the University faculty. The purpose of the meeting was to show the business man what plastics can and cannot do and to introduce him to methods of processing and fabrication. This work has been aided by a grant of $11,200 from Arizona Research Foundation, Inc.

While these invasions of new areas are significant proof that the University is determined to meet the challenges of the atomic age, it must be remembered that research is not new on this campus. Ever since it opened its doors, the University of Arizona has been meeting the challenge of new ages. Research began here in agriculture and mining in 1891, and the dollar contribution returned to the people has been many times their investment in higher education.

Other divisions followed agriculture and mining into research work. Among them were anthropology, astronomy, and dendrochronology—all three of which have made such tremendous contributions to human knowledge that scientists the world over have paid them high tributes. Nor can one dismiss the possibility that these sciences may yet make material contributions to the effort to compel desert areas to serve the expanding needs of man.

As the registration increased at the University, new buildings were erected to provide more classrooms, laboratories, offices, and dormitories. One result was that the boundaries of the original forty acres of desert campus became little more than an old stone wall and memories. Following the dedication of the Student Union in 1951, a total of eighteen new buildings went up in nine years, and eight more were remodeled or rebuilt. Twenty of these projects were crowded into the critical years between 1954 and 1960 inclusive.

By 1959 the campus had spread to Speedway Boulevard on the north; crossed Cherry Avenue on the east; crossed Park Avenue on the west; and reached Sixth Street on the south.

The dignified building occupied by the College of Law was now far too small for the classes that were on the way, and the Board of Regents authorized architects to make plans to replace it with a six-story $871,000 structure on the southeast corner of East Fourth Street and Park Avenue. Physics and mathematics had outgrown their quarters in the College of Liberal Arts building by 1958, and the new emphasis given to their sciences meant that by 1960 the space available for them would be wholly inadequate. Room in which to grow was also necessary to the Institute of Atmospheric Physics, and all of these needs called for an appropriation of $1,300,000 for a five-story building to be located on East Fourth Street between Park Avenue and Mountain Avenue.

In addition to the two large buildings, the program included long awaited remodeling and expansion of Steward Observatory that would provide a classroom, laboratory, and offices for the Department of Astronomy. The coming need was also recognized for a University of Arizona observatory on Kitt Peak where the huge national observatory was in process of construction, and provisions were made to move the famous Steward thirty-six-inch reflecting telescope to the peak where it would no longer be handicapped by the night illumination and atmospheric vagaries of the city of Tucson.

The certainty of future expansion of the University in the area between Fourth and Sixth Streets was recognized in plans for a tunnel which would carry utilities from the physical plant at Mountain Avenue and Fourth Street to the law and mathematics-physics buildings.

It was common knowledge now that students would continue to knock on the doors of the University in growing numbers. There were 159,473 students in the public schools of Arizona in the college year of 1953–54. Four years later the public school enrollment was 211,720, which is an increase of thirty per cent. When this gain was coupled with such factors as the rising birthrate, the growing number of vocations that demand the training and discipline presumably acquired at a University, and the social benefits inherent in the possession of a degree, the answer was clear enough to be understood by anyone who could read.

Most state universities and colleges faced the same problems but not to the extent that they existed in Arizona in 1959–60. In 1959 the Valley National Bank estimated that the 1960 census would credit Arizona with a population of 1,300,000. This would be a gain of 550,000 over the census reports of 1950 when the University had approximately 6,000 students, or half as many as it had registered in 1959. Further, as was pointed out by Mrs. Evelyn Jones Kirmse, while she was President of the Board of Regents,

> All reliable forecasts of population trends for this area indicate that the period of unprecedented influx will extend indefinitely. The industrial growth in this area has placed Arizona in the national forefront of population increase.

Superimposed on the problem of providing for the education of the country's youth was a growing obligation to step up adult education, and the University did not push it aside but met it by establishing a new division known as the Division of Continuing Education. Summer sessions, night classes, and extension work were correlated in this division, and placed under the administration of Dean Francis Pendleton Gaines, Jr., a former president of Wofford College and member of the staff of The Fund for the Advancement of Education. Under his guidance the division began to function early in 1959 and before the year was over the results were apparent.

Seven thousand students enrolled for the summer sessions, 100 students attended the summer courses offered by the College of Fine Arts in Prescott, sixty-five studied art at Douglas, and 400 students enrolled for University courses given at a summer school in Guadalajara, Mexico. The annual archaeological classes also reopened at Point of Pines, and the University sponsored a Humanities tour of Europe. In addition to these figures and activities must be added the 2,000 students who enrolled for evening courses on the campus and 1,000 others who took courses in Fort Huachuca, Phoenix, Ajo, Morenci, Benson, Hayden, Douglas, and other localities.

Dr. Gaines summed up the future of Continuing Education at the University of Arizona for this history in one definitive paragraph in which he said:

> The whole problem of adult education, which is the responsibility of this division, is an increasingly important one, and it seems to me that in the years ahead as floods of students come pouring over the shoulders of this University that we must operate economically, we must operate at all hours of the clock, we must operate in the morning, the afternoon, at night. We must have maximum utilization of our facilities, we must extend our services in every possible way. It is necessary to break away from old, traditional, academic patterns of three 50-minute periods, of classes just in the morning and all that sort of thing, and in this era of what we call adult education the greatest future of our State Universities lies ahead.

Leaders in the field of education, including The Carnegie, Rockefeller, and Ford foundations, see higher education as a dual obligation. The first is the obligation to the vast and growing generation of young people who realize that a bachelor's degree is only a stepping stone toward the training they need if they are to be well prepared for the future.

The second obligation is to the adults who find themselves with more and more leisure hours as the average work-week shortens. Thoughtful educators believe that what these adults do with free time can well become one of the crucial social problems in the United States. If the older generations can be persuaded to take an interest in a good book, in languages, art, history, or economics, then the general level of adult education will rise, and may make contributions in many fields.

This is a challenge the University accepted and then added a new teaching tool to help do the job. With the aid of approximately $60,000, a grant from the Ford Foundation, the new Division of Continuing Education began teaching five courses over the University television station, KUAT-TV, in September 1959. Further to develop television teaching, The National Educational Television and Radio Center made a grant of $40,000 for an audio-visual recorder which tapes both the classroom picture and the voice of the teacher. This tape, like motion picture film, may be used repeatedly and may be lent to any number of public schools.

Dr. Gaines, who is an ardent advocate of the use of television as an educational technique, believes that it will open a completely new field of co-operation with the high schools of Arizona. He plans audio-visual tapes that will make lectures and classroom teaching of various subjects available to the high schools. He has had no fear for the future of TV teaching, and of this he said:

> I think it will be a revolutionary method, but I don't share the traditional academic fear that television or radio will replace the classroom instructional method. I agree with the foundations which feel that we must reach out for persons we have never touched before in the area of education and that we must operate economically and utilize fully all our resources. The dialectic method of teaching will never be replaced by any mechanical device, but in large discussion classes on the freshman and sophomore level there is no reason why a great teacher cannot lecture to 1,000 students by means of television as effectively as he lectures to 50 or more in a large classroom.

Another advancement introduced with the opening of the 1959–60 University year was the arrangement of sequences of degree-granting courses that could be taken at night. While there had always been many courses offered to night-school students, it had never before been possible to get a master's degree wholly at night. It was expected that this change would be of great value to young executives and teachers who need and want higher education but cannot leave their work to attend daytime classes.

These imaginative advances are characteristic of the educational programs at the University, which is constantly reaching out for new ways to serve. The establishment of a wildlife research unit on the campus in 1951 is a case in point. Studies and research there lead to both B.S. and M.S. degrees, and graduates are in demand by state and government wildlife conservation agencies.

No one can now doubt the great value of the School of Nursing which was organized in 1957. A division of the College of Liberal Arts, the school provided four-year courses for high-school graduates and two-and-one-half-year courses for registered nurses. Both lead to the degree of Bachelor of Science in nursing. Simultaneously with the opening of the School of Nursing, the University announced a new medical technology program in the Department of Bacteriology.

With the appointment of Sidney W. Little as Dean of the College of Fine Arts in 1958, President Harvill recommended and the Board of Regents created a department of architecture. In speaking of the service to be rendered by this department, which he heads as director, Dean Little said:

> There are special problems of architecture that are found only in semi-arid regions and those who plan a future as architects should be acquainted with weather conditions, solar energy, radiation and air conditioning.
>
> We hope to train our students so that they will be able to plan and build the type of homes that will be going up in this area in 1970.

The courses in architecture offered the first year were greeted by eighty-six students, and the full program was underway by 1960 with a curriculum that included natural science, climatology, cultural anthropology, and special electives in sociology.

Total enrollment in 1958–59 of students in residence, including those in night classes, was 13,050, or better than a ten per cent gain over the previous year. Every state in the nation, the District of Columbia, and fifty-three foreign nations were represented in the regular enrollment. The administration, however, made no effort to drive for a marked gain in 1959–60; in fact it took the opposite course.

Past practice had been to admit all graduates from Arizona high schools to the three state institutions of higher learning, irrespective of their grades; but in 1959 the rules for admission were changed, and only those students whose scholarship placed them in the upper three-fourths of their class were accepted. To avoid injustices, however, tests and interviews were provided as additional measures of ability and motivation of students being considered for admission.

At the same time, undergraduates were informed they must have a grade average of 3.0 to qualify for graduation. The former over-all average had been 3.2.

These were not isolated instances but the reflection of a general policy in the direction of improving standards.

President Harvill's annual report on the University for 1958–59 made this policy very clear. He said in part:

> A source of real academic strength is reflected in the curricula of the University and, more significantly, in the philosophy from which these curricula evolved. The University has a tradition from which it has not departed in a year when pressures for such departures were widespread. The trend towards specialization of curricula solely to prepare students in the detailed operations of a great many modern occupations is not viewed with favor at the University of Arizona. This is not to say that specialization in many fields does not exist. The complexities of contemporary life demand specialists, and the University takes pride in the qualifications of graduates of its professional schools. In all cases, however, emphasis is upon thorough knowledge of fundamental principles underlying but not necessarily peculiar to a particular field of specialization. The emphasis remains upon understanding and only secondarily upon the acquisition of special skills. We assume the student will continue to learn after leaving the University and that the technique can be acquired more easily than can the fundamentals.

Continuing, the President pointed out:

> The academic strength of an institution of higher education cannot be assessed accurately without considering the degree to which its teaching-research programs are interrelated and complementary. We cannot in good conscience isolate and view the progress of one college or department without relating it to that of other component parts of the institution. If our goal is education in the classic sense—greater knowledge of all things—as it is at the University of Arizona, then we should not lose sight of the fact that expediency and the unrelated activities it produces have no place in such academic surroundings.

University strength during this period may be observed in the individual registrations in the College of Liberal Arts in English, history, philosophy, psychology, political science, French, German, Spanish, and the general humanities, which increased from 12,272 in 1954 to 16,813 in 1959; this was a gain of approximately 27 per cent. Equally impressive was the increase in the number of courses catalogued and taught in the Liberal Arts College. In 1951–52 there were 311 courses offered in twenty fields, while in 1959 559 courses were available in twenty-three fields.

This growth in the curricula included new special fields in mathematics, entomology, medical technology, nursing, and oriental studies. Ph.D. degrees were also offered in psychology and zoology, and more programs established in the new graduate fields.

There are times when totals are more impressive than percentages and this is true of the student credit hours, because the figures rose from 76,352 hours in 1954–55 to 108,514 in 1958–59.

As is always the case, the College of Liberal Arts for 1959–60 was the largest college on campus with an enrollment of 3,907. The College of Business and Public Administration was second, the College of Engineering was third, and the Graduate College advanced to fourth place.

Such educators as Dr. Ralph W. G. Wyckoff, Dr. Francis P. Gaines, and Dr. Reuben Gilbert Gustafson, formerly Chancellor of the University of Nebraska, vice-President and Dean of Faculties at the University of Chicago, and President of the University of Colorado joined the University in 1959, greatly strengthening the faculty in their particular fields. President Harvill called attention to this in his report and added that as a whole the faculty was young and dynamic and had been a tremendous factor in the progress of the educational program. In the estimation of the President the increase in salaries between 1951 and 1960 was inadequate. Feeling the future of higher education in Arizona was at stake he made his plea an urgent one. He said:

> I wish to speak frankly on a subject that represents the only retarded element in an otherwise progressive and fruitful year. Despite the encouraging comparative picture presented by our educational and research programs, the University of Arizona does not, in my opinion, measure up to comparable publicly-supported institutions elsewhere with respect to faculty salaries. During the past year the University experienced the greatest difficulty in its history in recruiting faculty personnel.
>
> I hope that the Board of Regents may give primary consideration during the coming year to the urgent needs for increasing salaries.

In this report on salaries the President was re-emphasizing what he had told the Board of Regents in April of 1959 when he said in part:

> It is already clear that unless a very drastic change is made in the points of view of those responsible for higher education, the zeal to take care of increased numbers will cause a lack of support and a consequent diminution in the quality of education. . . . In brief, the State faces a problem of advancing sufficient funds to be competitive with other states in quality of educational effort in the institutions of higher learning. It would be far better to suffer smaller enrollments than to sacrifice quality. Students of quality and industry ought to come first if the opportunity cannot be offered to all. . . .
>
> The state cannot afford to determine the allocation of the amount of expenditure necessary for higher education on the basis of number of students enrolled, without reference to whether these students are part-time or full-time students; undergraduate or graduate students; students taking general courses requiring little capital equipment and highly specialized teaching talent or students pursuing programs involving large outlays of specialized capital equipment and scarce critical talent. Allocation of funds should reflect more adequately the proper weighting of these factors.

In closing the President declared that:

> It is just as important that Arizona maintain the same competitive level in its system of higher education as it does in all other fields of activity. . . .

The President spoke highly in his report of the reputations achieved in the fields of anthropology, archaeology, mining, geology, and engineering and praised the progress in agriculture. The records for the College of Agriculture in 1959 showed that the thirteen University State farms covered 2,144 acres. Three of these farms were near Tempe and Mesa, three at Yuma, one at Safford, one at Marana, and another was near Oracle Junction. In addition there was a highway farm at Casa Grande, a Campbell Avenue farm at Tucson, and a dairy research farm on the Crocker tract north of Tucson. The types of branch research stations on these farms covered citrus, cotton, dairy farming, poultry, beef and sheep breeding, field crops and vegetable plant pathology, dairy research, irrigation, and ranch research. There were approximately thirty buildings and sixty men involved.

The chart on page 256 shows the type of research and the location of the farm and acreage involved as of 1959–60:

In addition to this widespread experimental work, the College of Agriculture covers the fourteen counties with twenty-six county agents and ten assistants, and twelve home demonstration agents with five assistants.

One of the newer colleges, but one highly esteemed professionally, is the College of Pharmacy. Among its many other activities were the nineteen poison-control centers, maintained in co-operation with the Arizona Medical Association and the Arizona Pharmaceutical Association, and supplying information on poison control to twenty-four hospitals. This public service reaches Ajo, Douglas, Flagstaff, Grand Canyon, Globe, Holbrook, Kingman, McNary, Mesa, Miami, Nogales, Phoenix, Prescott, Safford, Tucson, Wickenburg, Winslow, and Yuma.

A great deal can be learned by reading the biennial catalog for 1959–60. As a matter of fact it is one of the greatest testimonials that could be paid to the University preparing to enter the last quarter of its first century. In 452 pages the institution presented its academic and scientific teaching programs, its research work that benefits the State, the nation, and the world, and finally its contributions to the taxpayers who support it. The full story is too long to be told in narrative form, and tables have a limited value.

For a summary of the work that will be done in 1959–60, it is probably sufficient if these paragraphs from the official announcement are repeated:

> The organizational changes include the grouping of some existing and new courses to provide seven new undergraduate majors in the fields of watershed management, geography, Oriental studies, fisheries management, aerospace engineering, engineering mathematics, and engineering physics.
>
> Reflecting the growth of course offerings, student enrollment and size of faculty, five new departments have been created for existing academic areas, to aid in the administration of work in these fields. The former department of history and political science will become two departments,

TYPE OF RESEARCH	*FARM*	*ACREAGE*
Citrus	Citrus Research Farm (Tempe)	40
Field and vegetable crops research	Mesa Farm	160
Cotton	Cotton Research Farm (Tempe)	265
Field and vegetable crops and studies in irrigation	Yuma Valley Farm	160
Citrus	Yuma Citrus Farm Sturges Land	113
Field crops and livestock feeding	Gila Project Farm Yuma Mesa	80
Field and vegetable crops and nuts	Safford Farm	63
Field crops (anticipating livestock and field crops)	Marana Farm	228
Beef and sheep, breeding, feeding, field crops, plant pathology studies and irrigation	Campbell Avenue Farm (North Tucson)	80
Dairying	Dairy Farm (Ewing) (North of Tucson)	70
Poultry, livestock and field crops	Casa Grande Highway Farm	75
New dairy research experiments	Crocker Tract (North of Tucson)	10
Range research	Page Ranch (Northeast of Oracle Junction)	640
Total		2,144

> with political science falling under a new department of government, and history courses only being assigned to the department of history.
>
> The other four new departments include: accounting and marketing, both formerly in the department of business administration; watershed management; and nuclear engineering, which will offer a program for graduate students only.
>
> Eight new options open to students working for existing master's degrees include: aero-space engineering, under the department of mechanical engineering; engineering mechanics, under civil engineering; chemical engineering; metallurgy; marketing; plant breeding; watershed management; and government, which replaces the former option in political science.

The catalogue revealed that the members of the voting faculty had risen to 948 and that the entire faculty and staff totaled 1,165. An interesting note here is that faculty and staff now outnumber the total student enrollment of 1919–20.

Lists of loans, scholarships, and honors available to students filled twenty-four pages, and President Harvill referred to the fact that only a few years ago a detailed list would have taken but a few typewritten pages whereas in 1959 such a list would have doubled the size of his entire annual report.

One of the most significant sections of the President's report reflected the growth of confidence and respect among individuals, groups, business enterprises, agencies, foundations, and government. In the last academic year such donors contributed a total of $2,758,963.97. Of this sum $2,245,839.33 was for research grants and contracts. Gifts for scholarships amounted to $200,956.47, and miscellaneous gifts and grants reached the high figure of $312,168.17.

Broad as the coverage of the annual report was, there were effects that could not be assessed and yet are important in a general history of the University. Year by year the President's report makes note of new buildings, their purpose and costs. But this chapter of history is dealing with almost a decade rather than a single year, and so a realization of the extent of the building program carried on by the present administration can be found only by going back to 1951. The Student Union, power plant, and addition to the library belong in this period, although they were inaugurated by President McCormick. The "brick and mortar" period of the Harvill administration actually covered the

BUILDING	*YEAR*	*APPROXIMATE COST*
Student Union	1951	$1,158,000
Power Plant	1951	520,000
Library Addition	1951	246,000
Physical Plant Shop	1952	157,000
Business and Public Administration	1952	876,000
Home Management	1953	87,000
Administration Addition	1953	130,000
Bookstore	1953	111,000
Coconino Dormitory	1954	472,000
General Stores and Garage	1955	150,000
Engineering Annex Remodeling	1955	51,000
Graham-Greenlee Dormitory	1955	1,000,000
Art and Drama	1955	823,000
Engineering Annex, Park Avenue	1956	69,000
Dairy Lab Remodeling	1956	43,000
Biological Sciences	1956	1,167,000
Music	1956	195,000
Apache-Santa Cruz Dormitory	1957	900,000
Engineering East Wing & Aero	1957	394,000
Remodeling Engineering	1958	254,000
Biological Sciences—Animal Quarters	1958	107,000
Huachuca-Kaibab Dormitory	1958	1,016,000
Remodeling Education	1958	231,000
Geology	1958	1,153,000
Manzanita-Mohave Dormitory	1958	1,204,000
Home Economics	1959	731,000
Law (new)	1959	831,000
Physics-Mathematics (new)	1959	1,276,000
Total		*$15,352,000*

years 1952–1960 and constituted a program that had involved the spending of approximately $15,350,000 for additions, remodelings, and new buildings. One cannot devote space to full descriptions of the twenty-eight major projects, but they should be noted here for the purposes of historical reference. The list, costs, and purposes appear on page 258.

It has been a long time since Governor Goodwin told the First Territorial Legislature in 1864 that "self-government and education are inseparable" and his Legislature authorized a University and a Board of Regents.

Higher education, however, was not to be achieved easily. There were dark and perilous days when the pioneers fought for their lives. Poverty ruled a pioneer land embittered by the desertion of the federal government. Education had to climb a steep and rugged path, fighting always to overcome the understandable apathy of a people who had all they could do to keep alive. Then the mountains began to give up their store of treasures, irrigation projects made the desert bloom, cities opened small schools, and finally, in 1885, the Legislature completed the work Governor Goodwin had hoped to do and instituted the University of Arizona.

This would not mean, however, that the immediate following years would be easy. Sixteen presidents, scores of Regents, and thousands of faculty and staff members have struggled to make the University what it is, guarding it as one of the state's most precious assets.

The next quarter-century will present a tremendous challenge. But remembering the past seventy-five years of dedication and progress, one cannot fail to believe that when the University celebrates its centennial, the flame will be burning with growing brilliance in the Lamp in the Desert.

HOW THE UNIVERSITY GREW

Academic Year	Faculty	Students	Books	Buildings
1891–1892	6	32		1
1892–1893	12	38		1
1893–1894	9	57		5
1894–1895	9	47		9
1895–1896	14	100	2,000	9
1896–1897	14	151	2,600	10
1897–1898	15	155	3,100	12
1898–1899	17	133	3,600	12
1899–1900	15	161	5,000	13
1900–1901	16	225	6,000	14
1901–1902	16	215	7,000	14
1902–1903	19	198	7,500	14
1903–1904	22	204	7,240	15
1904–1905	22	193	8,128	16
1905–1906	25	226	8,865	16
1906–1907	26	215	9,640	16
1907–1908	26	237	10,696	16
1908–1909	28	201	12,880	16
1909–1910	32	222	14,260	17
1910–1911	30	195	15,893	17
1911–1912	37	301	17,583	17
1912–1913	37	254	19,131	18
1913–1914	40	249	21,160	18
1914–1915	47	308	22,359	18
1915–1916	70	463	24,045	19
1916–1917	70	519	27,060	17
1917–1918	84	474	28,431	18
1918–1919	78	705	30,214	20
1919–1920	86	1,088	33,363	20
1920–1921	95	1,171	34,325	21
1921–1922	107	1,369	37,867	21
1922–1923	116	1,456	43,223	21
1923–1924	122	1,578	49,129	21
1924–1925	130	1,617	53,934	21
1925–1926	131	1,766	57,609	23
1926–1927	137	1,843	61,493	23
1927–1928	157	2,033	65,871	23

ACADEMIC YEAR	FACULTY	STUDENTS	BOOKS	BUILDINGS
1928–1929	170	2,261	68,706	23
1929–1930	175	2,164	74,457	24
1930–1931	182	2,164	78,978	24
1931–1932	179	2,272	85,097	24
1932–1933	182	2,170	89,848	24
1933–1934	166	2,291	94,134	24
1934–1935	172	2,620	99,254	24
1935–1936	247	2,735	108,517	31
1936–1937	224	2,743	114,292	32
1937–1938	267	2,827	120,039	32
1938–1939	274	2,873	125,339	32
1939–1940	275	2,906	131,365	34
1940–1941	281	2,922	138,804	35
1941–1942	284	2,789	148,204	35
1942–1943	286	2,523	156,618	35
1943–1944	279	1,860	164,530	35
1944–1945	258	2,239	174,591	35
1945–1946	279	3,445	182,042	38
1946–1947	365	5,062	189,247	38
1947–1948	382	5,676	195,909	40
1948–1949	390	6,044	205,496	43
1949–1950	445	6,502	214,570	45
1950–1951	468	6,227	221,559	46
1951–1952	467	5,588	229,226	47
1952–1953	498	5,568	237,974	49
1953–1954	533	5,843	246,758	50
1954–1955	557	6,435	255,118	50
1955–1956	695	7,332 *	264,232	55
1956–1957	827	8,186 *	271,005	58
1957–1958	913	11,545 *	281,038	58
1958–1959	948 †	13,058 *	296,106	59

Statistics between 1891 and 1934–1935 are from the records of Librarian Estelle Lutrell. After that date the figures are from the office of the President, the Director of Buildings and Grounds, and annual library reports.

* Complete on-campus enrollment including night classes.

† Totals represent the voting faculty.

SUMMARY OF EARNED DEGREES CONFERRED

YEAR	TOTAL DEGREES			BACHELOR'S			MASTER'S			PROFESSIONAL			JURIS DOCTOR			PH.D. & ED.D.		
	M	W	T	M	W	T	M	W	T	M	W	T	M	W	T	M	W	T
1895	1	2	3	1	2	3												
1896																		
1897	3	1	4	2	1	3				1	1							
1898	2	2	4	2	2	4												
1899	1		1	1		1												
1900	2	2	4	2	2	4												
1901	2	1	3	2	1	3												
1902	6	3	9	6	3	9												
1903	8	1	9	6	1	7	2		2									
1904	4	1	5	4	1	5												
1905		1	1		1	1												
1906	6	3	9	5	3	8	1		1									
1907	4	2	6	3	2	5				1	1							
1908	5		5	5		5												
1909	3	4	7	3	4	7												
1910	9	1	10	9	1	10												
1911	6	5	11	5	5	10	1	1										
1912	10	4	14	9	3	12	1	1	2									
1913	13	4	17	13	4	17												
1914	6	2	8	5	2	7	1		1									
1915	12	7	19	11	7	18	1		1									
1916	33	14	47	26	13	39	7	1	8									
1917	34	13	47	33	11	44	1	2	3									
1918	25	16	41	23	14	37	2	2	4									
1919	25	31	56	22	30	52	3	1	4									
1920	37	25	62	33	25	58	3		3			1		1				

1921	54	29	83	49	26	75	1	3	4	1	1	3		3				
1922	81	52	133	64	46	110	14	6	20				2		2	1		1
1923	86	53	139	77	47	124	6	6	12	2		2	1		1			
1924	129	85	214	115	80	195	10	5	15	2		2	1		1	1		1
1925	134	76	210	116	72	188	16	3	19	2		2		1	1			
1926	148	93	241	124	86	210	21	7	28	1		1	2		2			
1927	134	97	231	111	86	197	17	11	28	5		5				1		1
1928	125	119	244	113	107	220	11	12	23	1		1						
1929	149	115	264	126	107	233	20	8	28	2		2	1		1			
1930	159	126	285	134	109	243	18	16	34	4	1	5	3		3			
1931	178	125	303	151	113	264	19	12	31	3		3	4		4	1		1
1932	188	145	333	151	121	272	28	24	52	5		5	4		4			
1933	203	136	339	146	109	255	45	27	72	3		3	7		7	2		2
1934	182	130	312	142	113	255	31	17	48	2		2	4		4	3		3
1935	228	139	367	180	124	304	39	14	53	4		4	4		4	1	1	2
1936	202	167	369	155	147	302	40	20	60	3	3	1	1					
1937	213	152	365	170	124	294	39	28	67	3		3				1		1
1938	250	132	382	198	111	309	43	21	64	5		5	1		1	3		3
1939	282	163	445	221	142	363	51	21	72	5		5	4		4	1		1
1940	294	166	460	237	145	382	55	21	76							2	2	
1941	279	167	446	215	149	364	60	18	78				1		1	3		3
1942	206	175	381	171	153	324	34	22	56							1		1
1943	134	154	288	123	140	263	10	14	24							1		1
1944	70	164	234	57	148	205	9	16	25	3		3				1		1
1945	69	170	239	57	158	215	9	12	21	2		2				1		1
1946	113	217	330	95	202	297	14	14	28	1		1	1		1	2	1	3
1947	283	245	528	248	233	481	25	12	37	5		5	1		1	4		4
1948	428	247	675	384	225	609	40	21	61	3		3				1	1	2
1949	547	287	834	496	269	765	43	18	61	2		2				6		6
1950	818	274	1092	764	253	1017	51	21	72	1		1				2		2
1951	861	280	1141	772	257	1029	84	23	107	3		3				2		2
1952	696	290	986	614	274	888	79	16	95	2		2				1		1
1953	646	282	928	525	252	777	115	30	145	3		3				3		3
1954	649	312	961	529	262	791	112	50	162	6		6				2		2
1955	647	295	942	520	250	770	113	45	158	7		7				7		7
1956	723	287	1010	591	249	840	117	38	155	7		7				8		8

YEAR	TOTAL DEGREES			BACHELOR'S			MASTER'S			PROFESSIONAL			JURIS DOCTOR			PH.D. & ED.D.		
	M	W	T	M	W	T	M	W	T	M	W	T	M	W	T	M	W	T
1957	794	331	1125	653	292	945	129	38	167	8		8				4	1	5
1958	933	399	1332	751	350	1101	168	49	217	7		7				7		7
1959	959	407	1366	792	352	1144	147	54	201	4		4				16*	1†	17**
GRAND TOTAL	13531	7428	20959	11368	6621	17898	1905	800	2705	120	1	121	45	1	46	90	5	95

* Includes 2 Ed.D.

† Ed.D.

** Includes 3 Ed.D.

ARIZONA GOVERNORS

	TERRITORIAL
1863–66	John N. Goodwin
1866–69	Richard C. McCormick
1869–77	Anson P. K. Safford
1877–78	John Philo Hoyt
1878–82	John Charles Fremont
1882–85	F. A. Tritle
1885–89	C. M. Zulich
1889–90	Lewis Wolfley
1890–92	John N. Irwin
1892–93	Nathan O. Murphy
1893–96	Louis C. Hughes
1896–97	B. J. Franklin
1897–98	M. H. McCord
1898–1902	Nathan O. Murphy
1902–05	A. O. Brodie
1905–09	Joseph H. Kibbey
1909–12	Richard E. Sloan
	STATE
1912–19	G. W. P. Hunt
1919–23	Thomas E. Campbell
1923–29	G. W. P. Hunt
1929–31	John C. Phillips
1931–33	G. W. P. Hunt
1933–37	B. B. Moeur
1937–39	R. S. Stanford
1939–41	R. T. Jones
1941–48	Sidney P. Osborn
1948–51	Dan E. Garvey
1951–55	Howard Pyle
1955–59	Ernest W. McFarland
1959 ——	Paul J. Fannin

UNIVERSITY PRESIDENTS

Theodore B. Comstock	1893–95
Howard Billman	1895–97
Millard Mayhew Parker	1897–1901
Frank Yale Adams	1901–03
Kendric C. Babcock	1903–10
Andrew Ellicott Douglass	December 20, 1910–March 10, 1911
Arthur Herbert Wilde	1911–1914
Rufus Berhard von KleinSmid	1914–21
Francis Cummins Lockwood	April 22, 1922–September 1, 1922
Cloyd Heck Marvin	1922–27
Byron Cummings	February 1, 1927–June 30, 1928
Homer LeRoy Shantz	1928–36
Paul Steere Burgess	1936–37
Alfred Atkinson	1937–47
James Byron McCormick	1947–51
Richard Anderson Harvill	1951 ——

UNIVERSITY VICE-PRESIDENTS

Robert Logan Nugent, Vice-President, 1947–1957
Robert Logan Nugent, Executive Vice-President, 1957
David Lyal Patrick, Vice-President for Academic Affairs, 1957
Norman Sterling Hull, Vice-President for Business Affairs, 1957–1959

MEMBERS OF THE BOARD OF REGENTS

(From the University of Arizona Register)

Babbitt, John G.	January 1, 1949–January 5, 1957
Bayless, Charles H.	October 24, 1904–February 10, 1910
Beck, Florence E.	June 12, 1945–January 3, 1947
Best, M. O.	January 9, 1939–January 3, 1947
*Billman, Howard	January 7, 1895–December 9, 1897
Bimson, Walter R.	February 6, 1947–January 1, 1955
Boysen, Mrs. Vivian Lahti	January, 1959 ——
Bradford, Elwood W.	February 24, 1957 ——
Bridge, George M.	January 31, 1927–December 28, 1932
Briscoe, James W.	March 12, 1945–May 15, 1945
*Brodie, Alexander O.	July 21, 1902–1905
†Brooks, M. L.	January 20, 1949–January, 1955 February 24, 1957–January, 1959
Brown, Herbert	May 8, 1889–October 10, 1889
Bruce, Charles M.	October 20, 1893–June 5, 1894
Bryan, William Jennings, Jr.	December 10, 1914–September 21, 1920
Campbell, John H.	March 26, 1919–September 13, 1926
*Campbell, Thomas E.	January 29, 1919–December 21, 1922
†Case, Charles O.	March 11, 1912–March 26, 1919 June 18, 1919–September 21, 1920 February 6, 1923–May 13, 1933
Chapman, J. H.	September 17, 1918–December 10, 1918
†Cheyney, George W.	January 11, 1890–1893
Compton, James G.	March 26, 1919–December 21, 1922
Corrigan, John J.	April 4, 1923–January, 1927
Crawford, Albert M.	April 4, 1935–January 4, 1943
Crider, Frank J.	January 31, 1927–April 4, 1935

* Governor
† Superintendent of Public Instruction

†Dalton, Thomas E.	1896–97
DeConcini, Evo	February 3, 1941–September 1, 1941
†Dick, W. W.	1959 ——
Drachman, Mose	September 9, 1921–April 4, 1923
Drake, Charles R.	April 1, 1899–March 21, 1901
Duffy, Frank	May 8, 1914–March 12, 1917
Egan, Mark J.	September 5, 1903–August 25, 1904
Ellinwood, E. E.	April 4, 1923–January, 1927
	May 13, 1933–January 6, 1941
Ellsworth, W. Ronald	February 8, 1943–January 8, 1951
*Fannin, Paul J.	January, 1959 ——
Fenner, Hiram W.	April 1, 1899–March 21, 1901
Fitch, Ferris S.	October 20, 1902–June 26, 1903
Finn, John	August 21, 1917–December 12, 1917
Ford, Rochester	May 1, 1893–April 1, 1895
*Franklin, Benjamin J.	1895–96; 1896–97
Franklin, Selim M.	July 7, 1888–August 5, 1897
Freeman, Merrill P.	December 3, 1889–October 19, 1894
Gardiner, John	March 30, 1891–March 11, 1912
*Garvey, Dan E.	July 30, 1948–January, 1951
Gentry, Martin	August 9, 1937–January, 1943
Goodwin, H. F.	October 10, 1899–March 4, 1891
Goodwin, Mrs. Garfield A.	June 12, 1945–January 3, 1947
Greenway, John C.	April 10, 911–January 10, 1912
Greer, Mrs. Joseph M.	February 3, 1941–January 20, 1949
Grossetta, Anthony V.	April 5, 1901–October 20, 1902
	June 5, 1907–May 18, 1911
Handy, John C.	November 27, 1886–November, 1888
†Harkins, Clifton L.	January 8, 1955–January 5, 1957
Heard, Dwight B.	September 9, 1921–April 4, 1923

* Governor
† Superintendent of Public Instruction

†Hendrix, Herman E.	1933–41
Hereford, Frank H.	March 11, 1912–August 15, 1917
Herring, William	September 6, 1898–October 6, 1902
Hilzinger, J. George	January 20, 1949–January 5, 1957
Hodges, Michael B.	April 4, 1895–July 15, 1896
Hodgson, Joseph P.	November 9, 1917–January 10, 1918
Houston, Clarence E.	September 8, 1941–January 29, 1949
Houston, Elbert T.	March 30, 1937–October, 1940
Hudson, Estmer W.	September 21, 1920–January 22, 1925
Hughes, John T.	January 10, 1918–January 29, 1919
*Hughes, Louis C.	1893–96
———	September, 1897–September, 1898 (Chancellor)
Hughes, Samuel	January 27, 1891–March 30, 1891
*Hunt, George W. P.	1911–12 through 1915–16 1923–24 through 1928–29 1931 through 1933
Jacobs, John M.	January 8, 1951–January, 1959
Jacome, Alexander G.	February 11, 1952 ——
Johns, Anthony A.	January 22, 1925–November 21, 1925
Johnson, Royal A.	May 8, 1889–November 12, 1889
*Jones, Robert T.	1939 through 1941
Joyner, W. C.	January 28, 1929–January 11, 1932
Kempf, Louis R.	January 31, 1927–November 10, 1928
Kennedy, Roderick D.	April 21, 1914–April 20, 1917
*Kibbey, Joseph H.	1904–05 through 1908–09
Kirkpatrick, Roy	June 2, 1925–December 28, 1932
Kirmse, Mrs. Evelyn Jones	January 8, 1951–January, 1959
Klemmedson, Linne D.	September 25, 1947–December 4, 1948
Knapp, Cleon T.	November 30, 1940–January 14, 1952
Laney, Lynn M.	June 12, 1945 ——
Layton, Charles M.	April 4, 1923–November, 1933
†Layton, N. G.	1901–02 1903 through 1905

* Governor
† Superintendent of Public Instruction

†Long, R. L.	1898 through 1901
	1905 through 1908
Mansfeld (Mansfield), Jacob S.	November 27, 1886–December 31, 1887
Marsh, Theodora	April 4, 1923–April 18, 1936
Marshall, Louise F.	September 17, 1918–March 26, 1919
Martin, Jack B.	April 4, 1935–January 3, 1947
Martin, John H.	April 5, 1897–March 20, 1899
Mathews, William R.	March 31, 1950 ——
McCluskey, Henry S.	January 28, 1918–January 10, 1919
	January 28, 1929–January 9, 1939
*McCord, Myron H.	1897–98
*McFarland, Ernest W.	1955–59
Millar, Robert T.	May 8, 1889–March 4, 1891
Miller, Halbert W.	May 13, 1933–January, 1941
Miller, O. D.	1959 ——
*Moeur, Benjamin B.	1933–34 through 1936–37
Monk, Edward R.	July 20, 1895–March 20, 1897
†Moore, Kirke T.	April 10, 1909–March 11, 1912
**Morford, N. A.	1892–93
Morgan, Joseph H.	February 8, 1943–January 15, 1945
Morris, Samuel H.	February 8, 1943–June 12, 1945
	1955 ——
*Murphy, Nathan Oakes	1898–1901
Murphy, W. J.	May 18, 1911–March 11, 1912
†Netherton, F. J.	February 5, 1894–September, 1897
Orme, John B.	September 20, 1917–January 22, 1918
Ormsby, John M.	April 22, 1889–July 1, 1890
	May 4, 1892–April 24, 1893
	October 20, 1902–May 5, 1905
*Osborn, Sidney P.	February 3, 1941–May 25, 1948

* Governor
† Superintendent of Public Instruction
** Territorial Secretary

Pattee, Samuel L.	March 29, 1934–February 28, 1935
* Phillips, John C.	1929–31
Pulliam, Nolan D.	February 6, 1947–July 26, 1947
*Pyle, Howard	1951–55
Randolph, Epes	March 26, 1919–September 9, 1921
Rasmessen, Rudolph	May 8, 1914–September 17, 1918
Ricketts, Lewis D.	March 30, 1912–23
†Ring, E. D.	February 3, 1941–January 3, 1947
Riordan, Timothy A.	March 26, 1919–April 4, 1923
Roberts, Madge	January 15, 1918–September 17, 1918
Roskruge, George J.	June 18, 1887–April 22, 1889
Samaniego, M. G.	November 27, 1886–May 13, 1889
	September 18, 1896–October 1, 1897
Scarlett, William J.	April 14, 1914–January 29, 1919
	March 26, 1919–May 21, 1921
Scott, John M.	June 12, 1945–February 27, 1950
†Shewman, Albert P.	1897–98
*Sloan, Richard T.	May 10, 1910–March 11, 1912
*Stanford, R. C.	1937–39
Stevenson, William W.	June 12, 1945–January 3, 1947
Stone, William R.	June 2, 1890
Strauss, Charles M.	November 27, 1886–January 31, 1889
Sweek, W. O.	February 23, 1932–June 1, 1937
Talbot, Walter	May 5, 1905–May 7, 1907
Tally, Robert E.	January 31, 1927–December 13, 1936
Tenney, Herbert B.	May 1, 1893–July 20, 1895
	April 1, 1899–October 20, 1902
Titcomb, Edward	August 21, 1917–January 15, 1918
†Toles, Elsie	February 24, 1921–December 21, 1922
Van Dyke, Cleve	April 4, 1923–January 28, 1929

* Governor
† Superintendent of Public Instruction

Waters, Albert L.	March 11, 1912–May 8, 1914
Wells, Edmund W.	January 29, 1919–January 22, 1925
Westover, William H.	April 4, 1935–January 4, 1943
Wheatly, Logan W.	March 11, 1912–December 10, 1915
White, Bettie	January 22, 1916–March 26, 1919
Whitmore, W. V.	October 1, 1897–March 20, 1899
	May 8, 1914–July 10, 1918
Wood, J. S.	June 18, 1887–July 1, 1889
Zabriskie, James A.	April 5, 1901–April 15, 1903

UNIVERSITY OF ARIZONA DEANS

THE COLLEGE OF AGRICULTURE

Robert Humphrey Forbes, 1914–1918
Daniel Webster Working, 1918–1922
John James Thornber, 1922–1928
Elmer Darwin Ball, 1928–1931
Paul Steere Burgess, 1931–1936
Ralph Sams Hawkins, 1936–1937 *
Paul Steere Burgess, 1937–1938
Ralph Sams Hawkins, 1938–1939 *
Paul Steere Burgess, 1939–1951
Ralph Sams Hawkins, 1951–1952 *
Phil S. Eckert, 1952–1955
Ralph Sams Hawkins, 1955–1958 *
Harold Edwin Myers, 1956

THE COLLEGE OF BUSINESS AND PUBLIC ADMINISTRATION

Elmer Jay Brown, 1943–1957
Shaw Livermore, 1957

THE COLLEGE OF EDUCATION

James Willis Clarson, Jr. 1927–1950
Oliver Kelleam Garretson, 1950–1959
Curtis Bradford Merritt, 1959 *

THE COLLEGE OF ENGINEERING

Gurdon Montague Butler, 1940–1951
John Callaway Park, 1951–1958
Thomas Lyle Martin, Jr., 1958

THE COLLEGE OF FINE ARTS

Charles Fletcher Rogers, 1928–1935
Arthur Olaf Andersen, 1935–1951
John B. Crowder, 1951–1957
Andrew W. Buchhauser, 1957–1958 *
Sidney Wahl Little, 1958

* Acting Dean

THE COLLEGE OF LAW

Samuel Marks Fegtly, 1925–1938
James Byron McCormick, 1938–1947
John Daniel Lyons, 1947

THE COLLEGE OF LIBERAL ARTS

Andrew Ellicott Douglass, 1915–1917
Byron Cummings, 1917–1921
Francis Cummins Lockwood, 1921–1926
Frank Mann Life, 1926–1927
Francis Cummins Lockwood, 1927–1930
Emil Richert Riesen, 1930–1944
Robert Logan Nugent, 1944–1947
Richard Anderson Harvill, 1947–1951
Francis Albert Roy, 1951—

THE COLLEGE OF MINES

Thomas Garfield Chapman, 1940–1957
James Donald Forrester, 1957

THE COLLEGE OF PHARMACY

Rufus Ashley Lyman, 1947–1950
Haakon Bang, 1950–1952
Willis Ralph Brewer, 1952

CONTINUING EDUCATION AND THE SUMMER SESSION

Francis Pendleton Gaines, 1959

DEAN OF WOMEN

Ida Christiana Reid, 1914–1916
Anna A. Fisher, 1916–1920
Kate W. Jameson, 1920–1923
Anna Pearl Cooper, 1923–1927
Clara Seippel Webster, M.D., 1927–1929
Evelyn W. Jones Kirmse, 1929–1942
Emma K. Burgess Herrick, 1942–1945

Hazel F. MacCready, 1945–1951
Karen Louise Carlson, 1951

DEAN OF MEN

Byron Cummings, 1919–1920
Francis Cummins Lockwood, 1920–1921
Robert McNair Davis, 1921–1922
Franklin Cressey Paschal, 1922–1926
Elmer Lacey Shirrell, 1926–1927
Arthur Hamilton Otis, 1927–1946
Joseph LeRoy Picard, 1946–1947 *
Alter Louis Slonaker, 1947

THE GRADUATE COLLEGE

Raymond J. Leonard, 1934–1937
Thomas Garfield Chapman, 1937–1940
Robert Logan Nugent, 1940–1944
John Franklin Walker, 1944–1946
Richard Anderson Harvill, 1946–1947
David Lyal Patrick, 1947–1957
Herbert Dawson Rhodes, 1957

* Acting Dean

BIBLIOGRAPHY

Adams, Ward R., and Sloan, Richard E. *History of Arizona.* 4 vols. Phoenix: Record Publishing Co., 1930.

Arizona and Its Heritage. (General Bulletin, No. 3) Tucson: University of Arizona, 1936.

Arizona: A State Guide. New York: Hasting House, 1940.

Association of American University Professors. *Bulletins.*

Bancroft, Herbert Howe. *Works*, Vol. XVII: Arizona and New Mexico. San Francisco: History Co., 1889.

Board of Regents of the Universities and State College. *Minutes of Meetings.*

———. *Annual Reports.*

Coleman, Helen Turnbull Waite. *Banners in the Wilderness.* Pittsburgh: University of Pittsburgh Press, 1956.

Cosulich, Bernice. "The University in World War II." Unpublished manuscript, University of Arizona, 1950

———. *Tucson.* Tucson: Arizona Silhouettes, 1943.

Dodge, Ida Flood. *Our Arizona.* New York: Scribner's, 1929.

Douglass, Andrew Ellicott. *Dating Pueblo Bonita and Other Ruins of the Southwest.* (Technical Papers, Pueblo Bonito Ser., No. 1.) Washington, D. C.: National Geographic Society, 1935.

———. Researches in Dendrochronology. (Biological Ser., Vol. X, No. 1.) Salt Lake City: University of Utah, 1946.

Farish, Thomas E. *History of Arizona.* 8 vols. San Francisco: Filmer Bros., 1915–18.

Governor of the Territory of Arizona. *Annual Reports to the Secretary of the Interior.*

Granger, Byrd. *Will C. Barnes' Arizona Place Names.* Revised and enlarged. Tucson: University of Arizona Press, 1960.

Harvill, Richard A. *Arizona: Its University's Contributions to the Southwest.* New York: Newcomen Society, 1953.

Hinton, Richard J. *The Hand-book to Arizona.* Tucson: Arizona Silhouettes, 1954.

Kelly, George H. *Legislative History, Arizona, 1864–1912.* Phoenix: Manufacturing Stationers, 1926.

Kuhn, Madison. *Michigan State; the First Hundred Years, 1855–1955.* Lansing: Michigan State University Press, 1955.

Lockwood, Frank C. *Arizona Characters.* Los Angeles, Times-Mirror Press, 1928.

———. *Pioneer Days in Arizona.* New York: Macmillan, 1932.

Lutrell, Estelle. "A History of the University of Arizona." Unpublished manuscript, University of Arizona, 1935.

McClintock, James H. *Arizona, Prehistoric, Aboriginal, Pioneer, Modern.* 3 vols. Chicago: S. J. Clarke, 1916.

McClusky, H. S. "Messages of Governor G. W. P. Hunt to the Legislature." (Compiled by state historian from *Arizona Silver Belt*, Miami; *State Press*, Phoenix; and typewritten copies of speeches not in print.)

Miller, Joseph. *The Arizona Story*. New York: Hastings House, 1952.

Morrow, Robert D. "The Education of Deaf and Blind Children in Arizona." Unpublished Master's thesis, University of Arizona, 1941.

Richards, Joseph M. *The Birth of Arizona*. Phoenix, 1940.

Superintendent of Public Instruction. *Reports*.

Svob, Robert S. "History of Intercollegiate Athletics at the University of Arizona." Unpublished Master's thesis, University of Arizona, 1950.

Weeks, Stephen B. *History of Public School Education in Arizona*. Washington, D. C.: Government Printing Office, 1918.

Wyllys, Rufus K. *Arizona, the History of a Frontier State*. Phoenix: Hobson & Herr, 1950.

PERIODICALS

Arizona Alumnus. Tucson: Alumni Association.

Arizona Daily Star. Tucson.

Arizona Highways. Phoenix: State Highway Commission.

Arizona Historical Review. Tucson: The University and the Pioneers' Historical Society.

Arizona Progress and Arizona Historical Review. Phoenix.

Arizona Republic. Phoenix.

Cunniff, M. G. "The Last of the Territories," *World's Work*, Vol. XI (January, 1906), 7108–19.

Earth. Vol. VI, No. 8. Chicago, 1906.

Graham County Bulletin. Safford, Arizona.

"The Howell Code." Adopted by the First Legislative Assembly of the Territory of Arizona. Prescott: *Arizona Miner*, 1865.

Huber, Charlotte. "Mademoiselle's College Chart," *Mademoiselle*. Vol. X (April, 1940), 104–05.

Phoenix Gazette.

Saturday Evening Post. Vol. CXCV, No. 49. Philadelphia.

Tucson Daily Citizen.

University of Arizona. Publications including books, reports, bulletins, *The University of Arizona Record*, and publications of the College of Mines and the College of Agriculture.

INDEX